# Dollar GNPs of the U.S.S.R. and Eastern Europe

A WORLD BANK PUBLICATION

# Dollar GNPs of the U.S.S.R. and Eastern Europe

*Paul Marer*

PUBLISHED FOR THE WORLD BANK
The Johns Hopkins University Press
BALTIMORE AND LONDON

*Library of Congress Cataloging-in-Publication Data*

Marer, Paul.
  Dollar GNPs of the U.S.S.R. and Eastern
Europe.

  "Published for the World Bank."
  Bibliography: p.
  Includes index.
  1. Gross national product—Soviet Union.
2. Gross national product—Europe, Eastern.
I. International Bank for Reconstruction and
Development.  II. Title.  III. Title: Dollar
GNPs of the U.S.S.R. and Eastern Europe.
HC340.I5M29     1985       339.347       85-45101
ISBN 0-8018-3123-7

# Foreword

Centrally planned economies (CPEs) account for a significant share of the world's production and income. In view of their importance in the world economy, and to facilitate international comparative analysis, the World Bank has for many years included statistical data on these countries in those of its publications, such as *The World Bank Atlas*, that aim for universal coverage. Among these data, those relating to gross national product (GNP) and to GNP per capita are the most important, and the Bank also needs them for operational purposes for its member countries, which now include some CPEs.

In the CPEs prices are generally set administratively and are often loosely or not at all related to the relative scarcity and costs of production of goods and services. This is particularly true of the exchange rate. The World Bank normally uses exchange rates for converting GNP figures from national currencies into dollars (or into any other numeraire), an indispensable step for international comparisons. The choice of an appropriate conversion factor therefore poses particularly difficult problems for most CPEs. A further difficulty arises because the national accounts of the CPEs are based on the concept of net material product (NMP), which differs from the concept of GNP used in market economies. To derive the GNP numbers of those CPEs that compile only NMP accounts, various adjustments must be made. The data required for making these adjustments are not always fully available. Finally, a separate set of issues arises in relation to year to year comparisons within the same CPE. For these too—and the corresponding growth rates—official data are not strictly comparable to growth rates of the market economies.

In early 1982 a research project sponsored and financed by the World Bank was undertaken to assess alternative methods of computing the per capita dollar GNP levels and growth rates of CPEs. It covered eight countries: Bulgaria, Cuba, Czechoslovakia, the German Democratic Republic, Hungary, Poland, Romania, and the U.S.S.R. The purpose of this research project was to define the best among known methods that could be applied to CPEs *as a group and make use of available data.* It was not its aim to establish and define new computation methods, whose application would have required many more years of effort even if data had been available.

This research project has produced eleven reports. The present book is the main document; eight country studies and two background papers are published separately in the World Bank Staff Working Papers series. The main report provides highly valuable insights into the problems related to the estimation and comparison of the GNPs and GNP growth rates for the CPEs. It also gives the author's best estimates of the actual values of these indicators for the majority of CPEs covered by the project, that is, those for which there was some statistical basis for computing estimates or choosing between those already available.

This main report on the research project on CPEs concludes that adequate GNP data in national currencies can be derived for most CPEs by adjusting official information about net material product in the light of statistical and other information known to country experts. It further concludes that the best method *generally* applicable to CPEs for converting such GNP data from local currencies into dollars would use conversion rates based upon purchasing power parity (PPP) information. For comparison with corresponding World Bank data on other World Bank members, these conversion rates should be adjusted to correct for the expected differences between the PPP rates and the actual official exchange rates (the "exchange rate deviation index"). The needed adjustments are estimated econometrically from the actual differences observed at each level of per capita GNP among the thirty-one market economies participating in Phase III (1975) of the International Comparison Project (ICP). For Hungary, Romania, and Poland, PPP information is derived from Phase III (1975) of the ICP, while for Czechoslovakia, the German Democratic Republic, and the U.S.S.R., it is derived from private bilateral comparisons chain-linked to the ICP data. This method yields a range of per capita GNP estimates; for example, $2,700 to $5,700, with a midpoint of $4,190, for the U.S.S.R. in 1980. No PPP estimate was available and no GNP per capita figure in U.S. dollars was calculated for Bulgaria and Cuba.

The main report also concludes that the official estimates of growth rates of the CPEs "tend to yield varying degrees of upward bias." For all countries except Hungary, the experts lean toward preferring alternative indexes, constructed by outside experts with partial information, although these too present problems (especially for countries other than the U.S.S.R.), and the experts therefore fell short of endorsing them. The author of the study on Hungary leans toward preferring the official index at this time.

The country studies and background papers that are being issued in the World Bank Staff Working Papers series provide additional details on the CPEs studied and their exchange rates. Some of the country studies include the respective authors' estimates of per capita GNP in U.S. dollars. These estimates, however, are the individual authors' experimental computations based on methods that may not be consistently applicable to CPEs generally.

There remain major uncertainties about GNP conversions by means of "adjusted PPPs." In addition to numerous remaining theoretical and practical problems associated with calculating PPPs within the framework of the centrally coordinated ICP, private estimates such as those used in this study for three CPEs still appear to be subject to a wide margin of error. Furthermore, there is no other way to estimate the exchange rate deviation index than to derive it from observation of the countries covered by the ICP (almost all of which are market economies). The applicability of an index derived in this fashion to the CPEs, whose economic structures are very different, remains subject to reservations.

The present study used ICP Phase III data relating to the year 1975, extrapolated to 1980. Phase IV ICP data already published shows estimates directly relating to 1980 for European countries, including Hungary and Poland; Romania, a participant in early phases of the ICP, has not provided the data needed for participation in Phase IV. It is noteworthy that Phase IV estimates of Hungary's and Poland's per capita GNP in 1980 are lower than the 1975 results extrapolated to 1980, used by the research report on CPEs. These differences are due partly to the greater attention paid in Phase IV to quality differences and to other methodological advances.

During the course of 1983 the Bank, with the help of a distinguished panel of experts,[1] undertook a review of the methodological problems and issues related to the estimation of internationally comparable per capita GNP figures for all countries. The preliminary results of the research project on CPEs constituted an important input into that review, whose findings and recommendations were approved by the panel of experts. In light of the review, the Bank has decided that for the time being (that is, at least until problems of data availability and other matters related to PPP information are resolved), official GNP information converted at official exchange rates should generally continue to provide the basis of the per capita GNP estimates published in *The World Bank Atlas*. Exceptions to this rule are to be made only when official GNP data, in national

1. Abram Bergson, Harvard University, chairman; Andre Vanoli, Institut National de la Statistique et des Etudes Economiques; and Parmeet Singh, Commonwealth Secretariat.

currency, are exceptionally bad or compiled in ways which diverge in an exceptionally large measure from the usual methods and standards, or when the official exchange rate is exceptionally far removed from the rate effectively governing foreign payments transactions. When there is a reason to believe that such exceptional circumstances prevail, and adequate information exists, appropriate adjustments are to be made. When adequate information does not exist and cannot be obtained, no estimates are to be published. At the time of writing this foreword, it seems likely that lack of information will for some time prevent the Bank from making estimates of the per capita GNP of most CPEs. Thus, *The World Bank Atlas* published in early 1985 contains an estimate of the values of GNP and GNP per capita for only one European CPE, Hungary.

Following the review endorsed by the panel of experts, the World Bank has adopted calculation methods and obtained results which, for a few countries, are different from those of the research project of CPEs. The Bank's general methodology must be applicable to all its member countries, including most market economies and only a few CPEs; the Bank could demand that its member countries provide additional information when needed; and it could, and did, decide not to estimate the per capita GNP of countries for which a minimal but still fairly extensive set of information could not be obtained. As noted earlier, however, the research project on CPEs has aimed at defining a method consistently applicable to all CPEs and one that could make use of available information. These differences in aims and constraints readily explain the differences in results.

The research project on CPEs, whose major findings are published in this book, has greatly enhanced the understanding of the CPEs' unique macroeconomic accounting frameworks and pricing systems. It has provided insight into many substantive issues, in particular the relationship of domestic and international prices. The individual country reports, published separately, shed much light on many important country-specific issues. The Bank will continue to build upon the valuable findings of the research project on CPEs in its future efforts to understand these important components of the global economy.

JEAN BANETH
*Director*
*Economic Analysis*
*and Projections Department*
*The World Bank*

*June 1985*

# Contents

# Preface

In the summer of 1981 the author of this study was invited by the Bank to submit a research proposal to identify and evaluate alternative methods for computing the levels and growth rates of the GNPs of centrally planned economies and to undertake illustrative benchmark year computations for 1980. Eight countries were included in the project: Bulgaria, Czechoslovakia, the German Democratic Republic, Hungary, Poland, Romania, the U.S.S.R., and Cuba. (China was not included in the study because an earlier Bank economic mission to the country had reviewed the national accounts statistics in detail and had found a way of estimating the country's gross national product in U.S. dollars.) A draft proposal was discussed informally with the staff and formally with the Bank's Research Committee during the second half of 1981. The project was approved to start in January 1982 and was to be completed in 1983. Much of the research was carried out by a team of independent experts assembled by the principal researcher and affiliated neither with the World Bank nor with the governments of the countries being studied. I served as liaison between the research team and the Bank, coordinated the country experts' work on individual CPEs or on special topics, was responsible for the general research methodology, prepared background papers for two workshops and thus helped to organize them, and wrote the preliminary and final reports on the project.

The research team consisted of the following independent experts: Abram Bergson (Harvard University), general consultant on methodology; Robert W. Campbell (Indiana University), country expert on the U.S.S.R.; Irwin Collier (University of Houston), country expert on the German Democratic Republic; Zbigniew Fallenbuchl (University of Windsor, Canada), country expert on Poland; Edward Hewett (Brookings Institution), country expert on Hungary; Marvin Jackson (Arizona State University), country expert on Romania; Friedrich Levcik and Peter Havlik (Vienna Institute for Comparative Economic Studies), country experts on Czechoslovakia; Carmelo Mesa-Lago (University of Pittsburgh), country expert on Cuba, assisted by Jorge Perez-Lopez, an independent consultant; and Thomas Wolf (Ohio State University), general consultant on exchange rates and purchasing power parity computations.

The expert commissioned to prepare a country study on Bulgaria, Ilse Grosser (Vienna Institute for Comparative Economic Studies), resigned in July 1982 because of ill health. Because it would have been difficult to find an independent expert to replace her on very short notice, two staff members of the World Bank, Shamsher Singh and Jong-goo Park (Economics and Research Staff, Economic Analysis and Projections Department), assumed joint responsibility for preparing a country study on Bulgaria. General administrative, logistical, and statistical support for the project was provided by Wharton Econometrics Forecasting Associates.

The project was fortunate in obtaining substantive contributions, offered without compensation, from the following experts, who participated in one or both workshops: Thad Alton (L. W. International Financial Research, Inc.); Jozef M. van Brabant (officer in charge, Centrally Planned Economy Section, United Nations); John P. Hardt (senior specialist, Soviet Union/ Eastern Europe, Congressional Research Service, Library of Congress); Alan Heston (Department of Economics, University of Pennsylvania); Michael Keren (Department of Economics, Hebrew University, Jerusalem, and University of Pennsylvania); Irving B. Kravis (Department of Economics, University of Pennsylvania); and Y. Ivanov (Statistical Office, United Nations).

During the spring of 1982 the Bank formally contacted the United Nations Statistical Office and the national statistical offices and central banks of the eight countries included in the study to inform them of the project and to ask for their cooperation in providing data and expertise. If a visit seemed feasible and potentially fruitful, the country experts were scheduled to travel to their countries to collect detailed basic data and to learn the views of national experts. Four countries responded. Bulgaria hosted the two country experts from the Bank and discussed the project with them during a short visit but did not make available information beyond the rather sketchy data already published in official sources. Hungary hosted the country expert and sent Piroska Horvath, an expert from its central statistical office, to participate in the second workshop. Poland sent Leszek Zienkowski, an expert from its central statistical office, to participate in the second workshop. Romania hosted the country expert and made available some previously unpublished data. The experts from the countries, however, played no role in drafting the report or the country studies and thus do not necessarily concur with the approaches, findings, and conclusions presented in this volume.

The Bank and I as the principal researcher organized two workshops at the World Bank in Washington, D.C. The first workshop, held June 12–13, 1982, discussed important conceptual and methodological problems, bringing together the project consultants, other invited experts, and interested staff from the Bank and the International Monetary Fund. The second workshop, held October 13–14, 1982, discussed the draft country reports and various technical issues relating to the project. Participants were the project consultants, the experts from Hungary and Poland, other invited experts, and interested staff from the Bank and the International Monetary Fund.

This book summarizes the main findings and conclusions reached at the two workshops, those of the team of experts commissioned to prepare country papers for this project, and those of the principal researcher. Statements made in the present tense throughout the book refer to 1983, unless otherwise specified. Further information and data can be found in the studies commissioned or made available for this project, which are published as World Bank Staff Working Papers and are listed in the references.

I wish to thank the members of the research team and the many people who contributed to the genesis and publication of this book. The research project was initiated under the administrative guidance of Sang E. Lee, then in the Economic Analysis and Projections Department of the World Bank. Bela Balassa and other members of the World Bank Research Committee gave support and guidance in getting the project under way. Jong-goo Park of the Economic Analysis and Projections Department, Comparative Analysis and Data Division, the World Bank, provided courteous and effective assistance on both administrative and substantive matters from the inception of the project to its conclusion. The publication of this book and of the related World Bank Staff Working Papers owes a great deal to Jean Baneth, director, Economic Analysis and Projections Department, the World Bank, for his personal involvement and his strong support of the idea of having independent scholars investigate the controversial issues that were dealt with in the project. Marcia Brubeck edited the book and did much to improve its presentation. Trina King prepared the index.

Neither the individuals who contributed nor the institution that sponsored the research should be held accountable for the shortcomings of the book.

# Abbreviations

| | |
|---|---|
| AFC | adjusted factor cost |
| CMEA | Council for Mutual Economic Assistance |
| CPE | centrally planned economy |
| CSO | central statistical office |
| ECE | Economic Commission for Europe of the United Nations |
| ECP | European Comparison Program |
| EEC | European Economic Community |
| EP | established prices |
| ER | exchange rate |
| ERDI | exchange rate deviation index |
| FTM | foreign trade multiplier |
| FTO | foreign trade organization |
| GDP | gross domestic product |
| GNP | gross national product |
| ICP | International Comparison Project |
| IER | internal exchange rate |
| IMF | International Monetary Fund |
| JEC | Joint Economic Committee, U.S. Congress |
| MPS | material product system |
| MTE | market-type economy |
| NBER | National Bureau of Economic Research |
| NCU | national currency unit |
| NEM | New Economic Mechanism |
| NMP | net material product |
| OECD | Organisation for Economic Co-operation and Development |
| PI | physical indicators |
| PPP | purchasing power parity |
| RPNI | Research Project on National Income |
| SEE | standard error of the estimate |
| SNA | system of national accounts |
| TPR | trade participation ratio |
| TR | transferable ruble |

# Dollar GNPs of the U.S.S.R. and Eastern Europe

# Chapter 1

# *Introduction*

Centrally planned economies account for about a third of the world's population and about a fourth of its output. In view of their importance in the world economy, they need to be included in international comparative studies. Their inclusion presents problems for several reasons, however. First, CPEs report net material product, not gross national product. Then, too, their prices and exchange rates are set administratively, so that conversion to dollars is problematic. Finally, they compute growth rates using methods that in most cases are strongly upward biased.

Until 1983 the World Bank included centrally planned economies in the *World Bank Atlas* and the *World Development Reports*, documents with universal coverage. The Bank's *Atlas* is the most frequently cited source of regular estimates of income per capita in U.S. dollars for nearly all countries of the world. These estimates are widely used by international organizations, governments, academic researchers, and firms in the private sector and are generally regarded as authoritative. Furthermore, several centrally planned economies are members of the Bank (Romania, Vietnam, Laos, China, and Hungary), representing more than one-third of the Bank's membership of developing countries in terms of population.

Per capita GNP figures in the *Atlas* are used as inputs for operational purposes by the Bank and by other agencies in determining eligibility for aid allocations. The *Atlas* GNP figures are used extensively also by bilateral and multilateral aid agencies. Hence individual CPE governments take the *Atlas* numbers seriously. One centrally planned economy, for example, was refused access to the Generalized Preference Scheme of the European Economic Community on the basis of the numbers published in the *Atlas*. Several other centrally planned economies, too, have expressed strong reservations regarding the level of their per capita GNPs as shown in the *Atlas* and also regarding the method of computation, which, they believed, resulted in overstatement of their per capita GNP.

Although the statistical offices of several centrally planned economies have carried out and in some instances published illustrative computations of GNP, no systematic effort has been made among centrally planned economies, or between them and any international organization, to produce a consistent set of GNP figures for them in dollars. The United Nations, for example, does not publish dollar GNP figures for CPEs (although it does make rough approximations strictly for internal purposes).

The CPEs' national accounts are based on the concept of net material product, which differs from the GNP concept used in market economies. Prices and exchange rates in CPEs are generally set administratively and to a considerable extent are not based on demand-and-supply relations. Some CPEs publish only fragmentary information, with very little explanation of the methods used to compile the data. The International Comparison Project has so far covered data for only three centrally planned economies, Hungary, Poland, and Romania. The chances that the ICP will undertake further computations for others seem remote. Through the 1981 edition of the *Atlas*, the Bank relied on a fairly rough and mechanical methodology for translating the official statistics of CPEs into concepts comparable with the standard system of national accounts, as explained in some detail in appendix A.

## GNP Estimates for 1980 in National Currency

After reviewing alternative approaches to the problem of obtaining GNP data, the research team for the present project concluded that scaling up from official NMP to gross national product is the best practical method for six CPE countries. In brief, this method adds to official (in some cases adjusted) net material product, depreciation, and net value added in nonmaterial services. Lack of data for Bulgaria necessitated use of another method, the estimation of GNP as the sum of the end uses of all goods and services produced. Neither of these methods could be applied in the case of Cuba, for which no comprehensive, reliable, and up-to-date statistical information on NMP or GNP could be obtained or reconstructed. The 1980 total and per capita GNP estimates for seven CPE countries in national currency units are shown in table 1-1. For six of the seven countries for which GNP could be computed via the scaling up method, the 1980 GNP/NMP ratios ranged from 1.24 for Romania to 1.31 for the German Democratic Republic, 1.28 being the average.

*Table 1-1. Total and per Capita GNP Estimates in NCUs for Seven CPEs, 1980*

| Country | Currency | Total GNP (billions) | Per capita GNP |
|---|---|---|---|
| Bulgaria | leva | 27.1 | 3,009 |
| Czechoslovakia | crown | 566.1 | 36,913 |
| German Democratic Republic | mark | 218.3 | 13,000 |
| Hungary | forint | 719.0 | 66,859 |
| Poland | zloty | 2,502.0 | 69,878 |
| Romania | lei | 619.9 | 27,838 |
| U.S.S.R. | ruble | 589.5 | 2,211 |

Sources: Total GNP: table 2-1; per capita GNP: total GNP divided by population reported in *World Bank Atlas* (1981).

## Converting GNP to Dollar Values

It is exceedingly difficult to find appropriate convertors for centrally planned economies, and the problem cannot be solved with a high degree of precision for a variety of conceptual and practical reasons. Traditionally, CPEs use a plethora of exchange rates and exchange-rate-type coefficients, largely for accounting purposes. Because traditional CPEs usually do not revise such rates or coefficients for long periods, their values are often unrealistic. ("Traditional CPEs" should be understood to mean CPEs whose economic system has remained essentially similar to that of the Soviet Union in the 1930s, which was copied in Eastern Europe and China in the early 1950s.) Beginning in the 1960s, some CPEs began to introduce economic reforms that often involved reductions in the number of exchange rates or coefficients and set them at more realistic levels. In a few cases, exchange rates serve as policy instruments much as they do in market-type economies. These developments suggest the possibility that the official commercial, tourist, or unified exchange rates might appropriately be used for GNP conversion, at least for some countries.

Detailed computations of purchasing power parity are also available as an option for six CPEs (Bulgaria and Cuba are again the exceptions); the International Comparison Project has computations for Hungary, Poland, and Romania, and unofficial bilateral computations have been made for the U.S.S.R. (with the United States), Czechoslovakia (with Austria), and the German Democratic Republic (with the Federal Republic of Germany). For some of the centrally planned economies, other PPP computations are available also.

One problem with using PPPs to achieve the conversion is that for MTEs, their exchange rates, not their purchasing power parities, are used in the *World Bank Atlas*. The task of the present project was to find comparable convertors for CPEs. Although it is the view of many experts and some international organizations that PPPs are the most appropriate convertors for ranking countries among the family of nations, a main purpose of this project was to find a set of convertors that would yield per capita dollar GNPs comparable to those for MTEs, based on exchange rates, as reported in the *Atlas*.[1]

Whatever the merits of using purchasing power parities or exchange rates as convertors for any country, this project provided a challenging opportunity to investigate some important facets of the economies of CPEs, including various ways of obtaining PPPs for their currencies. Inasmuch as exchange rates and PPPs have been found to diverge systematically even for market-type economies, PPPs will not be appropriate to use in *Atlas*-type comparisons of per capita gross national product. The solution proposed here is to adjust the PPPs computed for centrally planned economies by so-called exchange rate deviation indexes based on the relationship found between purchasing power parities and exchange rates for market-type economies at given levels of (PPP-based) per capita dollar GNPs.

Because the principal purpose of this project is to suggest ways of improving the international comparability of basic national income data of CPEs, we have sought to find a set of convertors that can be applied uniformly to CPEs as a group or to a significant subgroup of countries. The "adjusted PPP" approach, using the International Comparison Project's 1975 data for Hungary, Poland, and Romania as well as a variety of other unofficial PPP estimates for other centrally planned economies, all extrapolated to 1980, yields such a set of convertors for six of the European countries in the Council for Mutual Economic Assistance. No such estimates could be made for Bulgaria or Cuba.

The adjusted PPPs, per capita dollar figures, and income levels expressed as a percentage of the U.S. level for the year 1980 are shown in table 1-2. In view of the statistical uncertainties involved in determining exchange rate deviation indexes for centrally planned economies, the estimates shown above and in figure 1-1 are simply the "best" (midpoint) values within a comparatively wide range of possibilities.

There is no scientific test to assess the appropriateness of a set of convertors for CPEs; in fact, for any country the most appropriate convertor may depend on the purpose. That is, even for MTEs, often no single

---

1. See especially Kravis and others (1982) and the work of the Statistical Office of the European Community (1983), which computes PPPs for internal purposes.

*Table 1-2. Adjusted Purchasing Power Parity, per Capita Dollar GNP, and Relative Income Levels of Seven CPEs, 1980*

| Country | Adjusted PPP (national currency/ dollars) | Per capita GNP (dollars) | As percentage of U.S. per capita GNP |
|---|---|---|---|
| German Democratic Republic | 2.20 | 5,910 | 52 |
| Czechoslovakia | 7.78 | 4,740 | 42 |
| Hungary | 15.22 | 4,390 | 39 |
| U.S.S.R. | 0.53 | 4,190 | 37 |
| Poland | 18.73 | 3,730 | 33 |
| Romania | 10.40 | 2,680 | 24 |

*Sources*: Adjusted PPP and per capita GNP: table 3-18; as percentage of U.S. per capita GNP: table 3-21.

*Figure 1-1. Per Capita Dollar GNPs of the U.S.S.R., Eastern Europe, and Yugoslavia, 1980*

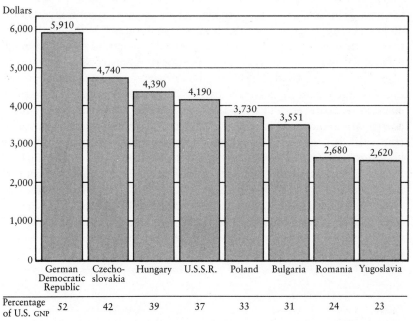

*Note*: Based on adjusted purchasing power parity (= proxy exchange rate), except for Bulgaria and Yugoslavia, for which the commercial exchange rate was used. See table 3-15.

convertor is best both as an equilibrium exchange rate and for use in obtaining the per capita dollar GNP that would rank the country "correctly" among the family of nations. Because the exchange rates of CPEs cannot undergo the test of being market determined, the appropriateness of a set of convertors is largely a matter of judgment. In this book, judgment is guided by (1) the availability or calculability of a similar set of convertors for all countries or for a large subgroup of them, to facilitate intercountry comparisons, and (2) the plausibility of the resulting per capita dollar GNP estimates.

Three possible sets of exchange-rate-type convertors are available or calculable for six CPEs: the commercial exchange rates, employed to link the foreign and domestic prices of at least some foreign trade commodity transactions; the tourist (noncommercial) exchange rates, used mainly for tourism, which presumably reflect approximately the PPP of a country's tourist basket; and the adjusted PPPs described above.

We established four criteria to assess the plausibility of alternative dollar GNP estimates. One is the set of comparisons of the intra-CMEA ranking of the member countries' per capita dollar GNP against the rankings that result from computations of relative income levels carried out by experts in the Council for Mutual Economic Assistance. Another is the findings of independent multilateral studies involving centrally planned and market-type economies and using the method of physical indicators to estimate their per capita dollar GNPs. The third method relies on foreign trade participation ratios, defined as exports plus imports divided by GNP. This third method is based on the following approach. The approximate dollar values of CPE trade can be determined readily.[2] Each set of convertors, however, will yield a different dollar GNP estimate. The trade participation ratios will therefore change, depending on the convertor employed. It has been independently established and documented in the literature that centrally planned economies typically have lower levels of trade—and thus lower TPRs—than market-type economies of comparable size and level of development. Accordingly, convertors that yield TPRs significantly higher than those of comparable market-type economies will be judged implausible. The fourth method relates to the fact that, in per capita energy consumption, centrally planned economies and market-type economies establish rankings that can be used as reference

---

2. The procedure involves reconverting to dollars East-West trade (always conducted in dollars or in other convertible currencies) and intra-CPE trade (whose initial value is set at bilaterally negotiated Western world market prices in dollars or other convertible currencies) at the same exchange rate at which these trade flows were converted to local currency units in the first place.

points, because energy consumption per capita has been found to correlate highly with levels of economic development (although the rankings of CPEs must be adjusted for the relatively wasteful use of materials that characterizes them).

The research team's main finding is that, of the three possible sets of convertors, the adjusted PPP set yields per capita dollar GNPs that are more plausible according to each of the four criteria than those derived using either the commercial or the tourist exchange rates. We do not claim that the adjusted PPP convertors necessarily yield the correct per capita GNP for each and every country in view of the unresolved questions concerning the accuracy of the PPP computations, especially as they are applied to CPEs, and in view of the theoretical and practical difficulties of determining exchange rate deviation indexes for CPEs. If our aim, however, is to rank centrally planned economies among market-type economies in terms of per capita dollar GNP levels, then the adjusted PPPs yield plausible outcomes.

It is difficult to say whether the prevailing exchange rate might for certain purposes be a better GNP convertor for one or another centrally planned economy than adjusted PPP. A difficult problem arises when a CPE has a prevailing exchange rate substantially different from that derived via the adjusted PPP method, as did Hungary in 1982. In deciding which convertor to accept for operational or *Atlas* purposes, an important question is whether the country's prevailing exchange rate performs several of the basic *economic* functions that exchange rates fulfill in MTEs. Key issues are whether the country has a uniform or multiple exchange rate system, whether and to what extent its prevailing exchange rate actually links foreign and domestic prices, whether enterprises have significant freedom to export and import, and whether their trade decisions are made largely on the basis of profitability. (These issues are discussed in country-specific detail in chapter 4, which focuses on the determination and role of prices in CPEs.) On the basis of these considerations, an argument can be made that Hungary's prevailing and (since 1981) uniform exchange rate may be acceptable for operational purposes, even though the resulting per capita dollar GNP is implausibly low. A similar situation often arises for many developing countries also.

A comparative analysis of the price and exchange rate systems in place in the CPEs during the early 1980s reveals that there was apparently no direct link between foreign and domestic prices in the U.S.S.R., the German Democratic Republic, and Cuba; some linkage in Bulgaria, Czechoslovakia, Poland, and (since 1981) Romania; and substantial linkage since 1980 in Hungary. Hungary differs from market-type economies chiefly in exhibiting seemingly only a weak link between the foreign and domestic prices of goods other than those actually traded, but in this respect Hungary may resemble many developing countries.

As previously noted, centrally planned economies use different types of conversion coefficients that link *some* foreign and domestic prices directly. Bulgaria, Hungary, and (since 1982) Poland rely on their commercial or unified exchange rates, whereas Czechoslovakia and Romania employ multiple rates, depending on the type of transaction, although there appears to be movement in both countries toward unifying the exchange rates.

The U.S.S.R. set its exchange rate in 1961 on the basis of the purchasing power parity of its net material product vis-à-vis that of the United States, but the small adjustments made since that time have not reflected differences in inflation rates between the two countries. The basis for the exchange rates of Bulgaria and the German Democratic Republic is not known. Hungary's 1968 exchange rate was based approximately on its export foreign trade multiplier, that is, on the average domestic cost of earning a dollar or its equivalent in other convertible currencies. Since 1968 the rate has been adjusted approximately to reflect differential inflation rates in Hungary and in its main trade partner countries. Romania's commercial exchange rate since 1981 is approximately the same as its foreign trade multiplier; Poland's new unified rate introduced in 1982 is based on its foreign trade multiplier plus a large markup (that is, currency depreciation). Chapter 3 (see "Exchange Rates and Purchasing Power Parities, by Country") tabulates and discusses, separately for each country, the different kinds of exchange rates, exchange-rate-type coefficients, and PPP computations available since 1970.

Analysis of the price systems in centrally planned economies provides informaton that helps explain the puzzlingly large differences between the values of PPPs and exchange rates based on foreign trade multipliers for some countries. A very important feature of the Hungarian price system, for example, is that the producer price level is exceedingly high because of the country's system of taxation, whereas the consumer price level is exceedingly low because of its system of subsidization. As a result the producer and consumer price levels are about equal, whereas in most MTEs consumer price levels are typically much higher. This anomaly has important implications for Hungary's dollar exchange rate, which essentially represents its export foreign trade multiplier, so that, in the numerator of the multiplier, Hungarian exports in effect are valued at retail prices. The appropriate analogue in the denominator, if PPP computations were to be made, would therefore be Western retail prices. In the denominator of the foreign trade multiplier, however, the dollar prices used are those that Hungary actually receives for its exports, which are very much lower than Western retail prices, because five layers of markups—which could amount to several hundred percent— separate the dollar prices Hungarian exporters receive from the Western retail prices. Thus it is not surprising to find very large differences between Hungary's foreign-trade-multiplier-based exchange rate (high number of forints per dollar) and purchasing power parity (low number of forints per dollar) even for traded goods; the PPP for all tradables and nontradables combined (that is, GNP) would of course be even lower than the PPP for traded goods because of the relatively low prices of services. Although Hungary may be an extreme case, similar problems are involved in comparing the PPPs and the FTM-based exchange rates in other centrally planned economies also.

In CPEs, investment goods are relatively expensive, and agricultural products and services relatively inexpensive, by comparison with those in MTEs. Consumer prices, on average, are also relatively low in CPEs— one reason for the low level of wages as well—with basic necessities priced very inexpensively and all other goods quite dearly.

One conclusion of this project, elaborated in chapter 3, is that centrally planned economies differ fundamentally from each other and from market-type economies in methods of price and exchange rate determination. Also, for several CPEs, data are increasingly difficult to obtain. These constraints on obtaining or computing reliable converters from NCUs to dollars are bypassed by the physical indicators method, an approach to estimating the per capita GNPs of CPEs that does not rely on prices and currency convertors. A detailed examination of the method and its results, its relatively simple data requirements, and the fact that it also yields internationally comparable growth rates suggests that, even though international organizations have discontinued using this approach to estimate the per capita dollar GNPs of countries—and thus no up-to-date estimates for CPEs were available for this project to consider as an option—the physical indicators method has much to recommend it.

## Growth Rates

The official NMP growth rates of centrally planned economies are calculated with distorted prices and according to methods of index number construction that tend to yield varying degrees of upward bias. The degree of bias is considered by independent experts to be so substantial for some centrally planned economies as to invite the conclusion that the official NMP growth rate or the NMP-based GNP growth rates of CPEs *taken as a group* cannot be compared meaningfully with the GNP growth rates of MTEs.

Centrally planned economies rely on the double-deflation method: both the value of gross output and the value of material purchases and depreciation are deflated separately by the relevant price indexes. Gross value is typically overstated, and the price indexes used to deflate them are downward biased so that the resulting constant price series will be upward biased. CPE price indexes are downward biased primarily because of their method of introducing "new" products. Enterprise plan fulfillment is measured in "constant" prices, and products are therefore often redesigned slightly by firms and labeled new products, then introduced at significantly higher prices, so that constant-price output will have a higher value. More generally, new products tend to be priced at higher introductory prices rather than at lower serial production prices. Lack of a strong, independent scientific tradition in the central statistical offices of some countries may encourage the subordination of statistical integrity to political considerations. To be sure, there are significant differences among the CPEs regarding the presence and importance of these factors, with corresponding impact on their growth rate statistics.

As a result of such shortcomings in the official CPE growth rate statistics, considerable effort has been devoted in the West to developing alternative measures, using official data exclusively but as much as possible replicating commonly accepted standards of valuation and index number construction in MTEs. The basic Western approach is to aggregate the official physical output series into branch, sector, and GNP indexes using weights constructed from official data according to the adjusted factor cost standard pioneered during the 1950s by Abram Bergson.

To be sure, the implementation of this alternative approach is hindered by gaps in published data that are very serious for some countries. Lack of published data on physical output for some branches often leaves researchers with no alternative but to rely on official constant-price indexes to estimate the growth rate of those branches, a practice that tends to impart an upward bias to the recomputed indexes also. A further problem is that recomputed branch indexes based on physical output may not adequately measure quality improvements and the introducton of new products, so that the resulting growth indexes may be downward biased.

There was no consensus among the country experts in this project as to whether the official or the independently computed growth rates would be preferable for use. The view that the official growth rates are significantly upward biased is unequivocal for all CPEs except Hungary; the country expert on Hungary is not certain. Most country experts, however, stop short of endorsing the alternative growth computations, sometimes because it is believed that the figures may also be biased for the reasons mentioned, but more often because the experts have not been able to resolve satisfactorily concrete questions about the application of the method to their countries. For the U.S.S.R., the building block data available from official sources, although not without gaps, have been adequate, and considerable resources have been devoted to making the alternative estimates, which are well documented and evaluated against the official indexes and do include sensitivity analyses in the sectors that present especially difficult statistical problems. These considerations led the country expert unequivocally to prefer them to the official series. The country experts writing on Czechoslovakia, the German Democratic Republic, Poland, and Romania consider the recomputed Western indexes more plausible but stop short of endorsing their use until the questions raised about them have been resolved. The adjustments to the official data made by the experts on Bulgaria significantly reduced the official growth rates, but in the view of most members of the team, they are still upward biased. The country author on Hungary leans toward a preference for the official index at this time. In the case of Cuba, data were insufficient to permit the country experts to recommend any set of growth statistics.

It is hoped that in the future the Bank will have substantive cooperation from the central statistical offices of the CPEs and that progress will be made in rectifying the most serious statistical problems. Alternatively, internationally comparable growth rates for the countries of Eastern Europe might be obtained by improving the application, but especially the country-specific documentation and evaluation, of the adjusted factor cost method. The quality of the official growth statistics of Hungary *may* be judged to be on a par with those generally available for market-type economies. For centrally planned economies as a group, one possibility would be to rely on growth rates generated by the physical indicators method.

In view of the serious methodological and practical problems of obtaining reliable per capita dollar GNPs and growth rates for CPEs, it is not surprising to find that the estimating methods used to obtain these figures for publication in the *Atlas* have been altered several times since the early 1960s, sometimes causing very large changes in the CPE figures from year to year or from period to period. Appendix A presents a comprehensive description and evaluation of the statistical methods used to obtain per capita dollar GNP and growth rate statistics in the *Atlas*.

The Bank decided to discontinue publishing in the *Atlas* the per capita GNP and the growth rate data of those CPEs for which the data problems and methodological issues could not satisfactorily be resolved. In consequence, the *World Bank Atlas* that was published, for example, in 1985 included per capita GNP data for none of the countries studied in this book except Hungary. For the World Bank's operational work, as well as for the work of other international agencies, governments, and interested persons in the academic and private sectors, it would be exceedingly useful to have GNP levels and growth rates for CPEs that are internationally comparable.

# Chapter 2

# GNP Estimates for 1980
# in National Currency

The national income accounts of CPEs record productive activity taking place on their territory rather than income received by their residents. They are therefore in the spirit of GDP rather than GNP.[1] The difference between GDP and GNP is net factor income—that is, GDP plus factor income receipts from abroad (workers' remittances, profits remitted on foreign investment, and interest income) minus factor income payments to nonresidents equals GNP. Because CPEs do not have significant workers' remittances, and have little income from and few payments on foreign direct investment, and because the interest payments on foreign loans are of modest significance relative to their GNP, the difference between GDP and GNP is small and can be ignored for present purposes. The terms GDP and GNP are used interchangeably in the country studies; the term GNP is used throughout this book.

To be sure, benchmark GDP estimates could be adjusted to obtain improved GNP estimates by subtracting interest payments on net external debt. Good estimates of the convertible-currency portion of the debt and interest payments are available for all CPEs from Western sources in dollars, but we have little information about the debt and interest denominated in rubles. Net interest payments in dollars could be converted to national currency units by using whatever coefficients are selected to convert GDP in national currency units to dollars. Illustrative computations, however, show that net interest payments are small relative to GDP, so that, as a practical matter, they may be disregarded. In the case of the U.S.S.R., 1980 interest payments on convertible-currency debt are estimated at about 1.5 million rubles, in contrast to the GNP estimate of 590

---

1. According to the SNA, gross national product is a measure of the total domestic and foreign output claimed by residents of a country. At market prices, GNP includes compensation of employees, operating surplus, provision for the consumption of fixed capital (depreciation), and indirect taxes less subsidies to producers.

billion rubles (Campbell 1985, p. 31). In the case of Hungary, which probably has the largest interest payments relative to GNP of any CPE, 1980 net interest expenses on net convertible-currency debt were about $400 million (see World Bank 1984, table 6). Conversion to forints at the proxy exchange rates shown in table 1-2 yields 6.1 billion forints, less than 1 percent of GNP. Even if the prevailing 1980 commercial exchange rate of 32.43 forints per dollar were used, net interest payments would represent a less than 2 percent deduction from GDP to yield GNP.

## Approaches to GNP Estimation

Four main alternative approaches have been employed in the literature to estimate benchmark year GNPs in national currency units for centrally planned economies: (1) building a more or less complete set of national accounts from disaggregated data, computing GNP as the sum of value added in the production sectors—industry, agriculture, and the like; (2) scaling up from NMP to GNP on the basis of the average regression relationship found between NMP and GNP for a group of Western countries in a benchmark year (using the *Atlas* method between 1977 and 1980); (3) scaling up from NMP by adding net value added in the nonmaterial sectors plus depreciation and otherwise adjusting as necessary to make the GNP estimates for centrally planned economies comparable to those for market-type economies; and (4) deriving GNP as the sum of the various end uses of the goods and services—consumption, investment, government, and net exports. A fifth method, the physical indicators approach, may be used to estimate GNP directly in dollars; it will be discussed briefly in chapter 3.

The first approach, building a set of national accounts from detailed data, has been used extensively in the West, particularly in studies focusing on the U.S.S.R. (see works cited in Campbell 1985, p. 10) and also on the countries of Eastern Europe (principally Alton 1981 and 1982). The method involves developing an articulated set of accounts based on official production data aggregated according to some sort of factor cost valuation. In most of these calculations, the results are identical with or very close to official CPE data for that portion of the total where the two approaches overlap (that is, material production). The structure of an economy may be quite different, however, depending on the discrepancy between established and factor cost prices. Although the results of such detailed computations are very useful and do provide important details and checks on alternative estimates, this approach was not used here because it is far too time consuming and entails a long delay. Estimates of approximately comparable reliability can be obtained relatively simply for most CPEs by means of shortcut methods.

The second approach, scaling up from NMP to GNP on the basis of an average relationship found for Western countries, is not used or recommended because it lacks a theoretical foundation. Differences in economic systems as well as in levels of development, for example, would lead us to expect the service sector to be relatively less important in CPEs than in the West European countries.

The third approach, scaling up from official NMP on the basis of country-specific data, is the best practical method and is followed here for six of the seven CPEs for which GNP estimates could be made, Bulgaria being the exception. The main advantage of this method is its relatively modest data requirements. For countries for which clearly defined data are available from official sources, the method is not too time consuming because the adjustments needed to transform NMP to GNP are well documented in the literature. This project's country experts relied on the GDP computations made by the central statistical offices of the CPEs if they were available and documented or, if they were not, used shortcut methods devised by the experts themselves.

The fourth method—estimating GNP as the sum of the end uses of all goods and services produced—was employed for Bulgaria only because the sectoral production data available were insufficient to scale up to GNP from the official NMP figures. It was also used as a supplementary method for Czechoslovakia and the German Democratic Republic. None of these methods could be applied to Cuba because no comprehensive, reliable, and up-to-date statistical information on that country's NMP or GNP could be obtained or reconstructed (Mesa-Lago and Perez-Lopez 1985).

## GNP Estimation Using NMP: Methods and Problems

CPE national income accounts are based on the material product system, whose most important aggregate is NMP, and its derivation is fairly standardized. The NMP comprehensively covers value added in the "material" sectors of production, typically representing between 70 percent and 80 percent of GDP. The consensus of experts participating in the project is that NMP can be taken as a point of departure for estimating *total* GNP for a benchmark year but not for estimating GNP components or growth rates, for reasons that I will indicate.

Even when we scale up NMP to estimate total gross national product, NMP data must be assessed, and if necessary adjusted, for statistically significant problems of individual country deviations from the "standard" MPS, for the inclusion of certain services in "material" production, and for other reasons.


## Deviations from the Standard MPS

The nearest thing to a manual detailing the methodology of computing NMP is a document prepared by the secretariat of the Council for Mutual Economic Assistance and published by the United Nations (United Nations 1971). As even this document indicates, however, in practice the individual CMEA countries frequently depart from CMEA's MPS standard. Some of the departures are known or implied; others are not revealed. The treatment of passenger transport, communications serving persons, and nonmaterial production, for example, is different. These areas are included in NMP by Hungary, Poland, the German Democratic Republic, Romania (since 1971), and Bulgaria (since 1972), and are excluded by the U.S.S.R. and Czechoslovakia. For the U.S.S.R., the item represents 2.5 percent of GNP; for Czechoslovakia the item is not available separately, but it is probably less than 2.5 percent, because transport distances are shorter.


## Services Included in Material Production

The statement that NMP covers only the production of goods and excludes services is not fully accurate. First, freight transport and material communications and trade are services that are always included in NMP. Second, in moving from the gross output of any sector of material production to net product, the MPS subtracts material inputs and depreciation but leaves in the value of services purchased from firms in the nonmaterial sphere—such as research and development, banking, insurance, education, and health—which need to be removed because they will be included in the estimates of the value added in the nonmaterial sectors. Corrections for this shortcoming were made when possible by the country experts, the adjustments averaging 3 percent of GNP (table 2-1). Third, social services provided free of charge to employees in the material sectors, such as health care and reimbursement for business travel, are also left in as components of NMP and should be removed. These, however, are of much smaller magnitude, and correction for them was possible for only some countries.

Lack of data and sometimes also lack of knowledge of production boundaries or valuation in the NMP practices of some of the countries have made it difficult to know whether or how to adjust NMP in some

Table 2-1. NMP and GNP of Seven CPEs at Current Established Prices, 1980

| Item | Hungary (forint) NCU billions | Percentage of GNP | Romania (lei) NCU billions | Percentage of GNP | U.S.S.R. (ruble) NCU billions | Percentage of GNP | Czechoslovakia (Kcs) NCU billions | Percentage of GNP | Poland (zloty) NCU billions | Percentage of GNP | German Democratic Republic (mark) NCU billions | Percentage of GNP | Bulgaria (leva) NCU billions | Percentage of GNP |
|---|---|---|---|---|---|---|---|---|---|---|---|---|---|---|
| NMP | 581 | 80.8 | 516.6 | 83.3 | 458.5[a] | 77.8 | 474.9 | 84.5 | 1,956 | 78.2 | 187.1 | 85.7 | 20,509 | 75.7 |
| Adjustment | −24[b] | −3.3 | −18.0[b] | 2.9 | 14.5[c] | 2.5 | −36.5[d] | −6.4 | −20 | −0.8 | −20.3[e] | −9.3 | n.a. | n.a. |
| Adjusted NMP | 557 | 77.5 | 498.6 | 80.4 | 473.0 | 80.2 | 438.4 | 78.1 | 1,936 | 77.4 | 166.8 | 76.4 | n.a. | n.a. |
| Nonmaterial sectors | 69 | 9.6 | 61.2 | 9.9 | 65.9 | 11.2 | 62.1 | 10.3 | 286 | 11.4 | 24.1 | 11.0 | n.a. | n.a. |
| Housing (including imputed rent) | n.a. | n.a. | n.a. | n.a. | (4.2)[f] | 0.7 | n.a. | n.a. | n.a. | n.a. | (3.4) | 1.6 | n.a. | n.a. |
| Housing (communal and others) | n.a. | n.a. | (8.3) | (1.3) | (10.5) | 1.8 | n.a. | n.a. | (33) | (1.3) | n.a. | n.a. | n.a. | n.a. |
| Depreciation | 93 | 12.9 | 60.1 | 9.7 | 50.6 | 8.6 | 65.6 | 11.7 | 280 | 11.2 | 24.0 | 11.0 | n.a. | n.a. |
| Material sectors | n.a. | n.a. | (52.0) | 8.4 | n.a. | n.a. | (50.2) | (8.9) | (243) | (9.7) | (22.6) | (10.4) | n.a. | n.a. |
| Nonmaterial sectors | n.a. | n.a. | (8.1) | (1.3) | n.a. | n.a. | (14.3) | (2.7) | (37) | (1.5) | (1.4) | (0.12) | n.a. | n.a. |
| GNP, total (billions) | 719[g] | 100.0 | 619.9 | 100.0 | 589.5 | (100.0) | 566.1 | (100.0) | 2,502 | (100.0) | 218.3 | 100.0 | 27,105[h] | 100.0 |

| GNP, per capita (units) | | | | | | | | | | | | | |
|---|---|---|---|---|---|---|---|---|---|---|---|---|---|
| 66,859 | — | 27,838 | — | 2,211 | — | 36,913 | — | 69,878 | — | 13,000 | — | 3,009 | — |
| Ratio: GNP/original NMP | | | | | | | | | | | | | |
| 1.24 | | 1.20 | | 1.29 | | 1.19 | | 1.28 | | 1.26[i] | | 1.32[h] | n.a. |
| Ratio: GNP/ adjusted NMP | | | | | | | | | | | | | |
| 1.29 | | 1.24 | | 1.25 | | 1.29 | | 1.29 | | 1.31 | | n.a. | n.a. |

*Note:* n.a. = not available. Parenthetical estimates are less firmly based.

a. Includes considerable amounts of what is really intermediate product that should be netted out, for example, services sold to material sectors, geological exploration, land melioration, fire protection, research and development (Campbell 1985, p. 20).

b. Nonmaterial services purchased by the material sectors.

c. Nonmaterial transport and communication (9.2 billion wage plus 5.3 billion operating surplus).

d. Sum of payments for nonmaterial services in the material sector of 22.3 billion; material cost of business travel of 5.9 billion; transfers to the nonmaterial sector or provision of free services for employees of 6.3 billion; and losses on stocks of 2.0 billion.

e. Subtract: (1) intermediate services to material production of 3.7 billion and (2) retail price and rental subsidy adjustment, to keep valuation consistently in market prices, of 18.1 billion, and add capital repairs of 1.5 billion.

f. Housing valued at established prices: 2.5 billion rent on state owned (1.7 billion square meters × 1.47 rubles) plus 1.7 billion imputed on privately owned (Campbell 1985).

g. The figure represents GDP. In the 1982 statistical yearbook of Hungary, the 1980 NMP was revised to 583, so that GDP also changes to 721. Because the country study of Hungary issued by the World Bank in 1984 reported the unrevised figures, however, the same data are used in this study for the sake of consistency.

h. Estimate based on components of GDP utilized at *market prices*, which differs from the GDP estimate for other countries scaled up from NMP at *established prices* because of the distorting effect of subsidies and indirect taxes on consumption.

i. Ratio of GNP at purchase prices (i.e., before the retail price and rental subsidy adjustment) of 236.4 to NMP at current prices of 187.1 (Collier 1985, table XII).

*Sources:* Studies commissioned for this project (see references).

19

cases. These are notably serious problems for Romania and the German Democratic Republic.

## Valuation

In centrally planned economies, prices are established administratively and satisfy neither the factor cost standard, which best reflects production potential, nor the welfare standard, which mirrors most accurately the contribution of goods and services to welfare. If the goal is to find a figure for total GNP valued in dollars, however, then distorted domestic prices will not be a serious problem if the most usable NCU/dollar conversion coefficient is based on established prices (that is, those charged to final users). In this case, all components of GNP should be valued at established prices rather than at prices adjusted to a factor cost or to some other standard. Relatively high prices put on certain goods or services mean, by definition, that relatively low prices are placed on other items. One problem, however, may be the inconsistent methods of imputation used to account for production that takes place outside the normal buyer-seller relationships and hence has no monetary value assigned to it. In CPEs, the prime examples are agricultural production consumed in kind and the rental value of owner-occupied housing. Countries are not always consistent in valuing these activities at prices at which equivalent goods or services are sold. If such problems are known to exist, they are flagged in the country studies, but it has not been proved possible to make comparable adjustments for all countries. Be that as it may, the acceptance in this book of NMP evaluated at established prices means that items added to or subtracted from NMP to derive GNP should also be valued at established prices. For determining the structure or the growth of GNP, however, adjusted factor cost prices consistently applied are preferable to established prices, and I have relied upon the former to the extent that they were available. There is no inconsistency between the two valuation standards as long as established prices are used to obtain only *total* GNP in national currency units.

## Special Earnings on Foreign Trade

In many ways, the treatment of foreign trade is the most complicated matter in CPE national accounts, making this a real problem sector for estimates or for interpretations when numbers are officially given.[2]

---

2. This section is based in part on Wolf (1985) and on discussions with Thomas Wolf, a project team member, and Jong-goo Park of the World Bank. Their help in clarifying the issues was a valuable contribution.

The following symbols should facilitate the explanation:

$T$ = Net value added in the foreign trade sector by CPEs using the "basic method" of treating foreign trade statistics (factor incomes generated by firms engaged in foreign trade plus "special earnings from foreign trade")

$T'$ = Net value added in the foreign trade sector by CPEs not using

$e_o$ = Official exchange rate

$B$ = Trade balance in domestic prices

$B_t^*$ = Trade balance valued in foreign currency prices

$B_t'$ = Trade balance at valuta prices, or $B_t^* \, e_o$

$\alpha$ = Internal exchange rate, or average ratio of exports and imports valued at domestic prices to their value in valuta prices

$\alpha_x$ = Internal export exchange rate, or average ratio of exports valued at domestic prices to their value in valuta prices

$\alpha_m$ = Internal import exchange rate, or average ratio of imports valued at domestic prices to their value in valuta prices.

The net value added in the foreign trade sector $(T)$ includes, in addition to the usual wage and other factor incomes generated at the firms engaged in foreign trade, "special earnings on foreign trade." (The German Democratic Republic is reportedly the only exception in that it includes only the first component.) Gross output of the foreign trade sector comprises two items. The first item is the value of imports less the value of exports, both in domestic prices $(B)$. The second item is the value of exports less the value of imports in foreign prices converted at the official exchange rate $(B')$. It is very important to note, however, that because domestic prices of CPE tradables are not in general equal to their foreign currency prices converted at the official exchange rate $(e_o)$ except in Hungary since 1976, the trade balance valued in domestic prices $(B_t)$ is usually different from the trade balance in valuta prices $(B_t')$, obtained from the foreign currency balance using $e_o$. The difference between the two balances $(B_t' - B_t)$ is the net "price equalization" tax (subsidy) collected from (paid to) the foreign trade organizations by the state budget.

A consensus was reached by our experts that the CPEs' so-called basic method of treating foreign trade in national income is conceptually equivalent to the system of national accounts, so that there is no bias and no need for adjustment.[3]

If trade is in balance in foreign currency (valuta) prices, the net price

3. Irrespective of the economic system, the gross output $(O)$ of the foreign trade sector *equals* the difference between export receipts from foreign importers $(X_t)$ and payments to the domestic producers of the exports $(X_d)$ *plus* the difference between sales of imports to

equalization will typically be a large positive number (Romania is an exception, probably because of the relatively low domestic prices of imports). This figure may be viewed as a measure of the "gain" from trade, as a tax on imports, or as the net outcome of distorted domestic prices, which is of relevance only for the state budget. From the standpoint of national income accounting, a positive amount on *balanced trade* should be considered a net tax (duty) on imports that, like the SNA, is properly included in GDP (Wolf 1985, p. 10). If a CPE treats it in this way in reporting NMP, there is no problem.

A CPE's departure from the "basic method"—examples include the German Democratic Republic, the U.S.S.R., Bulgaria, and until 1975 Romania—is likely to introduce a bias into net value added in foreign trade $(T')$. The bias is created when there is a trade balance in valuta prices $(B'_t)$ *and* the surplus is added to (or the deficit is subtracted from) "the difference between imports and exports evaluated at domestic prices" after multiplying by the "internal exchange rate" $(\alpha)$. (The terminology was introduced by van Brabant [1985], who explains it.) The result is the following bias in "net value added in the trade sector," as well as in NMP (and GNP scaled from NMP) vis-à-vis the SNA concept:

$$\text{If an export surplus: } T - T' = B'_t (\alpha_x - 1).$$
$$\text{If an import surplus: } T - T' = B'_t (\alpha_m - 1).$$

The extent of the bias will thus depend on the size of the valuta trade balance and the degree of distortion between domestic and foreign prices, indicated by the extent to which $\alpha_x$ or $\alpha_m$ differs from 1. In 1980, for example, the U.S.S.R. had a 5.2 billion valuta-ruble trade surplus. The latest year for which $\alpha_x$ was estimated for the U.S.S.R. is 1978, when it was 0.81 (Wolf 1985, p. 16). The bias in that year, in other words, was negligible—less than 0.2 percent of GNP $[(5.2)(-.19)/590]$—so that the GNP estimate of the country expert (Campbell 1985) could properly ignore

---

domestic users $(M_d)$ and payments to foreign exporters $(M_f)$. In other words,

$$
\begin{aligned}
O &= (X_f - X_d) + (M_d - M_f) \\
&= (X_f - M_f) - (X_d - M_d) \\
&= B'_t - B_t
\end{aligned}
$$

(according to the notation in the text). From this gross output, the trade sector pays out intermediate costs, such as transport and communication, as well as factor costs, such as wages and salaries, interests, and rents. The remainder will be gross profit from which depreciation of the capital stock should be set aside. Gross output, $B'_t - B_t$, in CPEs is generally called "price equalization" tax, or subsidy. If the government pays out all the operating costs for the foreign trade organizations, then it may tax away all of the gross output.

it. (For the derivation of the formula, see Singh and Park [1985, appendix 1]; for a more detailed discussion see Wolf [1985, pt. 3].)

## Adding Nonmaterial Services and Depreciation

The usual procedure for estimating the contribution of nonmaterial sectors is to begin with published figures on employment, average wages, and wage-type taxes (social security) to derive the wage bill, then add operating surplus in the form of profits and other types of accumulation as reported or as can best be estimated. The operating surplus component is usually the most difficult to obtain and so estimates can differ by wide margins on this item, although it is more likely to be understated than overstated.

Estimating the value of housing services is also highly problematic, first, because an imputed value must be assigned for the services of privately owned housing and, second, because a decision must be made as to what value should be put on housing, both public and private. In the case of the U.S.S.R, the country expert applied the average (highly subsidized) rent in state housing to an estimate of the stock of private and cooperative housing (Campbell 1985, pp. 16–21). In the case of Hungary, the central statistical office estimated the contribution of public and private housing services on the basis of cost, that is, adding the subsidies but excluding operating surplus (Central Statistical Office of Hungary 1982). Conceptually the first approach is correct, for reasons indicated in the discussion of valuation. For the other countries, procedures roughly comparable to one method or the other were followed, as could best be determined.

Depreciation is a very difficult item to establish, both conceptually and in practice. The key conceptual questions are the way in which depreciation should be computed and the extent to which the assets on which it is to be charged should be covered. The simplest and most satisfactory method would be to apply established depreciation rates to capital stock valued in current prices to bypass the difficult problem of determining the meaning of depreciation series obtained from enterprise balance sheet data, which reflect the changing acquisition prices of assets. As a practical matter, however, this is not the usual method. The estimates for the countries are based on depreciation amounts published, and the amounts are often reported without detailed explanation. With regard to coverage, SNA conformity requires that depreciation on the capital assets of the not directly productive (so-called budgetary) organizations be excluded (as is the case in the U.S.S.R.), whereas depreciation on collective farm assets and on privately and cooperatively owned housing must be added because

official data may not include it (as in the case of the U.S.S.R.). There are
further problems; for example, in some countries (such as the U.S.S.R.),
published depreciation has two components: a portion intended to finance
capital repairs and a portion meant to recover the original value of an
asset. The former should be considered an intermediate product and
should be disregarded. If a country using this method does not report
the components separately, however, or if there is no explanation of the
method used to compute the depreciation, the depreciation estimate might
be biased. It was surprising to find, therefore, that the shares of depreciation in the GNPs across the six countries did not vary a great deal,
ranging from a low of 8.6 percent to a high of 12.9 percent (there were
no data for Bulgaria), so that even, say, a 25 percent bias in depreciation
would bias the GNP estimate by only 2.5 percent.

## The Second Economy

In a CPE, the term "second economy" normally refers to the entire
range of private productive activities, taking the form predominantly of
agricultural production, housing construction, and the rendering of various
services. Most such activities are legal (although the extent of private
activities legally permitted varies by country) and should conceptually
be covered in official national income accounts, although measuring and
valuing them accurately may well be problematic. In addition to the legal
activities, a wide variety of illegal "production" also takes place and is
not covered in national income, but the same is also true of market-type
economies.

# Main Findings and Confidence in the Estimates

The NMPs and GNPs in national currency units of seven countries for
the benchmark year 1980 are presented in table 2-1. The country experts
carried out alternative GNP computations whenever it was necessary to
check their estimate and whenever it was possible to do so (for example,
for Czechoslovakia, the German Democratic Republic, and Poland). Each
evaluated its GNP estimate and the resulting GNP/NMP ratio against whatever comparable figures could be found in the publications of the country
(which in many cases showed only the end results of computations) and
against estimates prepared outside the country.
    The degree of confidence the country experts place in the GNP estimates
shown in table 2-1 range from "very high" for Hungary (the only CMEA
country whose central statistical office routinely publishes well-docu-

mented GNP computations and has worked with the central statistical
office of France on a joint, practical reconciliation of the two countries'
SNA and MPS accounts), to "good" for the U.S.S.R. and Czechoslovakia
(probably with ±5 percent error margins), to "somewhat problematic"
for Poland, Romania, and the German Democratic Republic (probably
within ±10 percent), to "problematic" for Bulgaria (the error margin
may exceed ±10 percent). The main problems in the case of Poland and
Romania are uncertain definitions and incomplete data for the adjustment
of NMP, plus the fact that 1980 was a year of some upheaval in Poland.
For the German Democratic Republic, an additional problem is its treatment of foreign trade, because a significant bias probably results from
the apparent disregard of "special earnings on foreign trade." In 1967
(the only year for which an estimate could be made), this omission caused
an estimated 3 percent downward bias in the NMP (Collier 1985, sec.
II-D). Given the increased importance of foreign trade for the German
Democratic Republic's economy since 1967, the bias could have been
higher in 1980. For Bulgaria, the main problem is the almost complete
absence of data on nonmaterial services, which were needed to scale up
NMP (it is calculated apparently following the standard MPS method except
in foreign trade), forcing the country experts to estimate GNP from highly
aggregated end use components whose coverage and valuation could not
be checked. One possible reason for the high GNP/NMP ratio for Bulgaria,
unlike the other countries, is that the depreciation is charged on replacement value rather than on cost, so depreciation could be significantly
higher.

The GNP/NMP ratios may be computed using the NMP published by
each country (table 2-1, row 1) or the NMP after adjustment (table 2-1,
row 3), which presumably improves cross-country comparability because
the definition of the NMP is more uniform. In the first instance, for six
of the countries, excluding Bulgaria, the 1980 GNP/original NMP ratios
ranged from 1.19 for Czechoslovakia to 1.28 for Poland, 1.24 being the
average. The GNP/adjusted NMP ratios ranged from 1.24 for Romania to
1.31 for the German Democratic Republic, 1.28 being the average. The
ratios tend to be somewhat higher for the more developed countries than
for the less developed countries. Poland's ratio may be relatively high in
part because the amount subtracted from NMP for nonmaterial services
purchased by the material sectors is low (0.8 percent of GNP versus 3
percent to 4 percent for the other countries) and partly also because the
ratio increases rapidly during an economic downturn and declines during
rapid expansion, inasmuch as the business cycle affects material production more than nonmaterial production (Fallenbuchl 1985, pp. 28–29).

For all of the East European countries, the GNP/NMP ratios are significantly lower than those obtained by the Research Project on National Income (Alton 1982), an important reason being the latter's factor cost imputations on housing and returns to land (see chapter 5).

It was possible to determine that, for the U.S.S.R., Hungary, and Czechoslovakia, the GNP/NMP ratios had changed little during the 1970s, whereas for Poland the ratio declined until 1977 and increased rapidly thereafter for the reasons mentioned. Insufficient information is available for the other countries to establish trends in the ratios.

Experimental computations published by the United Nations show estimates of NMP for eight market-type economies that use the SNA and estimates of GDP for two countries that use the MPS (United Nations 1981). The work was carried out in close collaboration with the central statistical offices of the participating countries. Unfortunately, most of the computations refer to data more than ten years old and include only one CMEA country, Hungary. Yugoslavia, the other MPS country included, cannot be considered a representative centrally planned economy. The GDP/NMP ratios resulting from these calculations (from United Nations 1981, table A) are listed below.

| Developed countries | | Developing countries | |
|---|---|---|---|
| United States | | Peru | |
| 1963 | 1.47 | 1969 | 1.195 |
| 1967 | 1.47 | Philippines | |
| United Kingdom | | 1961 | 1.22 |
| 1963 | 1.36 | 1965 | 1.27 |
| 1971 | 1.43 | Zambia | |
| 1972 | 1.44 | 1969 | 1.13 |
| Finland | | 1971 | 1.35 |
| 1965 | 1.37 | | |
| Austria | | MPS users | |
| 1964 | 1.265 | Hungary | |
| Japan | | 1972 | 1.195 |
| 1965 | 1.295 | 1976 | 1.193 |
| 1970 | 1.260 | Yugoslavia | |
| | | 1962 | 1.245 |
| | | 1970 | 1.292 |

The ratios differ considerably from country to country and, in some countries, also over time. The ratios tend to be significantly higher for the developed MTEs than for developing countries and the CPEs.

# Chapter 3

# *Converting GNP to Dollar Values*

Traditional centrally planned economies are characterized by comprehensive government controls over domestic price formation and resource allocation; exchange rates play a largely passive role. There is a sharp dichotomy between domestic prices and prices actually observed in foreign transactions. Also, there is a dual system of producer (wholesale) and consumer (retail) prices, with levels and structures that are kept apart by varied taxes and subsidies. For information, accounting, and planning purposes, CPEs tend to use a plethora of exchange rates and exchange-rate-type coefficients. Because it is the common practice of traditional CPEs not to revise such rates or coefficients for long periods, their values are often unrealistic. Each different exchange rate is applied to a segregated market, in which arbitrage occurs only to a limited extent. Some exchange rates may be determined in ways that are largely arbitrary or unique to the country.

Beginning in the 1960s, some CPEs began to introduce various kinds of economic reforms. These often involved reducing the number of exchange rates or coefficients, setting them at more realistic levels, and starting to use them as policy instruments in ways that in some respects resembled their function in MTEs. Most exchange rates, however, are still tailored to specific types of transactions and are realistic only at or near the time when they first become effective.

The next section of this chapter lists and explains briefly the main types of exchange rates and exchange-rate-type coefficients that are typically found in a CPE. The discussion will suggest in general terms which exchange rates might be appropriate and which would be clearly inappropriate to use for GNP conversion. I shall identify recent PPP computations carried out in the West that involve comparisons between CPEs and MTEs and explain very briefly the methods used. Country-specific detail on exchange rates and PPP-type computations will be provided, and I shall examine the conceptual and practical problems relating to the choice between using exchange rates or PPPs for GNP conversion. I shall then discuss the relationship between PPPs and exchange rates in general terms before estimating that relationship for CPEs. A last section will present the main conversion options, showing their implications for comparative per capita dollar GNP levels; assess their plausibility in a variety of ways; and identify the most realistic and feasible conversion option.

## Exchange Rates and Related Concepts in CPEs

The main concepts are: official exchange rates; internal exchange rates; foreign trade multipliers; commercial exchange rates; and noncommercial (tourist) exchange rates. Several other types of conversion coefficients may also be found in some CPEs, such as the exchange rates used in foreign currency shops, those used for private remittances, and of course the black market rates. These are described briefly in van Brabant (1985); they are not directly relevant for this project. Only exchange rates vis-à-vis convertible currencies are discussed; information on intra-CMEA exchange rates can be found in van Brabant (1985).[1]

### Official Exchange Rates

All CPEs established the gold parity of their currencies during the early postwar period and set the dollar exchange rates on that basis. The precise reasons for setting the gold parities remain obscure, and sources differ in their explanations. In at least some cases, however, gold parities were set to yield exchange rates to help achieve equilibrium in external payments or to reflect the PPP of the currency. Still, even if a country's initial exchange rates were so determined, after traditional central planning had been introduced, prices were set and changed independently of price movements in other countries. Thus the official exchange rates of CPEs became arbitrary and unrealistic by the standards used to evaluate the exchange rates in MTEs. The rates also remained unchanged during the 1960s except in the U.S.S.R. and Bulgaria, where new rates were introduced in 1961 and 1962, respectively. The response of the CPEs to the dollar devaluations of 1971 and 1973 and to the subsequent floating exchange rate system was unsynchronized. Most countries appreciated their official rates after 1971 and 1973, first to the dollar and more recently to an individually determined basket of currencies. Poland and

---

1. This section is based on van Brabant (1985). Van Brabant's many contributions to this project are gratefully acknowledged.

Romania kept their 1973 rates unchanged until 1978; the German Democratic Republic did so until 1979. During the past few years, CPEs have gradually switched over to frequent (monthly, biweekly, or weekly) exchange rate quotations against the main convertible currencies, with the German Democratic Republic and Romania being the exceptions.

Mention should be made of the so-called transferable ruble, which was created in 1964, when the CMEA's International Bank for Economic Cooperation was established. At that time, the rate of the transferable ruble was set equal to that of the Soviet domestic ruble, and its value has been maintained at approximately the same level ever since. The TR is emitted only in response to payment imbalances among the CMEA members. It is an artificial bookkeeping unit that plays practically no role in the CMEA countries' currency relations.

Technical details should not obscure the fact that, after central planning was introduced, the official exchange rates of the CPEs became, and in many cases still remain, arbitrary, notional rates with little economic content or practical significance. The first CPE to depart significantly from this pattern appears to have been the U.S.S.R., which in 1961 set a new official exchange rate that was apparently based on the ruble's PPP against the dollar. The U.S.S.R. employs this same rate for noncommercial (that is, tourist) transactions also, but otherwise the exchange rate still has little significance for economic decisions. Since the late 1960s, several East European countries have carried out exchange rate reforms of various kinds, as explained below, that have had lesser or greater significance for their economic decisionmaking.

## Internal Exchange Rates

Foreign trade transactions effected in external prices and converted to national currency units at the official exchange rate yield "devisa" (or valuta) national currency values, which differ from the values of the same transactions evaluated at domestic prices.[2] The internal exchange rate is a coefficient that relates ex post facto the domestic wholesale price of traded goods to their devisa price (that is, the foreign currency price converted at the official exchange rate). The IER is not always an annual number; sometimes it is computed as a multiyear average, and the year for which it is published may not be the year for which it is computed. The IERs may be intended partly to serve as guides for microeconomic decisions on exports and imports in those countries where reforms provide

2. The difference between the trade balance evaluated at devisa prices and at domestic prices is a component of "special earnings from foreign trade," discussed in chapter 2.

some flexibility for decisions by producing and trading enterprises. They also serve as a policy instrument for central planners in making investment and trade decisions; in addition, in some countries the IER is used in the formation of domestic prices. In either case, the IER may remain unchanged for years even though it will have become out of date. Hungary's IERs introduced in 1968, for example, were computed on the basis of the average price relations of traded goods in earlier years. The IERs so computed were then used to help set the foreign trade multiplier introduced in 1968, which remained unchanged for several years (van Brabant 1985, p. 15).

If the IERs were available for all CPEs or for a large subset, they *might* be used, in conjunction with the official exchange rates, to convert GNP or a segment of GNP (that is, producer goods) to dollars, after adjustments for shifts in a CPE's domestic wholesale and foreign trade prices that had occurred since the reference base. To be sure, difficult conceptual problems would remain even then, as we shall see.

### Foreign Trade Multiplier

The foreign trade multiplier is a coefficient that relates the domestic wholesale price directly to the foreign currency price ex post facto; that is, it is a proxy exchange rate. (The term's meaning in this context is not to be confused with its meaning in the general international trade literature, where it refers to the expansion in income associated with an increase in exports.) Thus, once the internal exchange rate is known, the FTM can easily be calculated by multiplying the internal exchange rate by the official exchange rate. Because the FTM relates domestic wholesale prices to foreign prices obtained or paid in the country's external trade transactions, however, it cannot be used for converting local currency GNP, which is not evaluated in wholesale prices. Once computed, the FTM, too, may remain unchanged for years, although in some cases it will be adjusted to reflect changes in the official exchange rate, which in turn are generally based on changes in the external value of the dollar in terms of other convertible currencies. Thus, much like the IER, the FTM accurately reflects the ratio of domestic prices to dollar foreign trade prices only in the base year. If the FTM were to be used as a conversion coefficient, it too should be adjusted for changes that have occurred since the base year in domestic and foreign trade prices. If the IER and the FTM have the same base year, then the IER multiplied by the official exchange rate yields the FTM; in other years that relationship is only more or less valid.

*Commercial Exchange Rates*

Three CPEs quote commercial exchange rates publicly: Romania since 1973, Hungary since 1976, and Poland since 1980. At the time these rates were introduced, in Romania and Hungary they were based directly on the FTM. In Poland the rate is based on the FTM, with a fixed premium added. The commercial exchange rates initially reflected some realistic ratio between domestic wholesale and foreign trade prices for the pattern of trade prevailing in the socialist and nonsocialist groups of countries, respectively, in the base year. Thus the commercial exchange rate may in fact at first be calculated in the same way as the FTM. In countries where trade decisions are partly decentralized, however, the commercial exchange rates, as introduced or as subsequently changed, may be undervalued to help improve the balance of payments. (Such undervaluation is more likely for dollar than for ruble trade in view of the fact that ruble trade can be regulated less through price incentives and that transferable ruble deficits are more desirable than transferable ruble surpluses in intra-CMEA trade.) In any event, we typically find that the commercial exchange rates (and the FTMs) "depreciate" the commercial ruble vis-à-vis the commercial dollar in comparison with the ruble/dollar cross-rates implied by the official exchange rates. Because the domestic price ratios, trade patterns, and commercial exchange rate policies of CPEs differ, however, the ruble/dollar cross-exchange rates implied by each country's commercial exchange rates or FTMs will not be identical.

Since Western currencies began floating, the three CPEs' commercial exchange rates vis-à-vis Western currencies have been changed periodically to reflect movements in the value of the Western currency basket to which the CPE currency is tied; a CPE's commercial exchange rates may also be altered for policy reasons.

*Noncommercial (Tourist) Exchange Rates*

Noncommercial exchange rates are used mainly for tourism, personal remittances, and certain other invisible transactions. The rates may be published as official noncommercial exchange rates or as premiums or surcharges on the official exchange rates. They are often defined ambiguously and are rarely applied uniformly to all persons and types of transactions (for example, the residents of some countries may have to pay as much as 150 percent more than the rate given to Western tourists to obtain convertible currency for tourism). Nonetheless, even in a CPE the noncommercial exchange rate for Western tourists must approximate in some rough and ready way the purchasing power parity of the country's currency for a tourist basket of goods and services. Such computations are indeed said to serve as points of departure for determining the rate in a base period, although the rates may not be set at the PPP level. The reason is that political and economic attitudes will influence the rates favorably if the country wants to encourage the inflow of Western tourists and unfavorably if the country wants to discourage tourism. In 1974, I compared intra-CMEA tourist exchange rates (which in the 1960s were known to be set on the basis of PPPs) with tourist exchange rates for the West and found that, in 1970 (latest year for which calculations could be made), Bulgaria, Hungary, and Romania appeared to provide substantial "incentives," whereas Czechoslovakia, Poland, the German Democratic Republic, and the U.S.S.R. seemed to offer smaller or no incentives, and possibly even disincentives, to Western tourists (Marer and Tilley 1974). Furthermore, since countries are known to change policies, a fact in 1970 may no longer be one in 1980. Moreover, a commercial exchange rate may gradually become an incentive or a disincentive rate if domestic and foreign price levels and ratios change significantly while the exchange rate remains fixed.

Even if a country's noncommercial exchange rate were set to reflect the PPP of a tourist basket of goods and services, it would not be a good rate for GNP conversion, first, because the expenditure patterns of tourists are very different from those of residents and, second, because the retail prices of goods and services need not have the same relationship to wholesale prices in centrally planned economies as in market-type economies, as we shall see in chapter 4. Nevertheless, the tourist exchange rates are useful reference points in the spectrum of exchange rates and conversion coefficients available for each country.

## Conclusions

The discussion of exchange rates and exchange-rate-type coefficients in this section may be summarized in three points. First, CPEs have a bewildering variety of exchange rates and related concepts; in effect, they have multiple exchange rate systems. Second, as a rule, exchange rates do not link domestic and foreign prices directly. Even in countries that have introduced commercial exchange rates on the basis of the ratio of domestic prices to foreign prices for goods actually traded in a base period, there is no arbitrage in the foreign exchange or goods markets. Thus exchange rates do not serve the same function that they do in MTEs. To be sure, there are important similarities between a typical CPE and the MTE developing countries that impose extensive controls on domestic prices, exchange rates, and external trade transactions. Third, the exchange rates of most CPEs do not reflect a continuously realistic relationship between domestic and foreign prices of selected transactions even if the rates did correctly reflect the indicated relationship when they were initially determined.

The main conclusion suggested by these findings is that none of the exchange rates or coefficients commends itself as the appropriate one for GNP dollar conversion for *all* countries. Whether any particular rate may be acceptable for one CPE or for a subgroup of CPEs for converting GNP, or a component of GNP, must be determined for each country individually.

## Computations of Purchasing Power Parity Involving Several CPEs and MTEs

This section summarizes the methods and data availability of PPP studies that involve several centrally planned and market-type economies, providing background for the more detailed country-specific discussion in subsequent sections. The most important study is the International Comparison Project, which in its third phase included detailed PPP computations for 1975 for GNP and components for Hungary, Romania, and Poland, along with thirty market-type economies plus Yugoslavia (Kravis et al. 1982). A brief mention will also be made of the PPP computations for consumer goods and services routinely carried out by the central statistical office of the Federal Republic of Germany for sixty countries, including Hungary, Poland, Czechoslovakia, and the U.S.S.R., and the United Nations' cost-of-living comparisons between New York City and cities in nearly 150 countries where United Nations personnel live, including Bulgaria, Czechoslovakia, Hungary, Poland, Romania, and Cuba. To be sure, the results of the various studies have different probable error margins, so that caution must be exercised in comparing them. The results of bilateral PPP comparisons between individual centrally planned and market-type economies are discussed in the next section.

### Methodology of the International Comparison Project

The purpose of the International Comparison Project was to devise a method for comparing the GDPs and the GDP components of countries more reliably than had been possible either with exchange rate conversions or with bilateral PPP comparisons where the resulting dollar values (and the cardinal ranking of countries) are partly a function of the reference country chosen and its dollar exchange rate with the numeraire country, usually the United States.

By 1983 the International Comparison Project had completed three phases. They differ in terms of the number of countries included in the comparisons (ten in Phase I, sixteen in Phase II, and thirty-four in Phase III) and significantly in terms of methodology, which has continued to evolve, so that the results from one phase to the next may differ, sometimes by substantially more than can be explained by revision of the data. Early in 1984, as this study was being readied for publication, the results of Phase IV, covering about seventy countries and applying a methodology substantially different from those used earlier, became available, and they will be noted briefly here.

The ICP's approach involves making volume comparisons by means of price and expenditure comparisons. In Phase III, each country's price comparisons are made for carefully specified goods and services. The price data are established jointly by each country's central statistical office and the ICP team, whose standardized item specifications are priced after taking quality into account, sometimes after inspection of items in shops, testing of samples, and correspondence with the authorities to resolve queries. A key innovation is the computation of "international prices"— quantity-weighted averages of detailed PPPs. In the "international" price system developed in Phase III, each participating country's prices help form "international" prices by categories of GDP, weighted by the share in world GDP of those countries for which the sample country is considered to be "representative." "International" prices are thus heavily weighted by the prices of the developed countries, a fact that in the view of many experts presents problems when the "international" prices are applied to developing countries. The "international dollar" has the same purchasing power over the U.S. gross domestic product as a whole that the U.S. dollar does, but its purchasing power over individual categories is different, being determined by the structure of international prices. An especially difficult problem is the international comparison of education, health care, and government. Alternative ways of valuing these services were tried that, while often yielding substantial differences in the quantity comparisons, had only a small impact on overall GDP estimates.

For each country, category quantities (obtained by dividing category PPPs into category expenditures) can be summed to determine total GDP or any of 151 subaggregates. In principle, the quantity of each good is valued at the average international price. The ICP also found that, except for the most highly developed countries (those of the Organisation for Economic Co-operation and Development), the PPPs it obtained for MTEs were significantly lower than their exchange rates. That is, although country $X$'s exchange rate may be, say, thirty NCUs per dollar, the International Comparison Project may calculate its PPP as twenty NCUs per dollar, yielding an exchange rate deviation index of 1.5 (30/20). I shall discuss the reasons for the systematic deviation between PPPs and exchange rates shortly.

Phase IV is proceeding somewhat differently from the earlier phases. Instead of grouping together all countries in the sample, it has set up independent groups of countries that are not too dissimilar in their economic structures and consumption patterns and is carrying out ICP-type computations independently for each group; the groups will be linked together later. There are valid theoretical as well as organizational and financial reasons for this new approach, especially as the number of countries in the ICP increases in Phase IV to about seventy nations. For the participating European countries, Phase IV is carried out under the auspices of the Conference of European Statisticians of the Statistical Commission of the United Nations (Economic Commission for Europe 1983). In Europe, two groups were formed. Group I covered twelve West European countries.[3] Group II comprised Austria, Finland, Hungary, Poland, Romania, and Yugoslavia, but because Romania withdrew before the computations were completed, Group II now covers five countries only. So that the two groups can be linked, Austria is also participating in Group I as a "bridge" country. The work of the two groups is known as the European Comparison Program.

The methods employed by the ECP differ further from ICP's earlier phases by (1) increasing the number of commodity groups from 151 to more than 300; (2) relying on more detailed specifications of the goods and services to be priced in the different categories; and (3) expending greater efforts to improve comparability through adjustments, as appropriate, for differences in product quality; and (4) employing alternative methods of linking two groups—simply using Austria as the bridge while keeping the original group results unchanged or, alternatively, merging the two groups by using the prices of all seventeen countries to obtain price weights. Because the structure of international average prices is very different in the two groups, the results of the alternative linking are quite different. The first method provides a satisfactory basis only for aggregate volume comparison; for detailed structure and price comparisons the alternative method is preferable.

## Is There a Systematic Bias in ICP Computations for CPEs?

The experts from Hungary and Poland participating in the second workshop, as well as other people with whom we have talked in Hungary,

---

3. They were the Federal Republic of Germany, France, Italy, the Netherlands, Belgium, Luxembourg, the United Kingdom, Ireland, Denmark, Greece, Spain, and Portugal, with Austria as the thirteenth, "bridge" country.

Romania, and Poland, believe that the ICP Phase III results (Phase IV computations were not available at the time) are strongly biased, that is, that the ICP yields fewer national currency units per dollar than it should, so that the resulting per capita dollar GDPs are upward biased. There are said to be two main reasons. First, in the view of the program's critics, the ICP did not sufficiently take into account the relatively poor quality and availability of CPE products and services. Second, the price inputs were based mainly on official price lists and on the prices of goods sold in state retail outlets at fixed prices. In reality, a certain percentage of goods is sold, especially in the consumer sector, at much higher prices on the officially sanctioned free market and the illegal black markets. The results of bilateral PPP computations, such as those between Austria and Poland, yield NCU/dollar ratios significantly higher than those derived by the ICP because they reflect more accurately quality differences and because, some specialists claim, the comparisons involved much greater detail and effort. Other observers note that, even though these arguments might have merit, we must be cautious in making judgments about any kind of bias. In any event, however, the issue is whether there is a bias *relative* to many less developed and moderately developed MTEs.

Kravis and Heston, two of the principal architects of the ICP, discussed these issues during the project's workshops. They explained the safeguards that were built into the program precisely to avoid the kinds of biases with which the ICP has been charged. First, the ICP's product specialists had many years of experience in a large number of countries that provided a basis on which to make informed judgments about the technical parameters and the quality of a CPE's products. Second, the prices were supplied by the authorities of the CPEs themselves, and therefore they cannot reasonably argue that either the price or expenditure data incorporated are biased. Third, the architects of the ICP are not certain that their results are downward biased, because prices on the private markets may not have been properly factored into the computations. The ICP asked each country to provide the average national price of each specified item across all markets and outlets. The ICP also stressed the need to embody in the corresponding expenditure figure the same average price that was provided for purposes of price comparison. For a quantity to be exaggerated, the price would thus have to *exclude* the private market component, and the expenditure figure would have to *include* the value of transactions on the private markets. Even if such were the case, as some observers claim that it may have been in Poland, the magnitude of the error would be modest. If, for example, 15 percent of Polish GDP were purchased at double the ICP prices and were included in net material product at actual (high private market) expenditures, the

1975 PPP of 14.3 (see table 3-8 and subsequent discussion) would increase only to 15.4. Finally, Kravis noted further, no method—PPP, exchange rate, or physical indicators—reflects the adverse welfare effect of shortages and queuing. The different methods measure the bundle of GDP that each country gets, with varying but unmeasured degrees of ease in shopping.

It was noted by various workshop participants that, for systemic reasons, the goods and services produced in CPEs tend to have shortcomings relating to technical aspects and to quality that may not be readily apparent upon first examination, even to an expert. Moreover, specialists from the CPEs who are knowledgeable about the details of their country's participation in the ICP observed that, at the time the data were gathered, there may have been a tendency on the part of their experts to answer questions calling for judgment (such as whether a product should be considered of high, medium, or poor quality) in such a way as to introduce an upward bias in quality basically for reasons of national pride. Moreover, when the data for the ICP were gathered, between 1970 and 1975, spokesmen in at least some countries were inclined to highlight tendencies stressing the country's economic achievements and understating its problems. This climate may have worked to reinforce the bias resulting from national pride. To put it bluntly, the authorities were unaware at the time of how upward bias could backfire if the results of the ICP computations to establish dollar per capita GDP levels were used as criteria for decisions about granting trade preferences or access to loans on attractive terms. It has also been noted that, to the experts from CPEs, the ICP procedures were like a "black box": the experts answered the questions put to them but had no opportunity to discuss the preliminary results and computation procedures until years later, when they were presented with the final results, by which time it was difficult for them to identify the precise source of the bias, both because of the lapse of time and also because of their unfamiliarity with the data processing and manipulating procedures, which they viewed as complicated.

The consensus of the participants in the two workshops was that it will not be possible for this project to resolve the debate or to quantify the ICP's presumed bias.

## Intertemporal Extrapolations of PPP Data

There are two basic methods of extrapolating ICP or other PPP data over time. One is to extrapolate the benchmark PPP on the basis of the relative price movements between the country in question and the numeraire country and then to use the extrapolated PPP to convert the GDP of the country in question, expressed in current national currency units, to dollars (or whatever serves as the numeraire currency). The other method is to extrapolate the benchmark GDP in dollars directly by the real GDP growth rate of the country in question. Both methods are subject to the error that may arise from not incorporating changes in international relative prices. Still, the first method better reflects the changes in relative prices in the country in question and in the numeraire country than the second method; therefore the first method is used in this study wherever PPP extrapolations are made.

### West German Comparisons of Cost of Living

Since the mid-1950s, the central statistical office of the Federal Republic of Germany has calculated the PPP of the deutschmark against the currencies of about sixty countries for a basket of consumer goods and services of a typical private household in the Federal Republic in 1970 and, alternatively in some cases, also according to the weights of the other country's consumer price index, and the average. The computations are generally based not on the official price lists of the other country but on standardized surveys periodically carried out by the central statistical office, using personnel from its embassies and private persons. The sample consists of between 200 and 300 items. Valuation tries to take cognizance of quality differences between the German products and those of the country surveyed (Statistisches Bundesamt 1980); how often the sample is changed and repriced is not indicated. The U.S.S.R., Czechoslovakia, Hungary, and Poland are the CPEs covered; the results for the individual CPEs are given below, by country. The most probable purpose of these collections is to make cost-of-living comparisons to provide the basis for post allowances to diplomats in the various countries. The list of goods and the outlets in which they are priced are therefore those appropriate for people with significantly higher income levels than the average for the local population. Moreover, some of the price data are apparently gathered by the persons whose post allowance may be affected by the results. For these reasons, and also because of the much smaller scale of effort by the German central statistical office in terms of manpower skilled in making such comparisons, the results are likely to have much wider error margins than those obtained by the ICP. This difference should be taken into account when the results of the various studies are juxtaposed and interpreted.

### United Nations Comparisons of Cost of Living

The United Nations periodically surveys the cost of living in New York City and nearly 150 cities around the world for a basket of goods and services typical of the pattern of consumption of United Nations personnel (see the *Monthly Bulletin of Statistics*). Two indexes are computed, one including housing, the other excluding housing. Because the basket differs from that of the indigenous population in the countries surveyed, because New York City prices are not fully representative of U.S. prices, and because the other problems mentioned in the previous paragraph probably apply to the United Nations comparisons also, the indexes will not accurately reflect the relationship between consumer prices in the United States and consumer prices in the countries surveyed. Cities in Bulgaria, Czechoslovakia, Hungary, Poland, Romania, and Cuba have been included in the survey. The results appear in the next section, by country.

## Exchange Rates and Purchasing Power Parities, by Country

### U.S.S.R.

Table 3-1 juxtaposes five sets of conversion coefficients for the U.S.S.R. Column 1 shows the official exchange rate, which in the Soviet case is the same as the noncommercial rate, annually between 1961 and 1981. The Soviet Union introduced a new exchange rate in 1961 (0.9 ruble = $1.00), which, according to an authoritative Hungarian source, was based on the dollar PPP of the ruble at the time, using Soviet quantity weights (Botos 1980, p. 1082). The more customary geometric average of Soviet and U.S. weights, had it been used, would have *raised* the exchange rate (that is, there would have been more rubles per dollar). Soviet computations were for material production only; the inclusion of services would have *lowered* the ruble/dollar ratio. To some extent, at least, the two biases thus offset each other. The official exchange rate remained unchanged until 1972, when the ruble began first to appreciate and then to change roughly in accordance with the international exchange rate of the U.S. dollar.

Columns 2 and 3 show, respectively, the average ruble cost of earning one dollar's worth of foreign exchange in exports and the weighted average ratio of domestic and foreign prices of imports (the "foreign trade multiplier," in our terminology) for total, not convertible, currency trade. These figures were computed in the West (Treml and Kostinsky 1982). The very large—in recent years almost two-and-a-half-fold—difference between the FTM calculated for exports and for imports results from the arbitrary nature of relative prices in the Soviet economy, that

Table 3-1. U.S.S.R.: Ruble/Dollar Exchange Rates and Purchasing Power Parities, 1961, 1970–81

| Year | Official exchange rate (1) | Foreign trade multipliers Exports[a] (2) | Foreign trade multipliers Imports[b] (3) | Soviet-computed PPP for NMP, Soviet weights (4) | PPP computed by the United States for GNP Soviet weights (5) | PPP computed by the United States for GNP U.S. weights (6) | PPP computed by the United States for GNP Geometric average (7) | PPP computed by the Federal Republic of Germany for private consumption Soviet weights (8) | PPP computed by the Federal Republic of Germany for private consumption Fed. Rep. weights (9) | PPP computed by the Federal Republic of Germany for private consumption Geometric average (10) |
|---|---|---|---|---|---|---|---|---|---|---|
| 1961 | 0.90 | | | (0.90) | | | | | | |
| 1970 | 0.90 | 1.79 | 2.36 | 0.76 | | | | 0.85 | 1.11 | 0.97 (0.85)[c] |
| 1971 | 0.90 | 1.50 | 2.36 | | | | | 0.77 | 1.01 | 0.88 |
| 1972 | 0.82 | 1.40 | 2.36 | | | | | 0.67 | 0.88 | 0.77 |
| 1973 | 0.74 | 1.28 | 2.44 | | | | | 0.52 | 0.68 | 0.59 |
| 1974 | 0.76 | 1.12 | 2.21 | | | | | 0.48 | 0.62 | 0.55 |
| 1975 | 0.72 | 0.95 | 2.04 | | | | | 0.43 | 0.56 | 0.49 (0.57)[c] |
| 1976 | 0.75 | 0.88 | 2.12 | 0.62 (0.41)[b] | 0.40 | 0.60 | 0.49 | 0.42 | 0.55 | 0.48 |
| 1977 | 0.74 | 0.82 | 2.16 | 0.60 | | | | 0.37 | 0.48 | 0.42 |
| 1978 | 0.68 | 0.81 | 2.27 | | | | | 0.32 | 0.41 | 0.36 |
| 1979 | 0.66 | | | | | | | 0.28 | 0.36 | 0.32 (0.45)[c] |
| 1980 | 0.65 | | | | | | (1.40)[d] | | | |
| 1981 | 0.72 | | | | | | | | | |

Note: Parentheses indicate that an alternative convertor was used to obtain the ruble/dollar ratio. Blanks mean no information was available.

a. Western computed for all trade.

b. Weighted average of Soviet-computed PPP for net material product, Soviet weights, and United States-computed PPP for services, Soviet weights (Campbell 1985, p. 28).

c. Converted at the ICP-based rate.

d. Moved to 1980 by multiplying by the ratio of U.S.S.R. to U.S. GNP deflators, U.S.S.R. GNP deflator estimated as the difference between GNP growth in current prices (Campbell 1985, table 6) and in constant prices (U.S.S.R. 1982, table A-1).

Sources: Column 1: time-weighted average of official quotations reported in Ekonomiceskaja gazeta, shown in van Brabant (1985, table 2); columns 2 and 3: Treml and Kostinsky (1982, p. 15); Campbell (1985); columns 4–7: Campbell 1985, table 6) and in constant prices (U.S.S.R. 1982, table A-1). columns 8–10: Statistisches Bundesamt (1981), converted to dollars at the dollar/DM rate shown in Havlik and Levcik (1985, table 19, row 5).

is, from the relatively high Soviet domestic prices of manufactured goods, which compose much of the U.S.S.R.'s imports, and the relatively low domestic prices of energy and raw materials (especially after the 1973 price explosion on the world market), which compose much of the U.S.S.R.'s exports. This combination of very low domestic prices and very high foreign prices of Soviet exports yields an FTM in exports that in recent years is closer to PPP than it is for the countries of Eastern Europe.

Column 4 shows the implied results of the Soviet's own PPP computations. Until 1977, Soviet statistical yearbooks reported the dollar value of Soviet national income "in accordance with relative prices," using Soviet quantity weights. The parenthetical number shown for 1961 indicates that the new official exchange rates introduced in that year were probably based on PPP computations like those that produced the results shown in column 1. The number in parentheses for 1976 was computed by Campbell (1985) by combining the Soviet PPP for net material product and the PPP for services computed by the United States.

Columns 5–7 report the Central Intelligence Agency's purchasing power parity computations for GNP, showing the differences resulting from using Soviet or U.S. weights. It is striking that in table 3-1 the Soviets' own PPP computations, adjusted for differences in coverage, are very close to the U.S. results with Soviet quantity weights for the benchmark year 1976. To obtain results comparable to those of the International Comparison Project, we would admittedly want to use the geometric average of Soviet and U.S. weights shown in column 5, which has been moved to 1980 via Soviet and U.S. price indexes.

The last three columns present the ruble/dollar PPP for private consumption, based on the computations of the central statistical office of the Federal Republic of Germany. It is again striking how much the results for 1976 conform with the results of other PPP computations.

### Bulgaria

Table 3-2 presents the rather meager information available for Bulgaria. The country introduced a new official exchange rate in 1962 (1.17 leva = $1.00; prior to that date the exchange rate was lower, 7.56 leva = $1.00; Marer 1972, p. 346) without explaining (as far as I know) the basis for the new parity. That Bulgaria was the only East European country altering currency parities in the early 1960s—exactly one year after a similar change had been made in the U.S.S.R.—suggests that Bulgaria, following the Soviet lead, may have based its official rate on some PPP computation. (On the other hand, Bulgaria uses a different exchange rate for Western tourists, unlike the U.S.S.R.)

Table 3-2. *Bulgaria: Leva/Dollar Exchange Rates and Purchasing Power Parities, 1970–81*

| Year | Official exchange rate (1) | Foreign trade multiplier Exports (2) | Foreign trade multiplier Imports (3) | Tourist (noncommercial) exchange rate (4) | UN cost-of-living index Including housing[a] (5) | UN cost-of-living index Excluding housing[a] (6) |
|---|---|---|---|---|---|---|
| 1970 | 1.170 | 1.76[b] | 1.82[b] | 2.000 | | |
| 1971 | 1.170 | | 2.000 | | | |
| 1972 | 1.078 | | 1.843 | | | |
| 1973 | 0.988 | | 1.689 | | | |
| 1974 | 0.970 | | 1.574 | | | |
| 1975 | 0.969 | | 1.161 | 1.13 | 1.04 | |
| 1976 | 0.966 | | 0.966 | 1.10 | 1.02 | |
| 1977 | 0.948 | | 0.948 | 0.99 | 0.92 | |
| 1978 | 0.892 | | 1.024 | 0.96 | 0.90 | |
| 1979 | 0.865 | | 1.298 | 0.92 | 0.87 | |
| 1980 | 0.857 | (1.12)[c] | (1.16)[c] | 1.286 | 0.85 | 0.82 |
| 1981 | 0.922 | | 1.383 | 0.92 | 0.98 | |

*Note:* Parentheses indicate estimated figures. Blanks mean no information was available.

a. Housing consists of rent, utilities, and service.

b. Calculated for total exports and imports, that is, predominantly ruble-denominated transactions.

c. Estimated by moving 1970 data via the state retail price index (a proxy for the GNP deflator) and the U.S. GNP deflator.

*Sources:* Column 1: van Brabant (1985), table 2; columns 2 and 3 computed from values shown in domestic prices (United Nations 1980) divided by the values shown in devisa-leva prices in various issues of the Bulgarian statistical yearbooks (*Statisticheski godishnik na narodna republika bulgaria*), multiplied by the official exchange rate; column 4: van Brabant (1985, table 4); columns 5 and 6: calculated on the basis of the exchange rate and index, shown in *Monthly Bulletin of Statistics*, various issues.

The tourist exchange rates shown in column 4 were computed on the basis of the announced premiums over the official exchange rate. The premium was 70 percent during the early 1970s; in November 1974 it was reduced to 23.7 percent; a year later it was abolished altogether; and in June 1978 it was reintroduced at 50 percent (van Brabant 1985, p. 47b). These moves cannot be explained by fluctuations in Bulgarian domestic or West European consumer prices.

The FTMs shown in columns 2 and 3 are based on information available for 1970 on Bulgaria's total exports and imports evaluated in domestic leva and at devisa leva. Their ratio yields the internal exchange rate, which, multiplied by the official leva/dollar exchange rate, gives the foreign trade multiplier, conceptually a proxy for the commercial exchange rate. Because the FTM is computed on Bulgaria's total, not Western, trade, however, and about 75 percent of the total was with other CPEs (mostly with the U.S.S.R.), it is almost certainly significantly downward biased as a proxy for the dollar FTM. Around 1970, about half of Bulgaria's intra-CMEA trade was composed of manufactured goods (Marer 1972, pp. 80, 104) whose prices, especially those of machinery, were higher than West-West prices and were considerably higher than East-West prices for similar goods. In other words, the 1970 devisa leva figures are higher, and the internal exchange rates and the FTMs lower, than they would be if only trade with the West were included. The 1970 FTMs were moved to 1980 by the official state retail price index for Bulgaria and by the GNP deflator for the United States. Inasmuch as official consumer price indexes in CPEs tend to be downward biased, on that account, too, the estimated 1980 FTMs are downward biased. Bulgaria's 1980 FTMs therefore cannot be compared directly with the FTMs or the commercial exchange rates of the other countries.

Columns 5 and 6 are based on the United Nations' cost-of-living computations for 1981; if U.S. dollars were converted to levas at the official (not tourist) exchange rate, the cost of living for a basket of goods and services, including housing, typically consumed by United Nations personnel would have been the same in Sofia as in New York City; if housing were excluded, it would have been 6 percent higher.

In sum, without a great deal more information on Bulgaria's domestic prices or more comprehensive PPP computations, it is not possible to suggest a meaningful coefficient to convert Bulgaria's GNP to dollar values. There is no information as to how the official exchange rate was determined; the tourist rate has been moved up and down independently of Bulgaria's consumer price index; and the known FTM is for total trade and is available for 1970 only.

Table 3-3. *Czechoslovakia: Crown/Dollar Exchange Rates and Purchasing Power Parities, 1970–81*

| Year | Official exchange rate (1) | FTM (exports) (2) | Tourist (noncommercial) exchange rate | | Purchasing power parities for consumer goods and services | | UN cost-of-living index | |
|---|---|---|---|---|---|---|---|---|
| | | | A (3) | B (4) | By country experts[a] (5) | By CSO of Federal Republic of Germany[b] (6) | Including housing (7) | Excluding housing (8) |
| 1970 | 7.20 | 28.70 | 16.20 | 16.09 | 8.98 | 12.70 (11.10)[c] | | |
| 1971 | 7.20 | | 16.20 | 15.49 | 7.75 | 11.46 | | |
| 1972 | 6.61 | | 14.90 | 14.82 | 7.77 | 9.88 | | |
| 1973 | 5.86 | | 13.26 | 13.04 | 7.75 | 7.74 | | |
| 1974 | 5.86 | | 10.25 | 10.86 | 7.71 | 7.06 | | |
| 1975 | 5.58 | | 9.77 | 10.56 | 7.67 (7.59)[c] | 6.38[c] | 9.07 | 9.00 |
| 1976 | 5.77 | | 10.11 | 9.27 | 7.60 | 6.29 | 9.00 | 8.86 |
| 1977 | 5.67 | | 9.92 | 8.87 | 7.51 | 5.65 | 8.54 | 8.43 |
| 1978 | 5.43 | | 9.48 | 8.60 | 7.39 | 4.85 | 8.27 | 8.38 |
| 1979 | 5.32 | | 9.31 | 8.48 | 7.11 | 4.39 | 8.01 | 8.33 |
| 1980 | 5.38 | (19.23) | 9.40 | 10.53 | 6.91 (7.86)[c] | 4.27 (5.85)[c] | 7.73 | 8.35 |
| 1981 | 5.89 | | 10.29 | | | | 7.33 | 8.26 |

*Note:* Parentheses indicate estimates or alternative computations. Blanks mean no information was available.

a. Geometric average of Austrian and Czechoslovak weights.

b. Federal Republic weights.

c. Converted at the ICP-based rate.

*Sources:* Column 1: Havlik and Levcik (1985, table 19, row 1); column 2, 1970: *Politicka ekonomie* (1974, p. 744), moved to 1980 by Czech and U.S. price deflators, the former estimated by the country experts (Havlik and Levcik 1985, pp. 25–26); column 3: computed by applying the premiums to the official exchange rate (van Brabant 1985, table 4); column 4: Kcs/Austrian schilling rate converted at the prevailing schilling/dollar rate (Havlik and Levcik 1985, table 19, row 8); columns 5 and 6: Havlik and Levcik (1985, table 19); columns 7–8: calculated on the basis of the exchange rate and index shown in *Monthly Bulletin of Statistics*, March 1982, special table P.

## Czechoslovakia

Table 3-3 documents the exchange rate and PPP series available for Czechoslovakia. The official exchange rate can be found in column 1; the FTM for the year 1970 alone, culled from a journal article, in column 2. The FTM was moved to 1980 by a coefficient whose numerator is the country's consumer price index (Havlik and Levcik 1985), the denominator the U.S. GNP deflator. Columns 3 and 4 present two tourist exchange rate series. The first was computed directly by applying the compulsory tourist premium to the official exchange rate with the dollar; the second indirectly, by converting the tourist exchange rate with Austria to dollars at the prevailing schilling/dollar rate. The two series differ, owing to fluctuations in the said rate.

Columns 5 and 6 present two PPP computations for consumer goods and services. The first one was computed by the country experts, on the basis of a comparison of Austrian and Czechoslovak prices, the second by the central statistical office of the Federal Republic of Germany. The two series are compared in some detail in table 3-4, showing the Kcs/dollar PPPs derived under alternative assumptions from bilateral comparisons between Czechoslovakia and Austria (top) and Czechoslovakia and the Federal Republic of Germany (bottom). The comparison with Austria uses 1980 as the benchmark year. On the basis of prices taken from the official statistics of the two countries, supplemented by estimates of some missing Czechoslovak prices, a total of 130 items were priced, with occasional adjustments for quality differences. A geometric average of PPPs weighted by Austrian and Czechoslovak expenditure patterns yielded an exchange rate of approximately 0.5 Kcs = 1 AS. Converted at the official AS/dollar rate of 13.81, this formula yields the benchmark Kcs/dollar estimate of 6.91; at the ICP's AS/dollar rate of 15.80, it gives 7.86.[4]

The benchmark estimates may be backdated to 1975 by one of three methods to reflect price changes in Czechoslovakia, Austria, and the United States. The first method moves the Kcs/AS rate by the Czechoslovak inflation rate estimated by the country experts (higher than the official rate) and the Austrian rate and then assumes that the Austrian versus U.S. price changes are captured by the AS/dollar exchange rate or, alternatively, by the ICP's bilateral PPP between the two countries (shown in parentheses). Method 2 differs only in that it relies on the official Czech-

---

4. Subsequently the authors revised their PPP estimate for 1980, yielding a Kcs/dollar rate of 7.23 (at the AS/dollar rate of 13.81) or 8.27 (at the ICP's AS/dollar rate of 15.80) (see Havlik 1983), which we did not have a chance to take into account in this book, but the results are not affected significantly.

*Table 3-4. Czechoslovakia: Crown/Dollar Purchasing Power Parities Derived from Bilateral Comparisons with Austria and the Federal Republic of Germany, 1970, 1975, and 1980*

| Method of computation | 1970 | 1975 | 1980 |
|---|---|---|---|
| *Bilateral comparison with Austria benchmark year*[a] | | | |
| 1. Backdated by Czech inflation estimated by country experts, Austrian inflation, and official (ICP) AS/dollars | n.a. | 10.35  (9.66) | 6.91 (7.86) |
| 2. Backdated by official Czech and Austrian inflation and official (ICP) AS/dollars | n.a. | 11.23 (10.48) | 6.91 (7.86) |
| 3. Backdated by Czech inflation estimated by country experts and U.S. inflation | 10.26 *(11.74)* | 8.43  *(9.64)* | 6.91 (7.86) |
| 4. Backdated by official Czech and U.S. inflation | 11.90 (13.63) | 9.14 (10.46) | 6.91 (7.86) |
| *Bilateral comparison with the Federal Republic of Germany benchmark year* | | | |
| 1. CSO of Federal Republic series[b] converted at official (ICP) DM/dollar rates | | | |
|    a. Federal Republic weights | 12.70 (11.10) | 6.38  (7.47) | 4.27 *(5.25)* |
|    b. Est. average of Federal Republic and Czech weights | 10.67  *(9.32)* | 5.58  *(6.27)* | 3.73 *(4.91)* |
| 2. Updated by Czech inflation rate estimated by country experts and U.S. inflation | | | |
|    a. Federal Republic weights | 12.70 (11.10) | 10.64  (9.30) | 8.51 (7.44) |
|    b. Est. average of Federal Republic and Czech weights | 10.67  *(9.32)* | 9.30  (7.81) | 7.44 (6.25) |
| 3. Updated by official Czech and U.S. inflation | | | |
|    a. Federal Republic weights | 12.70 (11.10) | 9.80  (8.57) | 7.33 (6.41) |
|    b. Est. average of Federal Republic and Czech weights | 10.67 (9.32) | 8.57  (7.20) | 6.41 (5.38) |

*Note:* Numbers in parentheses are alternative estimates based on the AS/dollar and DM/dollar rates, respectively. Italics indicate the conversion coefficients used to compute the dollar estimate for a given year, as explained in text. n.a. = not available.

a. Average of Czechoslovak and Austrian weights.

b. The apparent method of updating 1970 base is to revalue the basket at Czech and Federal Republic prices.

*Sources:* Columns 1–4: see text; columns 5–6: first PPP computation by the country experts, second PPP computation by the central statistical office of the Federal Republic of Germany.

oslovak inflation rate. Method 3 bypasses Austria and backdates the 1980 benchmark estimate by a coefficient of Czechoslovak and U.S. inflation rates, relying on the country experts' inflation estimate in method 3a and on the official inflation rate in method 3b. For operational purposes, the ICP-converted 1980 benchmark estimate of 7.86 is selected and is moved to 1975 by method 3a, considered to be the most straightforward.[5]

The comparison with the Federal Republic of Germany was made by the central statistical office of that country, apparently with 1970 as the benchmark year. The Kcs/DM purchasing power parity was converted to Kcs/dollars using the official DM/dollar and the International Comparison Project (Phase I) DM/dollar rates, respectively (the latter appear in parentheses). Next an estimate was made of the 1970 benchmark PPP as it would be if the geometric average of weights for Czechoslovakia and the Federal Republic of Germany had been used—the $b$ series.[6] One of three methods may be employed to move the benchmark estimates forward. The first converts the annually published Kcs/DM purchasing power parities to Kcs/dollars via the official (or ICP) DM/dollar rate. The extremely rapid appreciation of the Kcs (decline in Kcs/dollars) is caused, first, by the fact that between 1970 and 1980 the Kcs appreciated vis-à-vis the DM by about 50 percent (which implies that the central statistical office either accepted or confirmed the low official Czech inflation rate) and, second, by the more than 100 percent appreciation of the mark against the dollar (the ICP-based bilateral purchasing power parity shows a much smaller appreciation).

Methods 2 and 3 bypass the Federal Republic of Germany and extrapolate the 1970 benchmark estimate by a coefficient of Czechoslovak and U.S. inflation rates, in method 2 using the country experts' estimate, in method 3 the official figures on Czechoslovak inflation.

The foregoing discussion suggests two general conclusions. One is that it is exceedingly difficult to compare alternative PPP estimates purporting to measure approximately the same basket if the benchmark years are

5. The country experts' estimate shown in table 3-3, column 5, cannot be the preferred one. First, the 1980 benchmark figure should be 6.87 (Kcs 0.4975/AS × AS 13.81/dollar). More important, it was backdated, using their estimate of Czechoslovak inflation, without accounting for U.S. inflation.

6. The estimate is based on the relationship found in the Federal Republic of Germany's comparable series with the U.S.S.R., where the PPP based on a geometric average is 87 percent of that based on Federal Republic weights (table 3-1) and the country experts' findings using Czechoslovak and Austrian weights, where comparable computations yielded 81 percent (Havlik and Levcik 1985, p. 26). The average of the two, 84 percent, is used in table 3-4.

far apart, because alternative methods may be used to update or backdate the series. Fluctuating official exchange rates between Western currencies can be a very important reason for the apparent differences between estimates. Second, the West German central statistical office's PPP series can be a useful check on alternative series or itself may be employed as a PPP estimate if (1) an adjustment is made to correct for the bias if only weights for the Federal Republic are used and (2) an ICP-based rate rather than the strongly fluctuating official DM/dollar rate is employed to convert the NCU/DM purchasing power parities to dollars.

As a practical matter, it may be noted that the benchmark PPP computed by the country experts for Czechoslovakia is less firmly based than those available for the other countries.[7] Therefore, we shall average the estimates of the country experts and the official estimates of the Federal Republic. In the former series, we are using method 3 to obtain backdated estimates of purchasing power parity from the bilateral comparison with Austria in 1980. In the latter series we are using method 1 to obtain updated estimates from the bilateral comparison with the Federal Republic of Germany in 1970. (The numbers selected are italicized in table 3-4.) This procedure yields a 1975 PPP estimate of 7.95 [(9.64 + 6.27) ÷ 2] and a 1980 PPP estimate of 6.38 [(7.86 + 4.91) ÷ 2]. These numbers will be used in our subsequent calculations.

What kind of bias is introduced if we rely on a consumer-based PPP as a proxy for the PPP for gross national product as a whole? Two main factors would appear to determine the PPPs of the omitted main categories of gross national product—capital formation and government— *relative* to the PPP for consumption: methods of price formation in the centrally planned economy and relative prices in the market-type economy being used for comparison. With respect to methods of price formation, the PPP of consumption as compared with PPPs of capital formation and government would be affected by the incidence of taxes and subsidies: if the government levies net taxes mainly on production (that is, the balance of turnover taxes and subsidies levied on consumption is small, as is the case, for example, in Hungary), then capital formation will be *relatively* expensive. In other words, its PPP will be higher (more national currency units per dollar) than that for consumption. In Czechoslovakia, in 1977 (the latest year for which data are available), retail prices of consumer goods shown in national income statistics were 26 percent higher than the same goods valued in the input-output table at producer

---

7. In reply to my query, the country experts stated that the degree of confidence in their estimates was lower than that of the results of the ICP because fewer items were available and more prices had to be estimated without detailed knowledge of comparable qualities.

prices (Havlik and Levcik 1985, pp. 20–21a). This average percentage markup after the goods leave the farm or factory may well be lower than the average markups typical in Western countries but higher than in some other CPEs, for example, Hungary, where (until the recent steep increases in consumer prices) the retail price level was about the same as the producer price level. Thus, other things being equal, the PPP of capital formation relative to the PPP of consumption will be lower in Czechoslovakia than in Hungary. More generally, the ICP has found that capital formation is relatively high priced in Romania, Hungary, and Poland, whereas the country expert on the German Democratic Republic (with which Czechoslovakia is often compared) found that capital formation is relatively low priced in that country (see note to table 3-5). Thus in Czechoslovakia, the PPP for capital formation may not be very much higher than that for consumption. On the other hand, all studies agree that government is relatively low priced in the centrally planned economies. Thus its PPP may be lower than that of consumption. On balance, there is not enough information to state whether the use of PPP for consumption does or does not introduce a systematic bias as an estimate of the PPP for the GNP total.

The other factor is relative PPPs between consumption and the other GNP components in the market-type economy with which Czechoslovakia is being compared, in this case Austria and the Federal Republic of Germany. This information is available in the International Comparison Project study, showing the ratio of PPPs in capital formation and in government, respectively, to PPPs in consumption, relative to the U.S. structure of prices (Kravis et al. 1982, table 1-9). For Austria, the project found that the PPP of the schilling against the dollar was 15.6 in consumption and 23.9 in capital formation, as compared with the purchasing power of one dollar in these categories in the United States. Thus the PPP of the Austrian schilling in capital formation is shown to be 1.53 times that in consumption (23.9/15.6). The relative PPP pattern revealed for Austria for capital formation is similar to that found for all market-type economies and centrally planned economies, although its ratio is the highest among the Group IV and V countries. In contrast, this ratio is the lowest among Group IV and V countries for the Federal Republic of Germany, where it is only 1.02. The fact that the prices of capital relative to consumer goods are very high in Austria and very low in the Federal Republic of Germany, as compared with other market-type economies, will tend to lower the PPP on capital goods for Czechoslovakia expressed in schillings but will raise it if it is expressed in marks. Thus there is no firm basis for assuming that the PPP of capital formation measured as an average against these two Western currencies would be significantly different from the PPP of Czechoslovakia's consumption. Although it may be some-what higher for capital formation, which accounts approximately for 30 percent of GNP, for government (10 percent of GNP) it is almost certain to be the same as for other centrally planned economies, that is, at least 10 percent lower. The assumption that the somewhat higher PPP of capital formation and the lower PPP of government may approximately offset each other does not seem unrealistic.

### German Democratic Republic

The official exchange rates shown in column 1 of table 3-5 are based on gold parity (obtained from a Czechoslovak source!) and appear to be arbitrary. The commercial exchange rates shown in column 2 are pro forma rates obtained by comparing the dollar data that the German Democratic Republic reports to the United Nations with official data in

Table 3-5. *The German Democratic Republic: Mark/Dollar Exchange Rates and Purchasing Power Parities, 1970–81*

| Year | Official exchange rate (1) | Commercial exchange rate (2) | Tourist (noncommercial) exchange rate (3) |
|---|---|---|---|
| 1970 | 1.17 | 4.20 | 3.66 |
| 1971 | 1.17 | 4.20 | 3.43 |
| 1972 | 1.08 | 3.87 | 3.18 |
| 1973 | 0.99 | 3.48 | 2.67 |
| 1974 | 0.97 | 3.48 | 2.59 |
| 1975 | 0.97 | 3.48 | 2.46 |
| 1976 | 0.97 | 3.48 | 2.52 |
| 1977 | 0.95 | 3.48 | 2.32 |
| 1978 | 0.89 | 3.48 | 2.01 |
| 1979 | 0.87 | 3.48 | 1.83 |
| 1980 | 0.86 | 3.30 | 1.82 |
| 1981 | 0.92 | 3.32 | 2.26 |

*Note:* Purchasing power parities for GNP and components: GNP, 1.96; consumption, 2.3; investment, 1.9; government, 1.5; trade balance, 4.0 (Collier 1985, table 11).

*Sources:* Column 1: gold parity quoted in Czechoslovakia's statistical year book, adjusted by the same relatives as the commercial rate changed, as shown in van Brabant (1985, table 2); column 2: implied average rate between dollar data reported to the United Nations and official trade data in valutamarks, in van Brabant (1985, table 3); column 3: no official tourist rate, but since tourist rates are normally quoted at parity with the deutschmark, the rate shown is that of the official DM/dollar, quarterly average.

valutamarks (VM). For the German Democratic Republic, the interpretation of trade flows evaluated in VM is problematic. For trade transactions with countries other than the Federal Republic of Germany, VM values are *probably* obtained by converting trade valued in foreign currencies at the official exchange rate shown in column 1. Trade with the Federal Republic of Germany (data which the Federal Republic does not publish, considering it "intra-German," not "foreign," trade), which accounts for a significant share of the German Democratic Republic's total trade, is probably priced in deutschmarks, but because the German Democratic Republic considers deutschmarks equal to valutamarks, it adds this trade to other VM values without conversion. To be consistent, the German Democratic Republic should convert intra-German trade to VM at rates that accord with the official DM/dollar and VM/dollar values, that is, multiplying by the coefficient VM/DM. Thus in 1970, intra-German trade should have been converted to VM using a coefficient of 0.32, with a coefficient of 0.47 used in 1980.[8] Published trade flows in VM thus appear to be overstated.

The other problem is that the pro forma commercial exchange rate shown in column 2 is not the FTM but still another kind of official exchange rate. When it was established in 1959, it was set equal to the exchange rate of the deutschmark (4.2 DM = $1.00), but since 1972 it appears to have been linked to the dollar (van Brabant 1985, pp. 25 and 46a). Thus for this reason also, the German Democratic Republic's commercial exchange rate is not comparable to those of the other centrally planned economies.

The German Democratic Republic does not publish official tourist exchange rates but applies the prevailing exchange rate of the mark shown in column 3, another manifestation of its desire for its currency to have a status equal to that of the deutschmark. Nonetheless, in 1980 the tourist rate was close to the mark's estimated PPP.

The purchasing power parities shown in the note to table 3-5 were computed by our project's country expert separately for the four main components of GNP. Their point of departure is the purchasing power parity calculations between the German Democratic Republic and the Federal Republic of Germany, carried out by experts at the Federal Republic's Deutsches Institut für Wirtschaftsforschung in West Berlin, the nation's leading research institute on the economy of the German Democratic Republic. The purchasing power parities were available for

8. The DM/dollar and VM/dollar rates are shown in table 3-5, columns 3 and 1, respectively. Thus in 1970, 1.17/3.66 = 0.32; in 1980, 0.86/1.82 = 0.47.

Table 3-6. Hungary: Forint/Dollar Exchange Rates and Purchasing Power Parities, 1970–82

| | | | | | ICP-computed PPPs | | | | Federal Republic–computed PPP | UN cost-of-living index | |
| Year | Official ER (1) | Commercial ER (2) | FTM (export) (3) | Tourist (noncomm.) ER (4) | GDP (5) | Consumption[a] (6) | Cap. form. (7) | Government (8) | (Federal Republic weights) (9) | Incl. housing (10) | Excl. housing (11) |
|---|---|---|---|---|---|---|---|---|---|---|---|
| 1970 | 11.74 | | 60.00 | 30.00 | | | | | 22.10 | | |
| 1971 | 11.74 | | 60.00 | 30.00 | | | | | 20.30 | | |
| 1972 | 10.81 | | 55.26 | 27.63 | | | | | 18.17 | | |
| 1973 | 9.39 | | 48.71 | 24.35 | | | | | 14.66 | | |
| 1974 | 9.15 | | 48.71 | 24.35 | | | | | 13.56 | | |
| 1975 | 8.60 | 43.97 | | 20.65 | 12.3 | 11.1 | 17.6 | 10.7 | 12.62 | | |
| | | | | | | | | | (14.77)[b] | | |
| 1976 | discont'd | 41.57 | discont'd | 20.80 | | | | | 13.00 | 19.83 | 19.21 |
| 1977 | | 40.92 | | 20.50 | | | | | 12.00 | 19.79 | 19.37 |
| 1978 | | 38.01 | | 18.94 | | | | | 10.56 | 19.23 | 19.23 |
| 1979 | | 35.58 | | 20.30 | | | | | 10.00 | 19.50 | 19.90 |
| | | | | | | | | | (14.00)[b] | | |
| 1980 | | 32.43 | | 22.14 | 11.8[c] | | | | | 19.30 | 20.92 |
| 1981 | | 34.34 | | 31.00 | | | | | | 20.40 | 23.90 |
| 1981d | 35.00d | 35.00d | | 35.00d | | | | | | | |
| 1982 | 38.00 | 38.00 | | | | | | | | | |

Note: Parentheses indicate alternative estimates.
a. Private consumption.
b. Converted at the ICP-based rate.
c. Hungarian consumer price index, U.S. GNP deflator.
d. As of October 1.

Sources: Columns 1–4: average monthly rates officially published by the Hungarian National Bank (direct communication received); columns 5–8, 1975: Kravis and others (1982, table 1-9); 1980: multiplied by ratio of Hungarian and U.S. price indexes; column 9: Statistisches Bundesamt (1981), converted at the official dollar/DM rate shown in Havlik and Levcik (1985, table 19, row 3).

the various components of the GNP for different but recent years and were interpolated to 1980. Generally, more confidence can be placed in the purchasing power parity for consumption than for the other components. To make the purchasing power parities as comparable as possible to those obtained for other CPEs via the International Comparison Project, the geometric average of the purchasing power parities between the mark and the dollar that resulted from the ICP's binary comparisons (yielding DM/dollar = 2.88, versus the average prevailing exchange rate of 2.46), moved to 1980 by the ratio of the implicit price deflators in the two countries, was used. The 1980 DM/dollar rate so obtained is 2.47 versus the average prevailing exchange rate of 1.82 (Collier 1985, pt. 5).

In sum, the German Democratic Republic does not have an exchange rate with a clear economic meaning, and therefore none of the rates can be considered for converting GNP to dollar values. The country expert was able to derive 1980 purchasing power parity for GNP that conforms to the ICP method. There is no claim that the resulting estimate might not contain significant error margins, but it must be evaluated in light of the fundamental statistical gaps in official data from the German Democratic Republic.

## Hungary

In 1946 a new currency was introduced, the forint. Its nominal gold content was set to yield an exchange rate of 11.74 forints per dollar, which approximated the international purchasing power of the forint at the time. As shown in table 3-6, column 1, the official exchange rate established in 1947 remained unchanged until 1972 (when it was adjusted according to changes in the international value of the dollar), even though until the mid-1970s the inflation rate in the enterprise sector was much higher in Hungary than in the main Western industrial countries. To be sure, various surcharges and later the foreign trade multiplier were introduced, so that de facto exchange rates deviated from the official rate.

When the New Economic Mechanism was introduced in 1968, two rates for the forint were newly determined. They were intended to play an active role, in contrast with the passive role that exchange rates typically play in a traditional centrally planned economy: the foreign trade multiplier for the foreign trade transactions of enterprises and a tourist rate for other transactions. The FTMs (column 3) introduced in 1968 were calculated separately for dollar and ruble trade, according to the average domestic-currency-to-foreign-currency price relations computed for several earlier years, which yielded approximately sixty forints per dollar and forty forints per ruble. Within the Western currency area, the forint value

of the various other currencies was calculated according to their official parities against the dollar.

Within the CMEA area, a foreign trade multiplier was calculated only for the so-called transferable ruble, because by agreement all intra-CMEA commercial transactions are denominated in this clearing currency. The forint is valued more highly vis-à-vis the transferable ruble (that is, in trade with the CMEA countries) than in trade with the convertible-currency areas. One result is that the direct forint/dollar rate is inconsistent with the forint/cross-rate obtained via the ruble's official dollar rate. At one point in 1983, for example, the official exchange rates were forty-four forints/dollar and twenty-six forints/ruble (approximately the same for the transferable ruble). The 0.72 ruble/dollar official rate established by the U.S.S.R. yields a forint/dollar cross-rate, via the ruble, of about nineteen forints/dollar, a 130 percent difference from Hungary's official rate.

Part of the large difference between the official rates and the cross-rates reflects the overvaluation of the transferable ruble in a purchasing power parity sense vis-à-vis the dollar at its official rate. Further reasons for the discrepant rates can be found in the peculiarities of the intra-CMEA and East-West foreign trade pricing. Recalling that Hungary's dollar and transferable ruble exchange rates basically reflect the domestic costs of earning a unit of the respective currencies via commodity exports, the forint/dollar rate is "high" partly because, as a centrally planned economy, Hungary obtains unusually low prices for many of its convertible-currency exports (see chapter 4, "Prices"). In contrast, the forint/TR rate is "low" because Hungary obtains relatively high prices for its exports to the CMEA, which are composed predominantly of manufactures that are relatively highly priced on that market (again see chapter 4). One result of the large difference between the official and the cross-rate forint/dollar ratios, combined with the lagged-price CMEA formula that causes the intra-CMEA prices of energy and raw materials to be priced relatively low when their world market prices rise steeply, is that the dollar prices of their imports from the CMEA will appear to be very low.[9]

Beginning in 1972, the foreign trade multiplier was periodically adjusted,

---

9. Let us assume, for example, that in 1983 the price of crude oil imported by Hungary from the U.S.S.R., fixed on the basis of the CMEA formula, was $30 per barrel. In the CMEA, the price therefore is 21.6 transferable rubles ($30 × .72, the official ruble/dollar rate), which is equal to 561.6 forints (21.6 TR × 26, the official forint/TR rate). At the official forint/dollar rate, the price *appears to be* $12.76 (561.6 ÷ 44), whereas in reality the price was $30. Thus to ascertain correctly the prices at which Hungary and other CMEA countries trade with CMEA members, the procedure should be to go from national currency units to transferable rubles to dollars using the official rates, not from national currency units directly to dollars at the official rate.

largely to neutralize the domestic impact of foreign inflation, but other policy purposes may have been served also. Although nothing of major significance happened in Hungary's economic mechanism in 1976, the authorities decided to discard the old official exchange rate as of the beginning of that year and designated the foreign trade multiplier as the new official exchange rate. More precisely, it became the official *commercial* exchange rate, applicable for converting foreign trade transactions, so that it was still distinct from the official *noncommercial* (tourist) rate. The tourist exchange rate (column 4) was reportedly calculated to approximate the purchasing power of the forint at the retail level for the typical tourist basket.

Until February 14, 1979, the tourist rate was always adjusted proportionately with the commercial rate so that the 100 percent difference between them was maintained; on that date the commercial rate was approximately Ft 36 = US$1.00 and the tourist rate was approximately Ft 18 = $1.00. By October 1, 1981, however, the commercial and tourist rates were unified at the rate of the former. Since that time, Hungary has had a single official exchange rate against the dollar.

To understand the meaning of this exchange rate, we need to trace its evolution since 1968. It is very important to note that the exchange rate was, and essentially remains, the FTM, although the Ft 60/dollar rate may have been an approximately accurate ratio of domestic and foreign prices only during the first or middle part of the 1960s. The key point, however, is that even in 1981, the Ft 35–38/dollar rate probably reflects quite closely the average domestic cost of gaining a dollar through commodity exports.

Until 1979, there remained a 100 percent difference in favor of the tourist rate. The significantly greater purchasing power until 1979 of the tourist forint as opposed to the commercial forint can be traced to several sources. It should be noted, first, that the commodity coverage of the commercial exchange rate is different from that of the tourist exchange rate. A very important reason for the difference is the large subsidization of many consumer items—more generally, the Hungarian system of internal taxation and subsidization. In most countries, the retail price level is considerably higher than the wholesale (or producer) price level, accommodating large distribution costs, substantial retail markups, and steep taxes levied on consumption. In Hungary, by contrast, the *intended* difference between the wholesale and retail price levels (when the New Economic Mechanism was introduced) was only 6–10 percent, and even that small difference had disappeared by the mid-1970s. A large part of net social income, that is, budget revenues in the form of taxes and other levies, is financed by levies on producers, which stand in contrast to the international practice of levying taxes on personal income or consumption. After the 1973–74 price rises on the world market, which were permitted to affect wholesale prices to a certain degree but retail prices only to a lesser degree (until 1979), the consumer price level actually became lower than the wholesale price level, giving Hungary a situation unique among the CMEA countries and possibly among countries anywhere in the world. Since 1980 the retail price level has once again exceeded the producer price level by small margins (see chapter 4 for details).

A further very important reason for the large difference between the two exchange rates is Western discrimination against Hungarian goods and poor marketing by Hungarian exporters, both of which depress the dollar prices obtained by Hungary. Many products manufactured in Hungary are not in strong demand in the West, so the export of these products must be "pushed" by offering them at very attractive prices as compared with the prices that similar but not necessarily fully identical products would fetch in trade between market-type economies.

Let us consider the relationship between the tourist exchange rate and the purchasing power parity of consumer goods until 1979. As the reader may recall, I noted earlier that, if we judge Hungary's 1970 Western tourist rate by intra-CMEA tourist rates, known to have been based on computations of purchasing power parity, Hungary's Western rates provided "incentives" for Western tourists, that is, offered more forints per unit of Western currency than its PPP. The purchasing power parities computed by the central statistical office of the Federal Republic of Germany and presented in table 3-6, column 9, confirm this point. We may note, furthermore, the computations by the International Comparison Project, whose PPP estimates for 1975 are very close to those obtained from the independent source in the Federal Republic of Germany. The ICP shows that, in *total* consumption, Ft 11.1 = $1.00, whereas the Federal Republic's PPP for *private* consumption yields Ft 12.6 = $1.00; 14.8 if the ICP-computed bilateral PPP coefficient is used; 12.4 if the figure is adjusted for the estimated bias that results from not using the geometric average of the PPPs obtained with Hungarian and Federal Republic weights (the estimated adjustment is the same as that made for Czechoslovakia; see above). The United Nations' cost-of-living computations, whose coverage is much more limited, show the tourist forint closer to its purchasing power parity.

Between February 15, 1979, and October 1, 1981—in just two and one-half years—the tourist exchange rate, which according to the computations of both the International Comparison Project and the Federal Republic of Germany was undervalued at the beginning of that period, was depreciated by 100 percent (from 17.79 to 35/dollar), even though during the same period Hungary's retail prices rose less than 25 percent, probably not significantly faster than the retail prices of the main West European countries. The purpose of the depreciation was to unify the two exchange rates in order to have a single yardstick for calculation and in preparation for the eventual introduction of financial convertibility. Why the exchange rate was unified at the foreign trade multiplier level rather than at some other level is difficult for an outsider to say, but it probably reflected first and foremost the need to mirror realistically what it takes to earn a dollar in convertible-currency trade.

In view of Hungary's severe hard currency balance-of-payments problems, there is no basis for suggesting that the forint pegged at thirty-five to a dollar may not be an equilibrium, or even below equilibrium, rate. It is quite a different matter, however, to say that that rate is an approximately correct reflection of the purchasing power parity of the Hungarian currency or, putting the matter the other way, that the ICP results were blatantly unrealistic. The data presented in table 3-6 confirm very clearly that the purchasing power parity and the foreign trade multiplier (which may be considered a proxy equilibrium exchange rate) may be very far apart.

## Poland

Table 3-7 lists the various exchange rates and table 3-8 the different PPP computations available for Poland. In table 3-7, column 1 shows the official exchange rate, established in 1950, when one zloty was declared to be equal to one ruble. Between 1972 and 1978 the rate was tied to the dollar. Between 1979 and 1981 it was tied to a basket of twelve convertible currencies; as of Janaury 1982 it was replaced by a new uniform rate of exchange.

Column 2 shows the special commercial rate introduced in 1957 for "planning and financial control" (Fallenbuchl 1985, p. 47). Between 1959 and 1971 this rate was used instead of the official rate as the basis for calculating "price equalization" in foreign trade. Also, for some time this rate was used for financial transactions. The dollar balance-of-payments figures released to the Western bankers during the second half of the 1970s, for example, were computed at this rate. At the end of 1981, the special commercial rate was abolished. Column 3 shows the commercial exchange rate. It was reportedly introduced in 1971, but until 1980 its value was considered a state secret. Various statements by Polish economists suggest that in 1971 the rate was about sixty and had declined gradually to about forty by 1978–79 before rising to forty-five in 1980 and fifty in 1981. Effective January 1, 1982, the commercial rate became

Table 3-7. *Poland: Zloty/Dollar Exchange Rates, 1970–82*

| Year | Official exchange rate (1) | Special commercial exchange rate (2) | Commercial exchange rate (3) | Foreign trade multiplier (exports) (4) | Tourist (noncommercial) exchange rate (5) |
|---|---|---|---|---|---|
| 1970 | 4.00 | 24.00 | — | — | 40.00 |
| 1971 | 4.00 | 24.00 | n.a. | 54.00 | 40.00 |
| 1972 | 3.68 | 22.08 | n.a. | 50.78 | 36.80 |
| 1973 | 3.36 | 20.18 | n.a. | 41.50 | 33.65 |
| 1974 | 3.32 | 19.92 | n.a. | 31.87 | 33.20 |
| 1975 | 3.32 | 19.92 | 50.00[a] | 31.21 | 33.20 |
| 1976 | 3.32 | 19.92 | n.a. | 38.84 | 33.20 |
| 1977 | 3.32 | 19.92 | n.a. | 40.17 | 33.20 |
| 1978 | 3.24 | 30.94 | n.a. | 38.94 | 32.44 |
| 1979 | 3.10 | 30.95 | n.a. | 35.83 | 30.95 |
| 1980 | 3.05 | 30.49 | 45.00 | 34.82 | 30.49 |
| 1981 | 3.35 | 33.50 | 50.00 | n.a. | 33.50 |
| 1982[b] | 80.00 | 80.00 | 80.00 | 80.00 | 80.00 |

*Note:* n.a. = not available. Dashes indicate that there was no such rate at that time.

a. The approximate value indicated by Polish economists to the author.

b. January 1, 1982.

*Sources:* Column 1: van Brabant (1985, table 2); column 2: van Brabant (1985, table 3); column 3, 1980: Fallenbuchl (1985, p. 495); 1981: average of old rate and new rate of 55 introduced on July 1, 1981; column 4: Fallenbuchl (1985, table IV-1); column 5: van Brabant (1985, table 4).

unified with the other rates at eighty. The commercial exchange rate was reportedly based on the foreign trade multiplier, which was increased by what might be called a "scarcity of foreign exchange" premium, said in 1980 to be 30 percent (Fallenbuchl 1985, p. 50). (The 1980 foreign trade multiplier was 34.82 × 1.3, or 45.3, practically the same as the commercial exchange rate during 1980.) Column 4 reports the foreign trade multiplier, evidently computed annually as the average domestic cost of earning a unit of foreign exchange. Since 1971 the FTM has been available in an eight-sector breakdown (Fallenbuchl 1985, table IV-1), showing that, since 1975, the cost of earning a dollar in exporting fuels was between one-half and one-third the costs in most other sectors. The costs are highest in agriculture and in light industry. Column 5 lists the tourist exchange rate, which since 1979 has been the same as the "special" commercial rate.

As of January 1, 1982, all previous exchange rates were abolished and a new unified rate of eighty zlotys per dollar introduced, applicable to all commercial and noncommercial transactions except basic raw materials and certain intermediate goods. Their prices had been fixed earlier, calculated at the rate of fifty zlotys per dollar, and were then left unchanged when the new unified rates of eighty and later eighty-three zlotys per dollar were introduced. These prices held firm for purely administrative reasons; it would be too big a task to revise all fixed prices with every change in the exchange rate. When the new prices were determined, sometime during 1981, an exchange rate was of course needed for the purpose. The foreign trade multiplier may have been used during the first half of 1981 (except for basic raw materials and intermediate products), according to a Polish source cited in van Brabant (1985, p. 28), or it may have been the commercial exchange rate, that is, the foreign trade multiplier plus a percentage markup (Fallenbuchl 1985, p. 50). In any event, the unified exchange rate introduced as of January 1, 1982, "evolved as a political compromise between what economic calculations tended to indicate and the perceived need for trade incentives," according to the Polish source cited in van Brabant (1985, p. 28). Changes in the value of the uniform rate are linked to a basket of nine convertible currencies, so that on June 30, 1982, for example, the rate stood at 85.53 zlotys per dollar.

Table 3-8 assembles the PPPs obtained from five independent studies. The International Comparison Project's 1975 results for GNP were moved to 1980 by a coefficient of Polish implicit net material product (official statistics) and U.S. implicit GNP deflators. Because Poland's official price indexes may be downward biased, especially during 1979–80, an alternative estimate of Polish versus Western inflation rates was made by

Table 3-8. Poland: Zloty/Dollar Purchasing Power Parities, 1970–81

| Designation | 1970 | 1971 | 1972 | 1973 | 1974 | 1975 | 1976 | 1977 | 1978 | 1979 | 1980 | 1981 |
|---|---|---|---|---|---|---|---|---|---|---|---|---|
| *ICP* | | | | | | | | | | | | |
| GDP | | | | | | 14.3 | | | | | 14.3(13.7)[a] | |
| Consumption | | | | | | 13.2 | | | | | | |
| Capital formation | | | | | | 19.6 | | | | | | |
| Government | | | | | | 11.3 | | | | | | |
| *Joint Polish-Austrian central statistical offices* | | | | | | | | | | | | |
| GNP | | | | | | 17.1 | | | 17.2 | | 17.2(19.2)[a] | |
| Consumption | | | | | | 17.6 | | | 17.7 | | | |
| Capital formation | | | | | | 18.3 | | | 18.7 | | | |
| Government | | | | | | 9.3 | | | 9.8 | | | |
| *Bilateral comparisons with France and Austria* | | | | | | | | | | | | |
| GNP | 22.5 | 24.7 | | | | 20.6 | | | | | 18.0(18.2)[a] | |
| Consumption | | 22.6 | 21.7 | 18.9 | 17.6 | | | | | | | |
| Capital formation | | | | | 31.7 | | | | | | | |
| Machinery and equipment | | | | | 40.1 | | | | | | | |
| Construction | | | | | 19.2 | | | | | | | |
| Government | | | | | 15.6 | | | | | | | |

60

| *Computed by Federal Republic of Germany* | | | | | | | | | |
|---|---|---|---|---|---|---|---|---|---|
| Private consumption (Federal Republic weights) | 23.0 | 20.7 | 18.1 | 14.3 | 13.7 | 12.7 | 13.0 | 12.0 | 11.0 |
| *Computed by United Nations* | | | | | | | | | |
| Cost of living, incl. housing | | | | (14.8)[b] | 15.7 | 16.1 | 14.9 | 24.2[c] | 23.9 | 23.2 | 23.6 | (14.7)[b] |
| Cost of living, excl. housing | | | | 18.3 | 18.5 | 16.1 | 22.2[c] | 23.6 | 23.2 | 24.2 |

*Note:* Parentheses indicate alternative estimates.

a. Moved to 1980 by index of unit labor costs.

b. Calculated using ICP-computed geometric average of bilateral purchasing power parities, moved forward by a coefficient of relative prices.

c. The large jump in the cost of living in zlotys from 1977 to 1978 (by 62 percent in the first series and 38 percent in the second) does not seem to be warranted by changes in prices in Poland or in the United States, suggesting the possibility of an error.

*Sources:* ICP, 1975: Kravis and others (1982, table 1-9), moved to 1980 by a coefficient of Polish and U.S. prices, the former represented by the implicit net material product deflator calculated from Fallenbuchl (1985, table III-8); joint Polish-Austrian central statistical offices, 1975 and 1978: Central Statistical Offices (1982, table 3), converted to dollars by the ICP's geometric average purchasing power parity between the schilling and the dollar (appendix table 7-1), moved to 1978 and 1980 by coefficients of Austrian and U.S. prices; bilateral comparisons with France and Austria, 1970–74: Fallenbuchl (1985, p. 48), moved to 1980 by the same method as that used for the ICP; computed by the Federal Republic of Germany: Statistisches Bundesamt (1981), converted to dollars at the official DM/dollar rate.

computing Poland's index of relative unit labor cost (Poland's unit labor cost in manufacturing and mining—wage payments as a proportion of net output plus depreciation—relative to the export-weighted unit labor cost in manufacturing in fourteen Western countries). The 1980 PPP in parentheses is based on extending the International Comparison Project figure for 1975 by estimates of inflation in Poland and in its trade partner countries from the index of relative unit labor costs. Surprisingly, this measure indicates a relatively lower rate of inflation for 1975–80, although not for the period of 1978–80, when wage inflation became substantial (see table 3-9).

The central statistical offices of Austria and Poland collaborated for an extended period to complete the first comprehensive bilateral study between a centrally planned economy and a market-type economy of prices and gross domestic expenditure levels in the two countries in 1975 and 1978, using methods generally patterned on the International Comparison Project but pricing a significantly greater number of items. (Presumably these bilateral computations became the basis for Poland's participation in ICP Phase IV.) With respect to the purchasing power parity of consumption, the study explains:

A list of representative items was jointly worked out in detail and verified, and individual product items were strictly defined. Only those products were chosen that were actually available on the market both in Austria and Poland in the reference periods. Products of very high or low quality and luxury items were not included. The representative items were selected in close cooperation by Austrian and Polish teams on the basis of mutually presented samples, catalogues, technical descriptions, recipes, and other evidence, in order to obtain better comparability. . . . Certain products were verified in shops in Vienna and Warsaw. . . . Despite the maximum effort to ensure full comparability of representative items, the differences in quality could not be taken adequately into account in all cases [Central Statistical Offices 1982, p. 81].

*Table 3-9. Indexes of Ratio of Polish Labor Costs to Western Labor Costs, 1975, 1978, and 1980*

| Year | Polish NMP deflator ÷ U.S. GNP deflator | Index |
|---|---|---|
| 1975 | 100 | 100 |
| 1978 | 103 | 86 |
| 1980 | 100 | 96 |

Source: Fallenbuchl (1985, table 15).

Regarding capital formation and government, the resulting purchasing power parities are considered less reliable than for private consumption. (The definition of "government" in table 3-8 is not the same as that used in the ICP, the joint Polish-Austrian, or the bilateral study, so the results are not directly comparable.)

The central statistical office of Poland compared Poland bilaterally with France and with Austria for 1974. Neither the methods employed nor the exchange rates used to obtain the estimated PPPs in dollars are available; we have only the summary results shown in table 3-8. An important contribution is the decomposition of capital formation into its two main components: machinery and equipment versus construction. This decomposition shows that machinery and equipment (which may account for anywhere from one-third to about three-fifths of capital formation, depending on year and on whether Polish or Western prices are used as weights) are relatively expensive—much higher priced in Poland than construction or consumption.[10]

The methods employed by the two additional studies to obtain the purchasing power parity of private consumption—the PPP calculations by the Federal Republic of Germany and the cost-of-living index computations by the United Nations—were summarized above.

The results of the five independent studies of the mid-1970s PPP of the zloty in private consumption yield results that do not greatly differ, especially if we take into consideration differences in the methods used, the sample coverage, comparison countries, and methods of currency conversion:

| | |
|---|---|
| International Comparison Project (1975) | 14.3 |
| Central statistical office, Federal Republic of Germany (1975) | 12.7 or 14.8 |
| United Nations (1975) | 15.7 |
| Polish-Austrian central statistical offices (1975) | 17.6 |
| Bilateral studies with France and Austria | 17.6 |

The studies made by the ICP and the Federal Republic of Germany yield lower PPP estimates and the bilateral studies yield estimates that are about one-third higher. According to this project's country expert, in the case of Poland the ICP is very likely to have underestimated the PPP of consumption because of the method's inability to capture the effect of the especially serious and growing shortages of foodstuffs. According to

10. The weights for 1974 are implied in the PPPs presented (machinery accounted for 60 percent and construction for 40 percent of capital formation) in the joint comparison with Austria; machinery accounted for 35 percent to 45 percent in 1975 and from 33 percent to 44 percent in 1978, depending on whether zloty or schilling prices are used as weights, as shown in Central Statistical Offices (1982), table 7.

Table 3-10. *Romania: Leu/Dollar Exchange Rates and Purchasing Power Parities, 1970–81*

| Year | Official ER (1) | Commercial ER (2) | FTM Exports (3) | FTM Imports (4) | Tourist (non-comm.) ER (5) | ICP-computed PPP GDP (6) | ICP Consumption form. (7) | ICP Cap. form. (8) | ICP Government (9) | UN cost-of-living index Incl. housing (10) | UN cost-of-living index Excl. housing (11) |
|---|---|---|---|---|---|---|---|---|---|---|---|
| 1970 | 6.00 | 24.00 | 24.00 | n.a. | 18.00 | | | | | 11.3 | 11.2 |
| 1971 | 6.00 | 24.00 | 24.00 | n.a. | 18.00 | | | | | 11.5 | 10.9 |
| 1972 | 5.52 | 24.00 | 24.00 | n.a. | 16.00 | | | | | 11.0 | 10.4 |
| 1973 | 5.04 | 20.00[a] | 22.60 | 20.30 | 14.58 | | | | | 10.8 | 10.6 |
| 1974 | 4.97 | 20.00 | 18.20 | 18.28 | 13.79 | | | | | 10.4 | 10.4 |
| 1975 | 4.97 | 20.00 | 18.84 | 19.86 | 12.00 | 8.8 | 7.6 | 12.9 | 6.7 | 10.2 | 10.2 |
| 1976 | 4.97 | 20.00 | 19.93 | 18.12 | 12.00 | | | | | 11.8 | 9.7 |
| 1977 | 4.97 | 20.00 | 18.51 | 16.60 | 12.00 | | | | | | |
| 1978 | 4.56 | 18.00[b] | 17.26 | 11.92 | 12.00 | | | | | | |
| 1979 | 4.47 | 18.00 | 12.73 | 11.92 | 12.00 | | | | | | |
| 1980 | 4.47 | 18.00 | 12.16 | 9.88 | 12.00 | 6.3 | n.a. | n.a. | n.a. | | |
| 1981 | Discont'd | 15.00 | 14.50 | 12.60 | 11.00[c] | | | | | | |
| 1982 | | 16.50[d] | | | | | | | | | |

*Note:* n.a. = not available.

a. Introduced December 3, 1973. If the foreign trade multiplier is considered the commercial exchange rate, the time-weighted average would be 20.25.

b. Changed to 18.00 on March 6, 1978, so that a time-weighted average for the year would be 18.36.

c. Changed February 15, 1981. The time-weighted average rate for the year is 11.125.

d. As of January 1, 1983; it was supposed to be changed to 17.50 on July 1, 1983, when the Romanians claimed the rates would be unified.

*Sources:* Column 1: 1970–72: van Brabant (1985, table 2); 1973–81: International Monetary Fund, as cited in Jackson (1985, tables 43 and 44); column 2: Jackson (1985, table 44), supplemented by information in van Brabant (1985, table 3); columns 3–4, 1970–72: van Brabant (1985, table 4); 1973–81: Jackson (1985, table 44); columns 6–9, 1975: Kravis and others (1982, table 1-9); 1980: adjusted for relative price movements (Romania's as shown in Jackson 1985, table 44); columns 10–11: *Monthly Bulletin of Statistics*, various issues; 1982: Marvin Jackson, personal communication with the author, May 1984.

the expert, an increasing portion of foodstuffs has been purchased privately at significantly higher prices. Thus there is reason to believe that the kind of CPE bias in the International Comparison Project that I mentioned above is a greater problem in the case of Poland (and possibly also Romania) than in Hungary, especially when the results are extended to 1980:

> The official price index shows that prices of consumption goods and services purchased by the population increased to 157.1 in 1980 (1970 = 100), food prices to 161.5, food prices in socialist trade to 143.0, in restaurants, etc. to 179.0 and in the [free] market to 280.7. Most of these increases occurred in 1975–80. A growing proportion of food and non-food consumption goods were transacted outside socialist trade at higher prices. This tendency is shown in official statistics (the share of non-socialist-sector was 3.4% in 1970 and 11.7% in 1980), but both the price indices and the level and trend away from the socialist retail sector are underestimated.[11]

In view of Poland's special situation, especially during the 1978–80 period, use of the Polish-Austrian central statistical office's study may be considered. Its basic methods are similar to those of the ICP, but there was more comprehensive involvement of the Polish authorities in the computations, the sample size is larger, and data are available for 1978, a more recent year, and can be extrapolated to 1980 realistically by the index of relative labor costs shown in table 3-9.

## Romania

Table 3-10 presents the set of exchange rates and PPP calculations available for Romania. Column 1 shows the arbitrary official exchange rate, which was abolished effective January 1, 1981. In 1982 Romania had two "official" exchange rates: the commercial (column 2) and the tourist (column 5). The commercial exchange rate was introduced on December 3, 1973, and was based on the foreign trade multiplier computed for an earlier period. The rate remained unchanged for four years and was then reduced, probably to reflect the decreasing trend in the foreign trade multiplier as Romanian prices rose less than external prices. Between 1977 and 1980, the FTMs became significantly different from the commercial exchange rate because Romanian domestic wholesale prices were not changed, whereas major changes took place in relative prices on the world market. Romania is the only country for which FTMs are available annually in exports as well as imports.

11. Zbigniew Fallenbuchl, personal communication with the author, May 1984.

The noncommercial exchange rate in column 5 is the relevant rate for tourism (other than group tourism) and other invisible transactions. The rates, evidently set on the basis of the PPP of a relevant basket (compare columns 5 and 10), tend to remain unchanged for long periods before being adjusted to reflect, among other things, changes in the relevant relative prices in Romania and Western Europe.

The ICP Phase III results for 1975 are presented in columns 6 through 9 and are estimated for 1980 on the basis of relative price movements. It is likely that in addition to any CPE bias that may be present in the 1975 ICP results, the 1980 estimates have a significant downward bias because official Romanian data do not adequately reflect hidden price increases that have occurred between 1975 and 1980. In addition, growing shortages of foodstuffs and consumer goods tend to bias the PPPs, as indicated above in the discussion of Poland.

## Cuba

Cuba has no trade and practically no invisible transactions with the United States. Its trade with other Western countries is settled in a convertible currency subject to bilateral agreement. The single official peso/dollar exchange rate is thus relevant chiefly for tourists. There is little reliable information on how its value is determined. The interpretation of the country authors (Mesa-Lago and Perez-Lopez 1985, pp. 70–74) is the following. From 1914 until 1971 the peso was exchanged at par with the U.S. dollar, but since 1961 the peso has not been a convertible currency. Between 1961 and 1974 the peso was linked to the British pound to establish its nominal value in terms of convertible currencies other than the dollar until 1971 and including the dollar after 1971. In 1976 the peso was pegged to a basket of convertible currencies; countries and weights were not specified. During 1970–81, the single official peso/dollar rate had the following values (Mesa-Lago and Perez-Lopez 1985, table 32):

| | |
|---|---|
| 1970 | 1.000 |
| 1971 | 0.921 |
| 1972 | 0.921 |
| 1973 | 0.815 |
| 1974 | 0.829 |
| 1975 | 0.829 |
| 1976 | 0.820 |
| 1977 | 0.794 |
| 1978 | 0.752 |
| 1979 | 0.725 |
| 1980 | 0.709 |
| 1981 | 0.781 |

Although the official exchange rate greatly overvalues the peso in terms of PPP, it is not possible to estimate meaningfully the extent of the overvaluation. The black market rates published regularly in *Pick's Currency Report* cannot be taken as a measure because there is little opportunity for commodity or currency arbitrage and there are serious penalties for violating currency restrictions in Cuba.

### Conclusions

Table 3-11 compares the exchange rate and PPP relatives in the seven countries of the Council for Mutual Economic Assistance in 1975 and 1980. The tourist exchange rate was chosen as the numeraire.

Column 2 confirms that in most countries the official exchange rates are arbitrary. Expressed in terms of each country's tourist rate, in 1980 they ranged from 10 percent in Poland to 67 percent in Bulgaria, excluding the U.S.S.R. and Hungary, which do not have separate official exchange rates. Column 3 shows the relationship between the commercial exchange rate (and/or the export foreign trade multiplier) and the tourist rate. In large part this relationship will be determined by (1) the commodity composition of exports; (2) the domestic price *systems* and policies of the country, including the incidence of taxes and subsidies; and (3) whether the tourist rates are set to provide incentives or disincentives to tourists.

The impact of these variables can be seen most clearly in the case of Hungary in 1975. The commercial exchange rate was about twice the tourist rate because (1) much of Hungary's exports to the West consisted of manufactured goods and agricultural products (sold in the EEC markets), for which it was getting significantly lower dollar prices than market-type economies were receiving for similar products in West-West trade; (2) domestic producer prices were relatively high and consumer prices relatively low as compared with those in other centrally planned and market-type economies; and (3) the tourist rates were quite favorable to Western tourists. By 1980 the commercial/tourist ratio declined, largely because in 1979 Hungary began the process of unifying the two rates by depreciating the tourist exchange rate by 100 percent in less than three years, even though the Hungarian rate of inflation was not much different from the average West European rate.

The 1975 Czechoslovak pattern is similar to the Hungarian. Much of the exports to the West consist of manufactured goods sold at relatively low prices. That Czechoslovakia does not provide incentive exchange rates to foreign tourists tends to increase the ratio. The decline from 1975 to 1980 probably reflects the more rapid rise in export prices in foreign

Table 3-11. *Exchange Rate and Purchasing Power Relatives, Seven CMEA Countries, 1975 and 1980* (tourist exchange rate = 100)

| Country | Exchange rates | | | Gross national product PPP | | Consumption (Federal Republic) PPP | | | Cost-of-living PPP, United Nations |
| | Tourist (1) | Official (2) | Commercial or FTM (export) (3) | ICP (4) | Other studies (5) | CPE weights (6) | Fed. Rep. weights (7) | Average (8) | (9) |
|---|---|---|---|---|---|---|---|---|---|
| **U.S.S.R.** | | | | | | | | | |
| 1975 | 100 | 100 | 132[a] | — | 65[b] | 60 | 78 | 68 | — |
| 1980 | 100 | 100 | 125[ac] | — | 58 | 41[d] | 53[d] | 47[d] | — |
| **Bulgaria** | | | | | | | | | |
| 1975 | 100 | 83 | 124[ae] | — | | | | | 97 |
| 1980 | 100 | 67 | 87[a] | — | | | | | 67 |
| **Czechoslovakia** | | | | | | | | | |
| 1975 | 100[f] | 57 | 246 | — | 85[f] | — | 76 | — | 93 |
| 1980 | 100[f] | 57 | 205 | — | 92[g] | — | 62 | — | 82 |
| **German Democratic Republic** | | | | | | | | | |
| 1975 | 100 | 39 | n.a. | — | n.a. | — | — | — | — |
| 1980 | 100 | 47 | n.a. | — | 108 | — | — | — | — |
| **Hungary** | | | | | | | | | |
| 1975 | 100 | 42 | 213 | 60 | | — | 72 | — | 95[b] |
| 1980 | 100 | — | 146 | 54 | | — | 69[h] | 45 | 47 |

| | | | | | | | | | |
|---|---|---|---|---|---|---|---|---|---|
| Poland | | | | | | | | | |
| 1975 | 100 | 10 | 151 (94)[i] | 43 | 52[i] | 62[k] | — | 45 | — | 47 |
| 1980 | 100 | 10 | 148 (114)[i] | 45 | 56(63)[d] | 59(60)[k] | — | 45[d] | — | 76[l] |
| Romania | | | | | | | | | |
| 1975 | 100 | 41 | 167 (157)[i] | 73 | | | — | — | — | 94 |
| 1980 | 100 | 37 | 150 (101)[i] | 53 | | | — | — | — | 85 |

*Note:* n.a. = not available. Parenthetical figures are alternative computations. Blank cells indicate that no estimate was made.

a. Foreign trade multiplier for exports to all destinations.

b. 1976.

c. Computed by assuming that the foreign trade multiplier in 1980 was the same as in 1978.

d. 1978.

e. Calculated by assuming that between 1970 and 1980 the foreign trade multiplier has a straight line trend.

f. Table 3-3, column 3.

g. Purchasing power parity as shown and computed in "Exchange Rates and Purchasing Power Parities by Country," section on Czechoslovakia in the text.

h. 1979.

i. The first number is based on the commercial exchange rate, the one in parentheses on the foreign trade multiplier (see text).

j. Joint Polish-Austrian computations; the number in parentheses corresponds to the number in parentheses in table 3-8.

k. Polish central statistical office's comparisons with France and Austria.

l. See table 3-8, note *c.*

*Sources:* Based on tables 3-1–10.

currency than in domestic prices that occurred as Czechoslovakia—like other CPEs—tried to stop or at least moderate the transmission of external inflation to domestic prices by increasing subsidies and taxes. For the German Democratic Republic, a pattern similar to that of Czechoslovakia would be expected, but there is no information.

Poland is a special case. First, its commercial exchange rate is based on its foreign trade multiplier of an earlier period plus a fixed markup (there is no markup in the other countries), for which there would appear to be two justifications. First, since the mid-1970s the high world market price of coal has made it possible to earn a dollar in this sector at a zloty cost only about one-third as high as the cost in other sectors (Fallenbuchl 1985, table IV-1). Therefore, the commercial exchange rate—if it had been set at the average cost of earning a dollar, which is heavily influenced by the production cost of coal (which excludes rent)—would have understated the true average cost of the whole country. The country's severe balance-of-payments difficulties also justify a markup. Poland's foreign trade multipliers (the numbers in parentheses in column 3) are low, especially in 1975, because of coal exports; without coal the ratio would have been about 50 percent higher. A further reason why the ratio is relatively low is that the tourist exchange rate is relatively high (as indicated by the relatively low PPP/tourist exchange rate ratios in columns 4 through 9) in comparison with those of other countries.

Romania's 1975 ratio is about what we would expect: not as high as Hungary's or Czechoslovakia's because it has relatively large energy-based exports. Between 1975 and 1980 the FTM declined considerably because Romania did not increase domestic prices even though its export and import prices in foreign currency rose substantially. The commercial exchange rate was revalued at much less, so that it went from two to eighteen, the reason why the decline in the exchange rate was smaller than that in the foreign trade multiplier.

No comparable ratios can be computed for the U.S.S.R. and Bulgaria. For both, the numbers shown cover total trade, including trade with the CMEA countries, where export pricing is different. Moreover, in both cases even the estimates for total trade involve assumptions, especially uncertain for Bulgaria. In any event, the export FTM/tourist ratio for the U.S.S.R. is expected to be much lower than the ratios of the other countries because the U.S.S.R. is an exporter predominantly of energy products.

We have thus found likely answers to several questions. Do CPEs have uniform exchange rates (or exchange rate proxies whose concept and measurement are clear), and if so, do they have reliable information on how the exchange rates are established? If the CPEs are taken as a group, the answer is negative in both cases. The official exchange rates clearly cannot be considered. The tourist rates would also be problematic. There is insufficient information about the way in which they are determined. Evidence suggests that they do not necessarily approximate the purchasing power parity of consumer goods and services, nor are they necessarily responsive to supply and demand pressures. Since 1961, for example, the U.S.S.R. has adjusted its single exchange rate only to follow the changing international exchange rate of the dollar but not to account for substantial differences in Western and Soviet rates of inflation. Bulgaria has moved the rate up and down, to all appearances somewhat arbitrarily. The German Democratic Republic always quotes the deutschmark rate, even though retail prices move differently in the two countries. Hungary has depreciated the tourist rate by 100 percent in less than three years for reasons unrelated to changes in relative price levels. Romania kept the rate fixed for six years, although its inflation rate was significantly lower than those of its trade partners.

To be sure, none of these situations is unique to CPEs. My only point is that there is uncertainty as to the meaning of the tourist rates and great divergence of practice in their calculation. Moreover, even if the rates accurately reflected the PPP of a tourist basket, their use for GNP conversion would not be appropriate if the centrally planned economies priced the other components of GNP relative to the tourist basket differently from market-type economies. The conclusion that the tourist exchange rate is not the uniformly appropriate rate to use for GNP conversion does not preclude the possibility that for this country or that one, at one or another time, the tourist rate might not yield "reasonable" dollar GNPs.

The commercial exchange rate—or its proxy, the foreign trade multiplier—would seem to be a better candidate as a conversion coefficient. First, we know what it measures and how it is calculated. Second, in some ways it is like an exchange rate in a market-type economy in that it equates the domestic and foreign prices of some traded goods, namely those of exports (in some countries, also of some imports). The exchange rate of a market-type economy without pervasive trade and exchange controls would approximately equate the domestic and foreign prices of all tradables, not just exports. Such is not the case in CPEs, where the domestic prices of imports may be significantly higher or lower than the actual import price multiplied by the commercial exchange rate or the foreign trade multiplier. In the U.S.S.R. in recent years, for example, imports have been priced two to three times higher than exports (table 3-1, column 2 versus column 3); in Romania, in 1980 exports were priced 23 percent higher than imports (table 3-10, column 3 versus column 4).

In contrast, effective January 1, 1980, Hungary introduced a system in which the user of imports pays the actual cost of imports, and Poland moved toward such a system effective January 1, 1982, except for important raw materials and intermediate products (Fallenbuchl 1985, p. 50). The other centrally planned economies apparently are more like the U.S.S.R. and Romania.

A further problem is that the value of an FTM-based commercial exchange rate will be strongly influenced by the composition of exports. If a CPE exports manufactures and agricultural products, it will face considerable difficulties in selling these in the West at internationally competitive prices because of problems of quality and service, lack of name recognition, poor marketing, need to fulfill the plan (so that the exporter may not have full control over the timing and direction of its sales), and, very importantly, Western discrimination, which will depress the export price further. Moreover, many CPEs tend to obtain much of the operating surplus the government needs largely from industry by setting relatively high prices for industrial products and relatively low prices on agricultural goods and on many consumer items, with the result that the foreign trade multiplier is further increased for CPEs with high manufactured exports. The commercial exchange rate (or FTM) will undervalue considerably the currencies of such countries in particular and, when used as a GNP convertor, will introduce a significant downward bias in the resulting dollar GNP as compared with the dollar GNPs of market-type economies.

In contrast, centrally planned economies selling mostly energy and raw materials to the West will have no difficulty marketing their products competitively, so the dollar price will not be depressed. Moreover, the domestic prices of these goods are typically set relatively low. Their FTMs will consequently also be comparatively low. The conclusion, therefore, is that using the commercial exchange rate, or its proxy, the foreign trade multiplier, would not yield per capita dollar GNPs that are uniformly comparable among the CPEs or between CPEs and MTEs. As a practical matter, furthermore, commercial exchange rates are available only for three CPEs and are unavailable for the U.S.S.R., Bulgaria, Czechoslovakia, and the German Democratic Republic.

Turning to the PPP computations, the most striking result in table 3-11 is that the PPPs are significantly lower than the tourist exchange rates, regardless of whether the PPP refers to gross national product or to consumption only and whether it is computed (according to methods that differ) by the International Comparison Project, the central statistical office of a CPE, the central statistical office of the Federal Republic of Germany, the United Nations, or this project's country experts. The single exception is the German Democratic Republic, where in 1980 the purchasing power parity of GNP is estimated to be slightly higher. This exception, however, can be explained at least in part by the fact that the German Democratic Republic sets the tourist exchange rate unfavorably from the standpoint of the West, for political reasons and because the largest number of tourists come from the Federal Republic of Germany to visit relatives, so that the longer-run demand for tourist services is probably quite price inelastic. The next highest ratio is for Czechoslovakia, probably in part because the country is not known for setting incentive exchange rates for Western tourists.

The purchasing power parities for GNP, and also for consumption, are very low relative to the tourist exchange rate in Poland, probably because Poland's balance-of-payments problems and the very high black market rate for the zloty have forced the authorities to set the tourist exchange rate relatively high. Each of the five independent PPP computations reveals a similar pattern (except the United Nations 1980 data, but the latter may be in error, as indicated in table 3-8, note *c*). The purchasing power parities are also low in Hungary, at least in part because of the incentive tourist rates maintained throughout the period, especially since 1979. In the case of Romania, the large decline between 1975 and 1980 in the ratio of its purchasing power parity for GNP to the tourist exchange rate is largely due to the fact that the tourist exchange rate remained unchanged even though prices in Western Europe rose faster than in Romania. The same explanation is valid for the U.S.S.R.

The evidence summarized in this section on exchange rates and purchasing power parities suggests that no particular type of exchange rate is uniformly suitable for use in GNP conversion for all CPEs. This is a key reason why the country experts on the U.S.S.R. (Campbell), Czechoslovakia (Levcik and Havlik), the German Democratic Republic (Collier), Hungary (Hewett), Poland (Fallenbuchl), and Romania (Jackson), as well as the project's consultants on general methodology (Bergson) and on exchange rates and purchasing power parities (Wolf), suggest that, *for the purpose of obtaining regionally and internationally comparable per capita dollar GNP values for CPEs, the conversion coefficient should be based on purchasing power parities for GNP, adjusted to make them comparable to prevailing exchange rates in market-type economies.* The country experts on Bulgaria (Singh and Park) made no recommendation regarding conversion.

## The Relationship between PPP and the Exchange Rate in MTEs

Although it is generally recognized that comparability among countries cannot be achieved for many reasons, many experts also believe that

purchasing power parities are the best conversion coefficients for obtaining internationally comparable and consistent data on the *volume* of
goods and services produced by a country. To obtain such convertors
was the intended purpose of the International Comparison Project, as
stated in the 1980 *Atlas*: "The ICP has developed reliable measures of
the real GNP on an internationally comparable scale. The work of the
ICP has covered 16 countries, is . . . complete for 34, and will ultimately
cover about 75 countries. . . . International agencies are engaged in research
on appropriate ways of extending the ICP-type comparisons to all countries of the world on an annual basis" (p. 22). Still, "until such coverage
is complete, exchange rates remain the only available means for conversion of GNP from national currencies to U.S. dollars" (ibid.).

There are several reasons for the continued use of the prevailing exchange
rates. One is that benchmark ICP results in Phase III were available only
for thirty-four countries and in Phase IV only for about seventy countries,
whereas comparable conversion coefficients are needed for all countries.
Another is that ICP results become available only with a long time lag.
To be sure, shortcut estimates are available for just about all countries
(see Kravis et al. 1978; Kravis, Heston, and Summers 1978; and Ahmad
1980). Although these estimates are subject to wider margins of error
than the benchmark estimates, the margins are much smaller than those
found in exchange rate conversions. The shortcut methods developed
thus far, however, rely on the availability of exchange-rate-converted
GDPs, which poses an insurmountable difficulty for their application to
centrally planned economies. A further reason for continuing to use the
prevailing exchange rates as convertors is that there continue to be methodological questions about the meaning of the international prices used
by the ICP as well as about certain other aspects of the ICP method. The
fact that the ICP results show significantly smaller dispersion in total and
per capita real incomes in dollars between the developed and developing
countries than does conversion based on exchange rates is also a factor.
Not all countries endorse a method that might graduate them from lower
to higher per capita income categories, with possible implications for
preferential tariff positions and concessionary loans from international
organizations. To be sure, it would be possible to resolve this problem
by preparing new guidelines based on both purchasing power parity and
exchange-rate-computed per capita GDPs, but a discussion of these issues
is beyond the scope of this book.

The systematic relationship between the PPP-converted and the exchange-
rate-derived dollar GDP appears to be largely a function of the per capita
GDP levels of countries, as shown in figure 3-1. The vertical axis in figure
3-1 is the ratio of the exchange rate to the PPP, called the exchange rate
deviation index. An ERDI greater than one means that the exchange rate

is "higher" than the PPP (so that the real value of the country's currency is higher in terms of PPP than in terms of its exchange rate). Thus for a country with an ERDI greater than one, conversion of its gross domestic product to dollars via PPP will yield a higher dollar figure than if its exchange rate were used. More generally, the higher the PPP or the exchange rate, the lower the resulting dollar GDP, and vice versa.

The authors of the ICP interpret the relationship between the exchange rate deviation index and real per capita gross domestic product shown in figure 3-1 largely in terms of the differences in the productivity gap between high- and low-income countries for tradable and nontradable goods. That is, international commodity arbitrage tends to drive the prices of similar tradable goods toward equality in different countries. With equal or nearly equal prices, wages in tradable goods industries in each country will be determined by productivity; similar wages will prevail in each country's nontradable goods sectors also. In nontradable goods

Figure 3-1. *Exchange Rate Deviation Index in Relation to Real GDP per Capita, Thirty-four Countries, 1975*

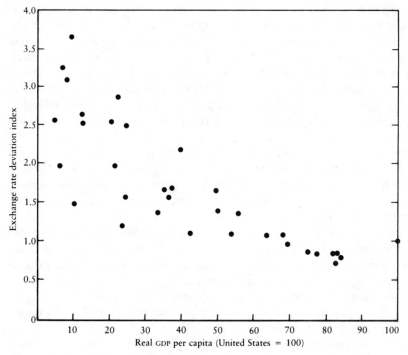

*Source*: Kravis and others (1982, fig. 1-1).

industries, however, international productivity differentials tend to be smaller. Consequently, in a high-productivity country high wages lead to high prices of nontradable goods, whereas in a low-productivity country low wages give rise to low prices of services and other nontradables. The lower a country's income, the lower will be the prices of its nontradable goods and the greater will be the tendency for exchange rate conversions to underestimate its real income compared with that of richer countries. In contrast, valuing nontradables at international prices or in the prices of a higher-income country (as in bilateral PPP comparisons) will tend to increase the real income of the poorer countries as compared with that of the richer countries (Kravis et al. 1982, pp. 11–42). To be sure, Kravis has shown that alternative treatment of services does not affect the overall GDPs very greatly (ibid., p. 138ff.). Moreover, experiments with different weighting systems, such as, for example, a system that assigns equal weights to prices in rich and poor countries, lowered the real per capita GDP of the eight poorest countries only by amounts ranging from 9 percent to 13 percent (Kravis 1984, p. 33). These differences are much smaller than those between exchange rate conversions and any PPP-based estimate.

Nevertheless, from the standpoint of developing countries, the abundance of services at low market prices is a sign of underdevelopment, reflecting the low marginal productivity of labor and the scarcity of alternative productive employment opportunities. Paradoxically, services are also relatively low priced in centrally planned economies, but (certainly in the European CMEA countries) for different reasons. In CPEs relatively low-priced services reflect their government's pricing decisions, even though labor is generally not in excess supply at the macro level and there is a shortage of many services at the prices prevailing. The relatively low prices of services appear to reflect a combination of low priority and low esteem in which such "nonproductive " (in Marxian terminology) activities are held by the planners. And even though the views regarding the unproductive nature of services may be changing in some CPEs, the relatively low prices of services persist as a legacy of pricing decisions made when traditional Soviet-type planning was introduced (see chapter 4 for further discussion of the pricing of services in CPEs).

Some researchers, including Kravis, have questioned the empirical validity of having relatively low-priced services as the main determinant of the ERDI. In his recent work, Kravis notes that the reciprocal of the ERDI for a country, that is, the ratio of the purchasing power to its exchange rate, is the same as its price level relative to that of the numeraire country. The low price levels that characterize low-income countries are thus the other side of the coin represented by high ERDIs. Kravis then shows that openness (exports plus imports relative to GDP) and the share of services in GDP as well as real per capita GDP contribute significantly to the explanation of price levels (Kravis 1984, pp. 28–29). Other researchers have suggested that several additional factors are likely to affect the ERDI of a country. Wolf, for example, has shown that, even if the exchange rate of a market-type economy were an equilibrium rate from the standpoint of the balance of payments, there would still be many reasons for the exchange rate to deviate from PPP, including differences among countries in (1) the relative prices of nontradables, (2) expenditure weights, (3) the terms of trade, and (4) explicit or implicit trade taxes (Wolf 1985, sec. 2). More recently, it has been shown also that the degree of openness (trade turnover divided by GNP), which is positively correlated with income levels, may explain the relationship between the ERDI and per capita GNP depicted in figure 3-1 (Wolf 1985, p. 10).

The conclusion is that, even though exchange rates may as convertors be only second best following PPPs, because the Bank and other international organizations will continue to employ them to convert GNPs to U.S. dollars, the aim here must be to find proxy exchange rates that would be appropriate for comparability between CPEs and MTEs. If we could ascertain empirically the relative importance of the factors determining the ERDI for market-type economies, we could use an equation to calculate a "comparable" ERDI for centrally planned economies. Unfortunately the causal relationships have not until now been fully established. Thus we are left with only the finding that the ERDI is strongly and negatively correlated with the level of per capita GNP, with a much better fit at relatively high income levels than at very low ones, as can be seen in figure 3-1.

## Estimating the Relationship between PPP and the Exchange Rate in CPEs

For 1975 the International Comparison Project computed the ERDI for thirty market-type economies, Yugoslavia, and three centrally planned economies (Hungary, Poland, and Romania). The ICP, however, does not yield meaningful ERDIs for the centrally planned economies because it is difficult to interpret these countries' official exchange rates, either the commercial or the noncommercial (the ICP has used the latter). Our previous discussion of the various exchange rates suggests very strongly that there is little basis for assuming that a centrally planned economy's commercial or tourist rates are truly comparable to the prevailing exchange rates of market-type economies used in the ICP study to compute ERDIs. The problem, therefore, is to find a method for plausibly estimating ERDIs for centrally planned economies in order to derive proxy exchange rates, first for 1975 (the latest year for which the ICP computed ERDIs for market-type economies), and then, by extrapolation, for 1980.

## Estimating ERDIs for CPEs for 1975

Various ways have been proposed of estimating for centrally planned economies ERDIs that will be comparable to those calculated for market-type economies. Some researchers have suggested applying to each centrally planned economy the ERDI of a market-type economy at approximately the same level of per capita income. A somewhat more sophisticated approach has been suggested by Wolf (1982). He notes that, as long as we have confidence in the basic ICP approach and its results for the three centrally planned economies included, there is no need to make assumptions about what would be "normal" ERDIs for centrally planned economies; it is sufficient to make an assumption for only one of the components of ERDI. Wolf (1982) has shown that the ERDI may be decomposed into two parts:

$$(3.1) \qquad\qquad ERDI = \frac{e_o}{e_p} = \frac{e_t/e_p}{e_t/e_o}$$

where $e_o$ = official exchange rate, $e_p$ = "overall" PPP, and $e_t$ = PPP for tradables. Because the data to obtain $e_t/e_p$ are generated internally by the ICP for all countries, including the three CPEs, without using an exchange rate, only the denominator, $e_t/e_o$, will have to be estimated for the CPEs, which can be done on the basis of the $e_t/e_o$ of "comparable" MTEs.

The selection of market-type economies "comparable" to centrally planned economies is to a certain degree judgmental, basically because there is no generally accepted explanation of what determines the ERDI, as previously noted. All we can say confidently at this stage of scholarship is that the ERDI is strongly and negatively correlated with the level of per capita GDP. Recalling from (3.1) that the ERDI has two components, this negative correlation is the outcome of a negative correlation between $e_t/e_p$ and income level and a positive correlation between $e_t/e_o$ and income level, as can be seen from the data in table 3-12. Because $e_t/e_o$ is positively correlated with the level of income, $e_t/e_o$ for CPEs may appropriately be estimated on the basis of MTEs at approximately the same level of income. There is no circularity in this approach once we accept the PPP-based per capita GDP figures for centrally planned economies as a point of departure, because we are concerned to estimate only $e_t/e_o$, *not* the level of dollar per capita income.

Two approaches have been suggested for selecting the reference group

Table 3-12. *Per Capita GDP and Exchange Rate Deviation Indexes, Selected MTEs and CPEs in 1975*
(United States = 1.00)

| Country | Per capita GDP (1) | $e_t/e_p$ (2) | $e_t/e_o$ (3) | (2) ÷ (3) (ERDI) (4) |
|---|---|---|---|---|
| **Group I** | | | | |
| Malawi | 352 | 1.44 | 0.565 | 2.55 |
| Kenya | 470 | 1.42 | 0.726 | 1.95 |
| India | 470 | 1.66 | 0.514 | 3.23 |
| Pakistan | 590 | 1.45 | 0.464 | 3.12 |
| Sri Lanka | 668 | 1.73 | 0.475 | 3.65 |
| Zambia | 738 | 1.43 | 0.955 | 1.49 |
| Thailand | 936 | 1.31[a] | 0.489[a] | 2.61 |
| Philippines | 946 | 1.55 | 0.615 | 2.51 |
| **Group II** | | | | |
| Korea | 1,484 | 1.35 | 0.531 | 2.54 |
| Malaysia | 1,541 | 1.51 | 0.766 | 1.98 |
| Colombia | 1,609 | 1.47 | 0.520 | 2.83 |
| Jamaica | 1,723 | 1.37 | 1.115 | 1.23 |
| Syria | 1,794 | 1.14 | 0.457 | 2.50 |
| Brazil | 1,811 | 1.34 | 0.849 | 1.58 |
| **Group III** | | | | |
| Romania | 2,387 | 1.55 | (0.804)[b] | (1.93)[b] |
| | | | (0.797)[c] | (1.94)[c] |
| Mexico | 2,487 | 1.40 | 0.822 | 1.70 |
| Yugoslavia | 2,591 | 1.29 | 0.828 | 1.56 |
| Iran | 2,705 | 1.30 | 0.761 | 1.70 |
| Uruguay | 2,844 | 1.32 | 0.605 | 2.17 |
| Ireland | 3,049 | 1.20 | 1.049 | 1.14 |
| **Group IV** | | | | |
| Hungary | 3,559 | 1.41 | (1.028)[b] | (1.37)[b] |
| | | | (0.928)[c] | (1.52)[c] |
| Poland | 3,598 | 1.44 | (1.028)[b] | (1.40)[b] |
| | | | (0.933)[c] | (1.54)[c] |
| Italy | 3,861 | 1.25 | 1.113 | 1.12 |
| Spain | 4,010 | 1.25 | 0.921 | 1.36 |
| **Group V** | | | | |
| United Kingdom | 4,588 | 1.18 | 1.060 | 1.11 |
| Japan | 4,907 | 1.04 | 0.951 | 1.10 |
| Austria | 4,995 | 1.11 | 1.112 | 1.00 |
| Netherlands | 5,397 | 1.06 | 1.186 | 0.89 |
| Belgium | 5,574 | 1.07 | 1.207 | 0.88 |
| France | 5,877 | 1.13 | 1.239 | 0.91 |

(*Table continues on the following page.*)

*Table 3-12 (continued)*

| Country | Per capita GDP (1) | $e_r/e_p$ (2) | $e_r/e_o$ (3) | (2) ÷ (3) (ERDI) (4) |
|---|---|---|---|---|
| Luxembourg | 5,883 | 1.10 | 1.205 | 0.91 |
| Denmark | 5,911 | 1.14 | 1.445 | 0.79 |
| Federal Republic of Germany | 5,953 | 1.10 | 1.260 | 0.88 |
| United States | 7,176 | 1.00 | 1.000 | 1.00 |

Note: My own estimates appear in parentheses.
a. One of these numbers must have a slight error, because they yield an ERDI of 2.68.
b. Obtained via the first approach (see text).
c. Obtained via the second approach (see text).
Sources: Columns 1 and 4: Kravis and others (1982, table 1-2); column 2: Kravis and others (1982, table 6-12, columns 8 and 10); column 3: Kravis and others (1982, table 6-12, column 8).

*Table 3-13. Centrally Planned Economies Matched with Market-Type Economies of Comparable GDP*

| Centrally planned economies | Reference market-type economies | $e_r/e_o$ of the reference group (unweighted average) |
|---|---|---|
| Hungary, Poland | Ireland, Italy, Spain | 1.028 |
| Romania | Iran, Mexico, Yugoslavia | 0.804 |

Source: Table 3-12.

of market-type economies. Wolf recommends the selection of those market-type economies whose per capita GDP in "international" dollars is "comparable" to that of a given centrally planned economy, say, within about ±20 percent. The results (from table 3-12) appear in table 3-13.

An alternative approach is to regress $e_t/e_o$ on per capita GDPs for all MTEs or for a subgroup of them, then substitute the per capita GDP of each of the three CPEs into the resulting equation to obtain estimates of their $e_t/e_o$. To select the statistical formula to depict the relationship, the data of all non-CPE countries are plotted in figure 3-2. The chart shows that the fit is not a very tight one. Using the least squares estimate yields:

$$(3.2) \qquad e_t/e_o = .529 + .0001122 \ Y/N$$
$$(R^2 = .66; \text{SEE} = .165)$$

where $Y$ = GDP in international dollars, $N$ = population, and $Y/N$ = per capita GDP.

*Figure 3-2. Price Level of Tradables in Relation to Real GDP per Capita, Non-CPE Countries, 1975*

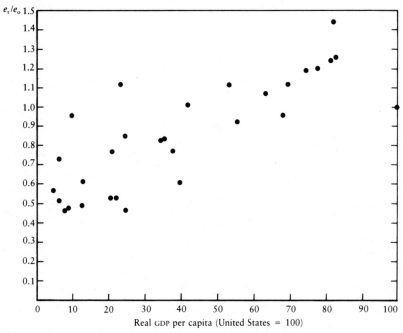

*Source*: Table 3-12, col. 3.

For the three CPES $e_t/e_o$ is obtained from (3.2) and is shown as the second set of estimates in table 3-12. For Romania, the two approaches yield practically the same numbers; for Hungary and Poland, the two estimates are reasonably close. The ERDIs are obtained by dividing column 3 into column 2. The second set of estimates is used in subsequent computations.

The country expert on Hungary has noted, however, that, when we are using a regression equation such as (3.2) to estimate either $e_t/e_o$ or the ERDI itself, the result is not a single number but a range within a confidence interval (Hewett 1985). On the assumption that the scatter in figure 3-2 is normally distributed, we can be 95 percent certain that the $e_t/e_o$ is within $\pm 2$ SEE ($\pm 0.33$) of the regression line. Thus if we want to provide a confidence band around the estimates, the ranges within which the ERDIs for the three CPES will most probably fall are those shown in table 3-14. Actually, inasmuch as the ERDI is inversely related to $e_t/e_o$, the intervals shown in table 3-14 for the ERDI range may be some-

*Table 3-14. ERDI Ranges for Romania, Hungary, and Poland, 1975*

| Country | Estimated $e_t/e_o$ | Range within $\pm 2$ SEE | ERDI range |
|---------|---------------------|--------------------------|------------|
| Romania | 0.797 | 0.467–1.127 | 1.38–3.32 |
| Hungary | 0.928 | 0.598–1.258 | 1.12–2.36 |
| Poland  | 0.933 | 0.603–1.263 | 1.14–2.39 |

*Source*: Computed on the basis of equation (3.2). The per capita GDP (*Y/N*) is obtained from table 3-12.

what underestimated. I shall discuss the implications of the ERDI range for estimating dollar per capita incomes shortly.

For centrally planned economies not included in the ICP, the ICP results can be used to obtain per capita "international" dollar GDP estimates and ERDIs because bilateral, PPP-based comparisons with market-type economies are available for the U.S.S.R. (vis-à-vis the United States), Czechoslovakia (vis-à-vis Austria), and the German Democratic Republic (vis-à-vis the Federal Republic of Germany), as discussed above. For Poland an alternative to the ICP estimate can be obtained on the basis of its bilateral comparison with Austria. Because the partner market-type economies have been included in the ICP, each centrally planned economy's 1975 per capita GDP can be estimated in international dollars through these bilateral links, as shown in table 3-15.

The ERDIs are estimated, as before, in two steps. On the basis of the limited sample of three centrally planned economies in the ICP, we obtain a relationship between CPE $e_t/e_p$ and MTE $e_t/e_p$ for a given "real" income group. In 1975 Hungarian and Polish "real" incomes were similar and so were their $e_t/e_p$ ratios: 1.41 and 1.44, respectively. Romania, with a lower "real" income, had a higher $e_t/e_p$: 1.55. The ratios of all three CPEs exceed those of their respective MTE reference groups by about 15 percent in each case. This characteristic suggests a systemic regularity: the relatively high level of prices of tradables to "overall" prices is explained by the fact that CPEs have relatively low prices for nontradables (for example, services). Let us assume, therefore, that the $e_t/e_p$ of each CPE is 15 percent higher than that of its MTE reference group, an assumption that is not likely to introduce a significant margin of error. The other component of the ERDI, $e_t/e_o$, is estimated as before, on the basis of equation (3.2) (see table 3-16).

## Estimating ERDIs for CPEs for 1980

PPP-based per capita dollar GDP figures are available for 1980 for six CPEs. What ERDIs should be applied to adjust these figures? One option would be to employ the ERDIs computed for 1975, without adjustment.

If we did so, however, we would be treating CPEs and MTEs asymmetrically, because between 1975 and 1980 the ERDIs of MTEs did not remain unchanged. The 1980 ERDIs of MTEs can be estimated by juxtaposing changes in exchange rates and inflation differentials between each country and the United States. If between 1975 and 1980, for example, an MTE's price level increased faster than the U.S. price level but its exchange rate depreciated (increased) by less than the price differential, then its ERDI declined. More generally:

$$(3.3) \qquad ERDI_{80} = \frac{(ERDI_{75})(e_{o80}/e_{o75})}{(P_{MTE80}/P_{MTE75}) \div (P_{US80}/P_{US75})}$$

where $e_o$ = official exchange rate against the dollar and $P$ = price index (GNP deflator if available, otherwise the consumer price index).

A comparison of the 1975 ERDIs of thirty market-type economies included in Phase III of the ICP yields remarkably consistent results: the ERDIs of twenty-five of the thirty countries had declined, the average ERDI of each of the five groups of countries classified by ascending real income level (see table 3-12) also declined, and so did every one of the sixteen market-type economies composing the three highest per capita income groups, with which the centrally planned economies can most readily be compared. The percentage change in the ERDIs of the individual countries in the five income groups (countries listed in the same order as in table 3-12) appears in table 3-17. There seems to be no correlation between the steepness of the decline in the ERDI and the level of per capita income: the average decline for Groups III, IV, and V was about 20 percent, with that for Groups I and II somewhat lower.

Whether we take the average change in the ERDIs of each group or the average of all of the countries individually, between 1975 and 1980 the average decline in the ERDIs was about 15 percent. This figure can be interpreted as the (unweighted) average decline in the effective exchange rate of the U.S. dollar against a representative basket of the world's convertible currencies. Therefore, to preserve the comparability of the per capita income levels of centrally planned and market-type economies expressed in current U.S. dollars, the 1980 ERDIs of the CPEs must be reduced by 15 percent also, yielding (the range within $\pm 2$ SEE appears in parentheses):

| | | |
|---|---|---|
| German Dem. Rep. | 1.12 | (0.85–1.67) |
| Czechoslovakia | 1.22 | (0.92–1.85) |
| Hungary | 1.29 | (0.95–2.00) |
| Poland | 1.31 | (0.97–2.03) |
| U.S.S.R. | 1.32 | (0.98–2.06) |
| Romania | 1.65 | (1.17–2.82) |

Table 3-15. Per Capita GNP and Exchange Rate Deviation Indexes for Six CMEA Countries and Yugoslavia, 1975

| Country | Purchasing power parity based | | ERDI in 1975 | Adjusted PPP (proxy exchange rate) | |
|---|---|---|---|---|---|
| | 1975 per cap. GNP (international dollars)[a] (1) | As percentage of U.S. per cap. GNP (2) | (3) | 1975 per cap. GNP (U.S. dollars)[a] (4) | As percentage of U.S. per cap. GNP (5) |
| German Democratic Republic | 4,230 | 59 | 1.32 | 3,200 | 45 |
| Czechoslovakia (bilateral with Austria and Federal Republic of Germany) | 4,000 | 55 | 1.44 | 2,780 | 39 |
| Poland (ICP) | 3,600 | 50 | 1.54 | 2,340 | 33 |
| Poland (bilateral with Austria) | 3,000 | 42 | 1.54 | 1,950 | 27 |
| Hungary (ICP) | 3,560 | 50 | 1.52 | 2,340 | 33 |
| U.S.S.R. (bilateral with United States) | 3,540 | 49 | 1.55 | 2,280 | 32 |
| Yugoslavia (ICP) | 2,590 | 36 | 1.56 | 1,660 | 23 |
| Romania (ICP) | 2,390 | 33 | 1.94 | 1,230 | 17 |

Note: Per capita GNP, based on adjusted purchasing power parity: column 1 divided by column 3 except Yugoslavia: official figures published in Atlas. ERDI: deviation explained in the text except Yugoslavia: calculated by the ICP.

a. International dollars (I$) and U.S. dollars are rounded to the nearest ten.

Sources: Per capita GNP, based on purchasing power parity. German Democratic Republic: sum of 1975 per capita consumption of DM 5,400, investment of DM 3,500, and government of DM 2,975 (Collier 1985, table 10 and sec. 5) is DM 11,875, which is 71 percent of the per capita GNP of the Federal Republic of Germany, which equals I $4,227. Czechoslovakia: total 1975 GNP of 474.4 billion Kcs, population of 14,918 million, and purchasing power parity of 7.95 Kcs/dollar yield per capita GNP of 56 percent of that of the United States, which equals I $4,000. Poland, Hungary, Yugoslavia, and Romania (ICP): Kravis and others (1982, table 1-2); Poland (bilateral with Austria): Central Statistical Offices (1982, table 1) shows that on a per capita basis, Poland's 1975 GNP was 60 percent of that of Austria (geometric average of calculations in Austrian and Polish prices), which yields I $2,997. U.S.S.R.: total 1976 GNP of 490 billion rubles, population of 256.674 million, and purchasing power parity of 0.49 rubles/dollar yields per capita GNP equal to 49.4 percent of that of the United States. Applying that percentage to the U.S. 1975 GNP yields I $3,545.

*Table 3-16. ERDI Ranges for the German Democratic Republic, Czechoslovakia, and the U.S.S.R., 1980*

| | | $e_t/e_p$ | | | |
|---|---|---|---|---|---|
| CPE | *Reference MTEs* | MTE | CPE | $e_t/e_o$ | *ERDI of CPE* |
| German Democratic Republic | Austria, Japan, United Kingdom, Italy, Spain | 1.16 | 1.33 | 1.004 | 1.32 (1.00−1.97) |
| Czechoslovakia | United Kingdom, Italy, Spain | 1.23 | 1.41 | 0.978 | 1.44 (1.08−2.18) |
| U.S.S.R. | Italy, Spain | 1.25 | 1.44 | 0.926 | 1.55 (1.15−2.42) |

*Note*: Ranges appear in parentheses.

*Sources*: The $e_t/e_p$ of the reference countries is from table 3-12 and has been adjusted by 15 percent, as explained in the text. The $e_t/e_o$ is computed on the basis of equation (3.2).

*Table 3-17. Percentage Change in the ERDIs of the Individual Countries in the Five Income Groups*

| *Group I* | *Group II* | *Group III* | *Group IV* | *Group V* |
|---|---|---|---|---|
| −15 | −20 | −12 | −13 | −32 |
| −20 | 2 | −12 | −24 | −21 |
| 9 | −26 | −36 | | −18 |
| − 8 | 2 | −40 | | −17 |
| a | −8 | −21 | | −17 |
| −13 | 16 | | | −14 |
| −11 | | | | −15 |
| −16 | | | | −16 |
| | | | | −15 |
| Average −11 | − 6 | −24 | −18 | −18 |

*Note:* Group IV excludes the two CPE countries; Group V takes the United States as the numeraire country.

a. Sri Lanka, which in 1975 already had the highest ERDI of 3.65, by 1980 had more than doubled it to 7.53, probably because noncomparable exchange rates were used in the two years. Whatever the reason, the figure is so implausible that the country was omitted from the computations.

*Sources*: Table 3-12, column 4, compared with results extrapolated to 1980 by applying formula (3.3). The official exchange rate and price index data for the countries are from *International Financial Statistics*, various issues.

Table 3-18 summarizes the results of computations of per capita GNPs of the European CMEA countries according to alternative convertors. Column 7 presents the estimates preferred by our team. The statistical uncertainty regarding the calculation of the ERDIs for CPEs, however, implies a corresponding uncertainty regarding the values of the adjusted PPP convertors and the resulting dollar per capita income estimates. If we

Table 3-18. *Calculations of per Capita GNP of the European CMEA Countries with Alternative Convertors, 1975 and 1980*

| Country | 1975 per capita GNP (international dollars) (1) | PPP convertor, 1980 | | | PPP scaled to exchange rate convertor, 1980 | | | GNP at prevailing exchange rates, 1980 | |
|---|---|---|---|---|---|---|---|---|---|
| | | Per capita GNP (NCU) (2) | PPP (NCU/ dollars) (3) | Per capita GNP (dollars) (4) | ERDI (5) | Adjusted PPP (NCU/ dollars) (6) | Per capita GNP (dollars) (7) | Commercial exchange rate or FTM (8) | Tourist exchange rate (9) |
| German Democratic Republic | 4,230 | 13,000 marks | 1.96ª | 6,630 | 1.12 | 2.20 | 5,910 | 3,940 | 7,140 |
| Czechoslovakia | 4,000 | 36,913 Kcs | 6.38ᵇ | 5,790 | 1.22 | 7.78 | 4,740 | 1,920 | 3,930 |
| U.S.S.R. | 3,540 | 2,211 rubles | 0.40ᶜ | 5,550 | 1.32 | 0.53 | 4,190 | 3,420ᵈ | 3,420 |
| Hungary (ICP, Phase III) | 3,560 | 66,859 forints | 11.80 | 5,660 | 1.29 | 15.22 | 4,390 | 2,060 | 3,020 |
| Hungary (ICP, Phase IV) | | | | 4,373 | 1.29 | | 3,390 | | |
| Poland (ICP, Phase III) | 3,600 | 69,878 zlotys | 14.30 | 4,890 | 1.31 | 18.73 | 3,730 | 1,553 | 2,290 |
| Poland (ICP, Phase IV) | | | | 4,081 | 1.31 | | 3,115 | | |

| | | | | | | | | |
|---|---|---|---|---|---|---|---|---|
| Poland | 3,000 | 69,878 zlotys | 19.20[e] | 3,640 | 1.31 | 25.15 | 2,780 | 2,010[f] | — |
| Bulgaria | n.a. | 3,009 leva | n.a. | n.a. | n.a. | n.a. | n.a. | 3,551[d] | 2,340 |
| Romania | 2,390 | 27,838 lei | 6.3 | 4,420 | 1.65 | 10.40 | 2,680 | 1,550 | 2,320 |

*Note:* n.a. = not available. A dash indicates that the survey was discontinued.

a. Bilateral with the Federal Republic of Germany.

b. Bilateral with Austria and the Federal Republic of Germany. The derivation of the PPP convertor is explained in "Exchange Rates and Purchasing Power Parities, by Country," under Czechoslovakia.

   c. Bilateral with the United States.

   d. Converted at the official exchange rate.

   e. Bilateral with Austria.

   f. Converted at the foreign trade multiplier.

*Sources:* Column 1: table 3-15; column 2: table 2-1; column 3: tables 3-1, 3-4 (and see "Czechoslovakia" in text), 3-5, 3-6, 3-8, and 3-10; column 4: column 2 divided by column 3 except Hungary and Poland ICP, Phase IV, whose derivation is explained under "ICP Phase IV Results for Hungary, Poland, and Selected MTES" in the text; column 5: see "Estimating ERDIS for CPES for 1980" in the text; column 6: column 3 times column 5; column 7: GNP per capita in national currency units shown in table 2-1 divided by column 6 and rounded to nearest ten, except Hungary and Poland, ICP, Phase IV, whose derivation is explained in text; columns 8 and 9: column 2 divided by exchange rates shown in tables 3-1, 3-3, 3-5, 3-6, 3-7, and 3-10.

set aside all other data and statistical problems, the uncertainties in estimating the ERDIs alone mean that we can be about 95 percent sure that, on the basis of the approach just described, the true estimates of 1980 per capita GDPs (equivalent to GNPs) lie within the range shown in table 3-19.

The extreme values presented do not of course mean that a country's GNP levels have an equal probability of being anywhere within the range; the highest probabilities cluster around the "best" (midpoint) estimates, which will be used in subsequent analysis.

## ICP Phase IV Results for Hungary, Poland, and Selected MTEs

As this book was being readied for publication, the results of ICP Phase IV for 1980 became available for the European countries participating in the European Comparison Program (United Nations 1983). Because of significant differences in country coverage and methods employed between Phase IV and Phase III, discussed earlier in this chapter, the results of Phase III extrapolations to 1980 and Phase IV computations for 1980 are not directly comparable.

Only two CPEs, Hungary and Poland, participated in the European Comparison Program (Romania, as previously noted, withdrew before the study was completed), and they did so as members of Group II, whose other participants were Austria, Finland, and Yugoslavia. It is important

*Table 3-19. Dollar per Capita GNP Range of the European CMEA Countries in 1980 at Alternative Exchange Rate Deviation Indexes*

|  | Convertor (NCUs/dollars) | | | Per capita dollar GNP | | |
|---|---|---|---|---|---|---|
| Country | Low | Best | High | Low | Best | High |
| German Democratic Republic | 1.67 | 2.20 | 3.27 | 4,000 | 5,910 | 7,800 |
| Czechoslovakia | 5.87 | 7.78 | 11.80 | 3,100 | 4,740 | 6,300 |
| Hungary | 11.21 | 15.22 | 23.60 | 2,830 | 4,390 | 5,960 |
| Poland | 13.87 | 18.73 | 29.03 | 2,400 | 3,730 | 5,040 |
| U.S.S.R. | 0.39 | 0.53 | 0.82 | 2,700 | 4,190 | 5,700 |
| Romania | 7.37 | 10.40 | 17.77 | 1,570 | 2,680 | 3,800 |

*Sources*: GNP per capita in national currency units shown in table 2-1 divided by the PPPs shown in table 3-18, column 6, adjusted by alternative estimates of the ERDI (the "best" estimate is based on the ERDI shown in table 3-18, column 5, the "low" and "high" estimates based on the range of ERDIs shown in the accompanying text).

to note that the international prices, and thus the PPPs and GDP volumes of these countries, are based on the average prices of the Group II nations, so that the outcomes are expected to differ from those that would be anticipated if the international prices were based on the average of all participating European countries.

Using Austria as the numeraire country and obtaining a linkage between Group I and II countries according to the first of two alternative methods indicated under "Methodology" above (that is, simply relying on Austria as the bridge while keeping the original, separate group results unchanged), we obtained the per capita GDP volume relatives shown below for 1980 (Austria = 100).

| | | | |
|---|---|---|---|
| Luxembourg | 121.7 | Finland | 94.4 |
| Federal Republic | | Italy | 89.2 |
| of Germany | 116.9 | Spain | 72.8 |
| Denmark | 112.6 | Ireland | 62.8 |
| France | 112.0 | Greece | 58.4 |
| Belgium | 108.1 | Hungary | 53.7 |
| Netherlands | 106.7 | Poland | 50.1 |
| Austria | 100.0 | Yugoslavia | 46.9 |
| United Kingdom | 94.6 | Portugal | 43.9 |

There is no unambiguous answer to the question of how these results for Hungary, Poland, and Yugoslavia would translate into U.S. dollars. Because the United States did not participate in the European Comparison Program, no direct conversion to dollars is available. The Organisation for Economic Co-operation and Development, however, extrapolated the GDP of the United States from 1975 to 1980 and estimated a ratio of per capita GDP between the United States and Group I countries. According to this estimation, in 1980 one Austrian "purchasing power" schilling (the common denominator in which the GDP volumes of the countries are expressed) was equivalent to $1.077. Computed on this basis, the dollar values of the per capita GDPs of the two centrally planned economies and Yugoslavia are:

| | |
|---|---|
| Hungary | $4,373 |
| Poland | $4,081 |
| Yugoslavia | $3,816 |

To move from these per capita GDPs evaluated in PPP dollars to per capita GDPs expressed in adjusted PPP dollars again presents a difficult problem because it requires the use of some "reasonable" exchange rate deviation index. The European Comparison Program did compute ERDIS, again finding that for the more developed countries the ERDIS were near or below one, whereas for the less developed European countries they were considerably above one. The study also notes, however, that the magnitude of the ERDIs depends greatly on the currency selected as the reference unit. Because in 1980 the exchange rate of the Austrian schilling was rather high in relation to the other currencies (that is, relatively few schillings per foreign currency), it imparts an upward bias to the ERDIs of the other countries when they are measured against the Austrian numeraire currency unit. For this reason, and because of the more comprehensive country coverage of Phase III on which the computations can be based, I shall apply the ERDIs obtained previously for 1980 in the case of Hungary and Poland. These, incidentally, are not very different from the ERDIs obtained from Phase IV for approximately comparable MTEs.

| | |
|---|---|
| Italy | 1.326 |
| Spain | 1.321 |
| Ireland | 1.240 |
| Greece | 1.414 |
| Portugal | 1.855 |

If we apply the midpoint ERDIs shown above, the "adjusted PPP" dollar per capita GDPs are:

| | |
|---|---|
| Hungary | $3,390 |
| Poland | 3,115 |

Inasmuch as Phase IV computations for Hungary and Poland depend to a significant extent on Hungarian, Polish, and perhaps Romanian and Yugoslav prices that are believed to embody greater distortions than the prices of most market-type economies (see chapter 4), and inasmuch as the results are available for only two centrally planned economies, and it is necessary, to obtain results in dollars, to estimate the PPP of the U.S. currency in terms of the Austrian currency, which introduces an additional element of uncertainty, our preference is for the adjusted PPP convertors obtained from Phase III ICP data through the method described in "Estimating the Relationship between PPP and the Exchange Rate in CPEs," above.[12]

## Comparison of Alternative Convertors

There is no acid test to evaluate the per capita dollar GNPs resulting from the application of alternative conversion coefficients. The only test

12. I do not know whether Group II's international prices were adjusted to reflect the withdrawal of Romania.

that can be applied is that of plausibility. One approach is to compare the per capita dollar GNPs with the results of independent studies that have themselves been judged plausible by experts. We may, for example, assess the per capita dollar GNPs in terms of the ordinal and cardinal ranking of the countries *within* the Council for Mutual Economic Assistance, comparing these with the results of similar computations carried out by experts in the CMEA countries. Alternatively, the results may be compared with the findings of independent multilateral studies involving centrally planned and market-type economies. A variation of this approach is to compare estimates against carefully performed bilateral or multilateral comparisons of an earlier period, when data may have been more readily available, moved forward to a current benchmark year by "reasonable" growth rates. Still another approach is to examine the plausibility not of the per capita dollar GNPs themselves but of their implications, for example, in terms of foreign trade participation ratios or in terms of such physical indicators as per capita energy consumption. Per capita dollar GNPs that are found to be more plausible according to the criteria just mentioned should be considered "better" than alternative estimates that are less believable.

I shall assess the plausibility of the alternative sets of estimates in light of four sets of reference points: studies by experts in the CMEA of the ranking of per capita incomes of the CMEA countries; the per capita dollar GNP estimates for centrally planned and market-type economies derived by the physical indicators method; implied trade participation ratios; and a comparison of per capita energy consumption of centrally planned and market-type economies at approximately the same per capita income levels. I shall first consider the method of calculation, evaluation, and interpretation of each of the four sets of reference points.

## Studies in the CMEA

For more than two decades, the central statistical offices of the CMEA countries have been carrying out ICP-type computations comparing the national income levels and structures of the member countries and, more recently, Yugoslavia, under the auspices of the CMEA Statistical Commission. (The project is formally called International Comparison of the Main Indices of the Levels of Development of the CMEA Countries and Yugoslavia.) Until now, the work on comparisons involved four phases: in Phase I, comparisons were made, with 1959 as the base year (using average 1958–61 values); Phase II, for 1966 (1963–66 average); Phase III, for 1973 (1970–73); and Phase IV, for 1978 (1974–78) (Szilágyi 1979). During the initial phases of the project, the participants were unaware of the OECD-sponsored Gilbert-Kravis study (the predecessor of the ICP) and independently designed an approach similar to the ICP method; in subsequent stages, the project benefited from the literature and practice of the ICP and other international comparison projects (Szilágyi 1979). Unfortunately, the empirical findings of the CMEA studies have not been published, presumably because of the politically sensitive nature of income-level comparisons.

A leading Hungarian expert, who has been participating in the work of the CMEA project, however, has published an article reporting the methodology and the results of his own independent calculations on comparing the national incomes of six CMEA countries and Yugoslavia in 1973 (Szilágyi 1978). (Reports of an earlier CMEA comparison, including the U.S.S.R., have also been published in the Soviet Union by Riboykov in the January 1967 issue of *Voprosi ekonomichki*.) Unfortunately, even Szilágyi (1978) omits the U.S.S.R., presumably because its level of income vis-à-vis that of the individual East European countries is a particularly sensitive matter. Although the comparisons are for 1973, refer only to material production, and include many caveats about the accuracy of the results (the author notes especially that the greater the difference between the structures of two economies, the greater the margin of error in the estimates of their development levels), it would seem reasonable to assume that Szilágyi's results would not be very different from those of the CMEA study. National income levels in 1973, expressed as a percentage of the Hungarian level, are listed below. (Estimates of absolute levels are given only in forints; Szilágyi 1978, p. 155.)

| German Democratic Republic | 124 |
|---|---|
| Czechoslovakia | 122 |
| Hungary | 100 |
| Poland | 100 |
| Bulgaria | 95 |
| Romania | 81 |
| Yugoslavia | 72 |

The results should be considered PPP scale.

## Physical Indicators Method

The main alternative approach to estimating per capita dollar GNP via currency conversion (for example, using the prevailing exchange rate or some type of PPP) is the physical indicators method. The essence of this simplified, or shortcut, approach is the determination of a regression relationship between a set of physical indicators of development and per capita dollar GDP. The statistical relationship obtained is then used to estimate the per capita dollar GDP both of the countries included in the sample and of CPEs for which neither GDP nor a meaningful dollar exchange rate could be found. The independent pioneers of this method were the Hungarian economist Jánossy (1963) and the English economist Beckermann (1966). Jánossy's associate, Éva Ehrlich, has continued to develop the original method in Hungary and is applying it to an increasing number of market-type and centrally planned economies. The latest version of the work that she and her associates have done covers seventy-nine countries, including the six East European CPEs and Cuba, the Democratic People's Republic of Korea, Vietnam, Mongolia, and China for 1977 (Pártos 1982).[13] A version of the Jánossy-Ehrlich method was adopted by the Economic Commission for Europe of the United Nations (United Nations 1980a, 1980b, 1983). The most recent ECE calculations, published in 1980, include thirty market-type economies and seven European CPEs for the benchmark years 1950, 1955, 1965, 1970, and 1973, relying on thirty physical indicators to make the estimates (United Nations 1980a). In the same study, an "extended exercise" was also undertaken, for 1970 only, including seventy-five additional countries, testing the extent to which results are affected by variations in the number of countries and indicators used (see appendix B). The World Bank itself relied on the physical indicators method to obtain the per capita dollar GNPs of the European centrally planned economies for 1973–76 and published the figures in the *Atlas* (see appendix A). Subsequently, however, the Bank stopped using this method because it had found results of the methods and some underlying assumptions unsatisfactory. The ECE also discontinued reliance on the physical indicators method without giving an explanation.

The basic assumption of the Jánossy-Ehrlich-ECE version of the method is that a country's level of per capita GDP is revealed in many areas of its consumption and the stock of certain assets. Although it is not possible to identify a *single* physical indicator that by itself is capable of indicating accurately the level of development of a country, a judiciously selected *set* of physical indicators, each providing an independent estimate of per capita GNP, can be averaged to achieve this goal. The basic method of estimating per capita dollar GNP according to the Jánossy-Ehrlich-ECE approach involves seven steps.[14]

13. The authors note that the data base for the Asian CPEs was so poor that only 50 percent or fewer of the required physical indicators were available, so the results for these countries are highly tentative.

14. The method was explained to me during my conversations with I. Borenstein, formerly with the ECE, in Geneva during the summer of 1982, and my conversations with E. Ehrlich and Gy. Pártos in Budapest during the summer of 1983. I am grateful for their assistance.

1. Select a group of MTEs and convert their official per capita GDP in national currency units to dollars, using the prevailing exchange rates.

2. Select the physical indicators that show a high correlation with the above per capita dollar GDP figures.

3. Determine individual regression lines between each physical indicator and the per capita dollar GDP of the sample countries. (The number and type of physical indicators as well as the method of determining the regression lines differ in the Jánossy-Ehrlich and ECE versions; for the latter reason especially their results are not directly comparable.)[15]

4. On the basis of the regression lines obtained in step 3, determine the predicted relationship between each physical indicator actually observed (official data deal mostly with intermediate and final consumption) and the estimated per capita dollar GDP.

5. There will be as many GDP estimates for each country as there are physical indicators with actual observations. The geometric average of all the GDP estimates for a given country will be the "adjusted" per capita dollar GDP estimate for that country.

6. Next comes a series of iterations intended to obtain a tighter fit between each indicator and the successively adjusted per capita dollar GDP estimates. The iteration consists of repeating steps 3 through 5 while substituting the latest adjusted per capita dollar GDP estimate for the original dollar GDP estimate. The iteration ends when the $n$th adjusted dollar per capita GDP estimate coincides with the estimate labeled $(n - 1)$. This last value is taken to be the corrected GDP estimate for each country. The final per capita dollar GDP estimate so obtained for the United States and the other countries is in effect valued not at domestic U.S. dollars but in a currency unit that reflects the dollar's realistic international purchasing power. The difference between the original and the "corrected" U.S. per capita GDP estimate in any given year is due largely to the temporary overvaluation or undervaluation of the U.S. dollar in terms of other currencies. The "international purchasing power dollar" obtained via this method is to be distinguished from the ICP's "international dollar," which has the *same* purchasing power over U.S. GDP as

15. The ECE selects one of ten mathematically specified regression relationships on the basis of the best fit, whereas the Jánossy-Ehrlich-Pártos approach determines the shape of the regression line on the basis of visual inspection, then specifies its mathematical function. Although the latter approach has been criticized as being somewhat subjective, its authors claim that it is better able to reflect economic reality, which may be quite dissimilar for countries at different income levels. The dissimilarity of the functional relationship at widely different income levels often cannot be captured accurately by one of the standard regression formulas. In any event, subjectivity is constrained by the application of the iterative procedure described in step 6.

a whole as the U.S. dollar and has a PPP-based *scale* vis-à-vis other currencies. It is very important to note, in contrast, that, although the physical
indicator method corrects the original GDP values for the undervaluation
or overvaluation of the dollar vis-à-vis other convertible currencies, it
still preserves the prevailing exchange rate *scale* in the regression lines.
For this reason, before we can meaningfully compare the results obtained
by the physical indicators method with the results of the ICP, we must
effect a scale transformation (similar to shifting from Celsius to Fahr-
enheit on a thermometer) via a standard procedure explained in Ehrlich
and Pártos (1979).[16] The PI results before scale transformation *can* be
compared directly with our "adjusted PPP" estimates because both
approaches rely on an exchange-rate-based scale. The PI results *after* scale
transformation can be compared directly with ICP results because both
rely on a PPP scale, as indicated in note 15.

7. The last step is to estimate the per capita dollar GDPs of CPEs by
substituting the physical indicators of these countries into the regression
equations obtained for the reference group of market-type economies.
The estimates obtained by the different versions of the physical indicators
method are shown in tables 3-20 and 3-21, below.

The physical indicators method is mainly useful as a way of deriving
per capita dollar GDP estimates for countries with no official or reliable
per capita GDP (or GNP, NMP, and so forth) values in national currency
units and no meaningful dollar exchange rate. A further advantage of
the method is that it generates information about differences in the
production or consumption structures of countries, some of which are
determined by the economic system. Finally, this method can also yield
internationally comparable GDP growth rates. The usual growth rate
computations made by the central statistical offices of the individual
countries are more or less able to eliminate changes in relative prices
within a given country but are unable to handle differences in relative
prices among the countries satisfactorily. For this reason growth rates
are not readily comparable across countries. The computation of growth
rates that are internationally comparable is not a simple task because it
must adjust for changes over time in the value of the dollar in which the
original GDPs are expressed, in the relationship between the dollar and

---

16. The scale transformation formula (Ehrlich and Pártos 1979, p. 99) is $1/K_v = a\ 1^n/K_x$, where $K_v$ = exchange rate scale, that is, the absolute ranking of the per capita dollar
GDPs of the countries obtained via prevailing exchange rates; $K_x$ = PPP scale, that is, the
absolute ranking of the per capita dollar GDPs of countries obtained via PPP computations;
and $n$ = directional tangent. In 1970, $a$ = 0.85 and $n$ = 1.41, according to the Ehrlich-
Pártos computations.

other national currencies, and in the relationship between the per capita dollar GDP and the different physical indicators. This last problem is analogous at the international level to the problem of changing relative prices in growth rate computations at the national level. Work is currently under way in Hungary to compute internationally comparable growth rates, but the results have not yet been published.

The physical indicators method is alleged to have several shortcomings when it is used to estimate the per capita dollar GDPs of centrally planned economies.

WHAT IS BEING MEASURED? As a perusal of the thirty physical indicators used in the latest ECE study (1983; see appendix B) shows, more than half cover aspects that are not, or are only partially, included in GDP estimates. Seven are welfare-type measures (for example, infant mortality); seven are stock measures (for example, rooms per thousand inhabitants); and two are employment statistics (manufacturing and agricultural employments, respectively, as percentages of total employment). Thus the estimates obtained may represent economic attainments that go beyond the conventional GDP measure. The advocates of the method reply that infant mortality is a proxy for annual health expenditures, the stock of housing is a proxy for the annual housing rent, and so on. The most basic defense regarding this matter, however, is that all thirty indicators have been found to correlate highly with the level of GDP—across countries and over time—and can therefore be used for estimating GDPs, especially those of countries for which alternative approaches yield clearly inferior results.

WEIGHTING. Because each estimate provided by each indicator is given equal weight (they are geometrically averaged to yield a composite per capita GDP estimate), some GDP activities are underrepresented and others are overrepresented, thus introducing bias. This criticism receives the following answer: at the practical level, experiments with more elaborate weighting systems do not yield obviously superior results, and with a large number of indicators, slight changes in the weighting system cease to be important; at the theoretical level, no weighting system is obviously superior to geometric averaging.

INDICATORS ARE NOT QUALITATIVELY COMPARABLE. No account is taken of large differences among countries in the quality of products used as a physical indicator, such as passenger cars, television sets, meat consumed, and so on. This omission introduces an upward bias into the GDP estimates of the lower-income countries as compared with those of higher-income nations because lower levels of development are associated with products of poorer quality. It would appear that this problem is especially serious for centrally planned economies, which are known to produce, on the average, products of lower quality than do market economies at comparable levels of development.

RELATIVELY INEFFICIENT PRODUCTION WILL INTRODUCE UPWARD BIAS. Some of the physical indicators represent final consumption, whereas others represent intermediate consumption. Inefficient use of materials—especially characteristic of CPEs—will be reflected in relatively high GDP estimates based on such indicators. That is, according to the logic of the method, the wasteful use of material inputs will yield GDP estimates that are significantly upward biased.

THE METHOD INCORPORATES RATHER THAN SOLVES THE EXCHANGE RATE BIAS. Because exchange rates do not accurately measure the relative purchasing power of currencies, using them for conversion of GNP to dollars tends to exaggerate real income differences between less developed and more developed countries. Inasmuch as the dependent variable in the regression equations is per capita dollar GDP obtained from national currency units via the prevailing exchange rates, the estimates of per capita GDPs of countries obtained via this method will incorporate the exchange rate bias. This built-in bias is indeed a problem but only for researchers who prefer to use a PPP-based convertor rather than prevailing exchange rates. For researchers who wish to rely on PPP-based convertors, or to compare the results of physical-indicator-based estimates directly with those of the ICP, the scale transformation method devised by Ehrlich and Pártos is available for use.

The alleged shortcomings mentioned first and second do not introduce any known bias. The third and fourth problems will cause an upward bias in the estimates for centrally planned economies, especially vis-à-vis high-income market-type economies, but should not affect intra-CMEA comparisons in a major way, because quality and production inefficiency are problems in all centrally planned economies. To be sure, these may be greater problems in the relatively less developed countries, whose estimates, therefore, could be biased upward relative to those of the other CMEA countries. The fifth issue, that the per capita GDP estimates are based on the adjusted exchange rates of MTEs, is not a problem because in this study we are seeking precisely such exchange rate proxies.

A detailed examination of the physical indicators method's logic, relatively simple data requirements, and comparative ease of computation (benchmark estimates should be computed, say, once every five years) suggest that its use should once again be seriously considered. The method has not been assessed in detail by our team and was not discussed extensively during the two workshops, basically for two reasons. As noted, the World Bank decided not to use the physical indicators method after having done so for several years. This decision, together with limitations of time and resources, prompted us to direct our efforts toward the exploration of alternative approaches. The second reason was that, even though until 1980 the ECE had devoted considerable resources to developing the methodology, carrying out computations, and publishing the results, it suddenly stopped all work on the method, apparently at least partly for political reasons. In view of the fact that it will not be possible to find a best method that is free from substantial controversies, however, and because centrally planned economies as a group are not likely to participate in ICP-type computations involving market-type economies also, several members of our team and the author of this volume conclude that the physical indicators approach has much to recommend it for comparing CPEs with each other and with MTEs.

*Foreign Trade Participation Ratios*

Because East-West trade is priced and settled in convertible currencies and intra-CPE trade is evaluated at average world market prices of the last few years, we may obtain the approximate dollar value of a CMEA country's exports and imports. To be sure, these are only approximate dollar values, because the prices in intra-CMEA trade may be significantly higher or lower than those on the world market or in East-West transactions (see chapter 4). Nevertheless, comparing their sum with the estimated dollar value of each country's GNP yields estimated trade participation ratios. Many studies have shown that such ratios are lower in CPEs than in MTEs of approximately the same size (population) and level of development (Hewett 1980). The reasons are largely systemic:

- Most foreign trade decisions are made by central planners; arbitrary domestic prices make it difficult for them to discern profitable trading opportunities.
- The central planner's desire for control promotes self-sufficiency whenever domestic production is a feasible alternative to imports.
- Within the CMEA, it has not proved possible to find an effective mechanism for promoting intraindustry specialization, which accounts for much trade among MTEs.
- Producing enterprises have little direct contact with customers and

suppliers in other countries. Because producing for the foreign market is more difficult than supplying the domestic market, which typically has excess demand for most goods, the majority of firms are fundamentally uninterested in exports. In most cases the firm's existence is not threatened by its inability to export.

To be sure, some offsetting pressures push up CPEs' trade participation ratios: the desire of central planners to overcome bottlenecks and to speed growth encourages imports. An excess of imports over exports can be supported temporarily by large loans, which were available and were taken up by all CPEs until the early 1980s. Nevertheless, the consensus of experts is that the trade participation ratios of CPEs are certainly not higher, and are most probably significantly lower, than those of MTEs of approximately the same size and development level.

### Energy Consumption

Per capita energy consumption is highly correlated with the level of economic development and whether or not development is oriented toward promoting a high rate of growth, so that a large share of GNP will be devoted to investment, or toward consumption, in which case the investment/GNP share will be lower. To be sure, the relatively wasteful use of inputs that characterizes CPEs is expected to drive their per capita energy consumption levels somewhat higher than those of MTEs at similar development levels. Still, even though there may be significant variations among countries in per capita energy consumption levels for reasons unrelated to development levels, the measure is useful as a rough and ready check on the plausibility of alternative per capita GNP estimates.

## Plausibility of Alternative Convertors

There are four main options for converting the 1980 GNP of CPEs to dollars: purchasing power parity; adjusted purchasing power parity, a proxy for market-determined exchange rates; the official commercial exchange rate or its proxy, the foreign trade multiplier; and the official tourist exchange rate. Countries with unified commercial and noncommercial exchange rates have only three main options. For earlier years, a fifth option is the physical indicator method.

Let us examine briefly the plausibility of the alternative results, in two steps. Intra-CMEA *relatives* will be juxtaposed first, then *absolute levels* of the per capita GNP of centrally planned economies and selected market-type countries will be compared.

Table 3-20. *Comparison of Alternative Calculations of per Capita Dollar GNP of the European CMEA Countries and Yugoslavia*
(Hungary = 1.00)

| | PPP based converters | | | | | | Exchange rate-based convertors | | | | Prevailing exchange rates | |
|---|---|---|---|---|---|---|---|---|---|---|---|---|
| | | | ICP Phase III 1975 | | | ICP Phase IV | | | | Adj. | | |
| | PI 1970 | CMEA 1973 | and other PPP | PI 1977a | PPP 1980 | 1980 | PI 1970 | PI 1973 | PI 1977 | PPP 1980 | Commercial 1980 | Tourist 1980 |
| Country | (1) | (2) | (3) | (4) | (5) | (6) | (7) | (8) | (9) | (10) | (11) | (12) |
| German Democratic Republic | 1.43 | 1.24 | 1.19 | 1.31 | 1.17 | | 1.67 | 1.36 | 1.59 | 1.35 | 1.91 | 2.36 |
| Czechoslovakia | 1.33 | 1.22 | 1.12 | 1.19 | 1.02 | | 1.50 | 1.29 | 1.34 | 1.08 | 0.93 | 1.30 |
| U.S.S.R. | n.a. | n.a. | 0.99 | 1.12 | 0.98 | | n.a. | 1.10 | n.a. | 0.95 | 1.66b | 1.13 |
| Hungary | 1.00 | 1.00 | 1.00 | 1.00 | 1.00 | 1.00 | 1.00 | 1.00 | 1.00 | 1.00 | 1.00 | 1.00 |
| Polandc | 0.92 | 1.00 | 1.01 | 0.97 | 0.86 | 0.93 | 0.90 | 1.01 | 0.96 | 0.85 | 0.75 | 1.00 |
| Polande | | | 0.84 | | 0.64 | | | | | 0.63 | 0.98d | 0.76 |
| Bulgaria | 0.83 | 0.95 | n.a. | 0.98 | n.a. | | 0.77 | 0.99 | 0.98 | n.a. | n.a. | 0.77 |
| Romania | 0.68 | 0.81 | 0.67 | 0.72 | 0.78 | | 0.59 | 0.83 | 0.59 | 0.61 | 0.75 | 0.77 |
| Yugoslavia | 0.74 | 0.72 | 0.73 | 0.84 | | | 0.66 | 0.74 | 0.76 | | 1.27 | 0.87 |

a. Transformed to purchasing power parity scale, as described in text (step 6) and note 16.
b. Converted at the official exchange rate.
c. ICP.
d. Converted at the foreign trade multiplier.
e. Bilateral with Austria.

*Sources*: Columns 1 and 7: Ehrlich and Pártos (1979, p. 99); column 2: Szilágyi (1978, p. 155); columns 3, 5, 10, 11, and 12: table 3-18; columns 4 and 5: Pártos (1982, pp. 12–13); column 6: United Nations (1983, p. 100); column 8: United Nations/ECE (1980a, p. 31).

## Intra-CMEA Relatives

Table 3-20 summarizes the alternative calculations. Only results that have the same "scale" can be compared directly, that is, PPP-based or exchange-rate-based convertors. Actually, the situation is a little more complicated because, among the exchange-rate-based convertors, those obtained via the PI method (columns 7 through 9) correct for the undervaluation or overvaluation of the dollar in terms of other currencies (described above), whereas our method (column 10) does not. In table 3-20, six independent studies are compared according to the PPP scale: physical-indicators-based computations for 1970, transformed from the original exchange-rate-based scale; the CMEA study (described above) for 1973; ICP Phase III and other purchasing power parity results presented earlier; another physical-indicators-based study for 1977 transformed to PPP scale; the purchasing power parities for 1980, extrapolated from earlier years or based on 1980 as the benchmark year; and ICP Phase IV results for 1980, available for two countries only.

The juxtapositions show that, in spite of the differences in methods, the concordance between the outcomes is quite strong. The pattern revealed generally accords with the experts' ranking of the CMEA countries' development levels. The top group comprises the German Democratic Republic and Czechoslovakia, with the German Democratic Republic's income being somewhat higher. The middle group is composed of the U.S.S.R., Hungary, Poland, and Bulgaria; the third group, of Romania and Yugoslavia. The only surprise is the ranking of Bulgaria at the low end of the middle group rather than at the top of the third group. Because the Szilágyi and the ECE estimates are both based on physical indicators (though their methods are very different; for example, Szilágyi compares only the CMEA countries and Yugoslavia), the reason for the relatively high income level of Bulgaria, and to some extent that of Romania as well, is pinpointed by the Hungarian pioneers of the method (Ehrlich and Pártos 1979, pp. 74–75):

> In the case of Bulgaria, exceedingly high estimates are obtained on the basis of indicators characteristic of the consumption of materials by producing units (lead, synthetic fertilizer, energy, kilowatt-hours used, tonnage of products). The unusually high cement indicator suggests large-scale investment and construction activity. We find it difficult to explain (even considering the climatic conditions of the country) that the natural-fiber textile indicator suggests a level of per capita GDP exceeding even that of the US ... However, other indicators connected with the standard of living suggest relative backwardness: grain consumption is relatively high whereas milk consumption is

relatively low. Among the stock-type indicators, relatively low are the proportion of flats with toilets, plumbing, and other living space indicators, and the number of radios. . . . Romania is also characterized by the high consumption of materials by producing units and the relatively low level of indicators linked to the standard of living and to infrastructure.

The results of the four studies according to the exchange-rate-based convertors (columns 7 through 10) are roughly consistent with those of the PPP-based results; the main difference is that the range of development levels is wider, as can be seen by comparing column 7 with 1, column 9 with 4, and column 10 with 5; the reasons were elaborated in connection with the discussion of ERDIS. In this respect, however, the ECE's physical-indicators-based 1973 results (column 8) represent an anomaly because that column compares better with PPP-based results even though its scale is exchange rate based. The apparent paradox is explained by the fact that in 1973—and only in that single year—the scale difference between PPP-based and exchange-rate-based convertors disappeared, owing to the combination of dramatic changes in exchange rates and domestic price relatives in many countries (Pártos 1982). The computations show that, as far as intra-CMEA relatives are concerned, Poland's ICP series fits much better than the per capita GNP estimate based on the PPP obtained in the bilateral comparison with Austria. In the International Comparison Project's 1975 PPP-based series, Romania's relative position is shown to be lower than in the other studies; the most likely reason was indicated in the quoted statement by Ehrlich and Pártos. The fact that by 1980 the German Democratic Republic had increased further in relative position vis-à-vis Czechoslovakia is explained in part by the former's growth, which was more rapid than that of Czechoslovakia and countries in the second tier, and in part by differences in the two countries' methods of computing purchasing power parity.

The relatives that result from either of the two possible kinds of official exchange rate conversions are much less satisfactory. The most striking problem is that both conversions yield relatives that place the German Democratic Republic's income level nearly 100 percent higher than Czechoslovakia's; another shortcoming is that in conversions at the commercial exchange rates, the U.S.S.R.'s income is 71 percent above that of Czechoslovakia. To be sure, if the German Democratic Republic is omitted, the tourist exchange rates appear to yield acceptable intra-CMEA relatives. Before too great a significance is attached to this observation, however, it should be noted that, if the relatives were computed according to exchange rates in effect at the beginning of 1982, they would show (Hungary = 1.00):

| | |
|---|---|
| German Democratic Republic | 3.00 |
| Czechoslovakia | 1.85 |
| U.S.S.R. | 1.61 |
| Hungary | 1.00 |
| Poland | 0.46 |
| Bulgaria | 1.18 |
| Romania | 1.32 |

The inordinately large change in the relatives is caused mainly by Hungary's and Poland's drastic devaluation of their recently unified exchange rates. The numbers for a given CPE differ significantly, depending on the conversion factor employed, because of the essentially arbitrary nature of the commercial and noncommercial exchange rates of several CPEs.

## Comparing CPEs and MTEs

Table 3-21 juxtaposes alternative calculations of per capita dollar GNPs of the centrally planned economies and selected market-type economies, and to facilitate cross-country comparisons, the dollar figures are expressed as relatives of the United States. Among the PPP-based convertors, it is interesting to note first that, for 1970, ICP Phase II and physical indicators both placed Hungary (the only centrally planned economy covered by ICP for that year) almost identically vis-à-vis the United States: 40 percent and 38 percent, respectively. The close concordance between the ICP-type computations and the physical indicators results can be observed in later years for other CPEs and MTEs also: compare, for example, PPP results for 1975 (column 3) either with physical indicators 1977 results (column 4) or with the ECE's results for 1973 (column 6). (The latter can be juxtaposed with PPP-based results even though the scale is exchange rate based, for the reasons indicated in the preceding section.) These findings increase our confidence in the results of both types of computations. Let us examine the results more closely on the basis of selected bilateral CPE/MTE comparisons.

ECONOMIC COMMISSION FOR EUROPE, 1973. The most relevant comparisons for the most-, medium-, and least-developed CPEs would appear to be the MTEs shown in table 3-22 (the numbers represent each country's per capita GNP relative to that of the United States, on the basis of table 3-21, column 6). The comparison between the German Demo-

*Table 3-21. Comparison of Alternative Calculations of per Capita Dollar GNPs, 1970, 1973, 1975, 1977, and 1980*

| | PPP based | | | | | | | |
| | PPP 1970 (ICP Phase II) (1) | | PI 1970 (2) | | PPP 1975 (ICP Phase III and other PPP) (3) | | PI 1977 transformed to PPP scale (4) | |
| Country | I $ | U.S. =1 | I $ | U.S. =1 | I $ | U.S. =1 | I $ | U.S. =1 |
|---|---|---|---|---|---|---|---|---|
| CPES | | | | | | | | |
| German Dem. Rep. | | | 2,623 | 0.55 | 4,230 | 0.59 | 4,309 | 0.56 |
| Czechoslovakia | | | 2,428 | 0.51 | 4,000 | 0.56 | 3,913 | 0.51 |
| U.S.S.R. | | | n.a. | n.a. | 3,560 | 0.50 | n.a. | n.a. |
| Hungary | 1,910 | 0.40 | 1,825 | 0.38 | 3,559 | 0.50 | 3,285 | 0.43 |
| Poland | | | 1,687 | 0.35 | 3,598 | 0.50 | 3,200 | 0.42 |
| Bulgaria | | | 1,518 | 0.32 | — | — | 3,243 | 0.42 |
| Romania | | | 1,255 | 0.26 | 2,387 | 0.33 | 2,382 | 0.31 |
| Cuba | | | | | | | 2,060 | 0.27 |
| Dem. People's Rep. of Korea | | | | | | | 1,506 | 0.20 |
| Mongolia | | | | | | | 1,617 | 0.21 |
| China | | | | | 883 | 0.12 | 777 | 0.10 |
| Vietnam | | | | | | | 494 | 0.06 |
| Selected MTES | | | | | | | | |
| Austria | 2,495 | 0.52 | 29.44 | 0.62 | 4,995 | 0.70 | 5,044 | 0.65 |
| Belgium | 3,449 | 0.72 | 3,262 | 0.68 | 5,574 | 0.78 | 5,841 | 0.76 |
| Denmark | 3,518 | 0.73 | 3,568 | 0.74 | 5,911 | 0.82 | 5,788 | 0.75 |
| Finland | — | — | 3,015 | 0.63 | — | — | 5,037 | 0.65 |
| France | 3,504 | 0.73 | 3,025 | 0.63 | 5,877 | 0.82 | 5,000 | 0.65 |
| Fed. Rep. of Germany | 3,747 | 0.78 | 3,398 | 0.71 | 5,953 | 0.83 | 5,802 | 0.75 |
| Greece | — | — | 1,504 | 0.31 | — | — | 3,087 | 0.40 |
| Ireland | 2,134 | 0.45 | 2,428 | 0.51 | 3,049 | 0.43 | 3,435 | 0.45 |
| Italy | 2,356 | 0.49 | 2,328 | 0.49 | 3,861 | 0.54 | 4,203 | 0.55 |
| Japan | 2,835 | 0.59 | 2,811 | 0.59 | 4,907 | 0.68 | 4,632 | 0.60 |
| Netherlands | 3,298 | 0.69 | 3,587 | 0.75 | 5,397 | 0.75 | 5,280 | 0.69 |
| Norway | — | — | 3,474 | 0.72 | — | — | 5,530 | 0.72 |
| Portugal | — | — | 1,437 | 0.30 | — | — | 2,482 | 0.32 |
| Spain | 1,904 | 0.40 | 1,874 | 0.39 | 4,010 | 0.56 | 3,569 | 0.46 |
| Sweden | — | — | 4,264 | 0.89 | — | — | 6,390 | 0.83 |
| Switzerland | — | — | 3,521 | 0.73 | — | — | 5,406 | 0.70 |
| Turkey | — | — | 714 | 0.15 | — | — | 1,506 | 0.20 |
| United Kingdom | 3,039 | 0.63 | 3,559 | 0.74 | 4,588 | 0.64 | 5,416 | 0.70 |
| United States | 4,790 | 1.00 | 4,800 | 1.00 | 7,176 | 1.00 | 7,698 | 1.00 |
| Yugoslavia | | | 1,354 | 0.28 | 2,591 | 0.36 | 2,780 | 0.36 |

*Note*: n.a. = not available. Dashes indicate when countries were not included in the ICP (so that no results exist for them). Empty cells indicate that no computations have been made.

a. Converted at the official exchange rate.
b. ICP Phase IV yields $3,390, equal to 0.30 of the U.S. level.
c. ICP Phase IV yields $3,115, equal to 0.27 of the U.S. level.

| PI 1970 (5) | | PI 1973 (6) | | PI 1977, unadjusted (7) | | Adj. PPP 1980 (8) | | Commercial 1980 (9) | | Tourist 1980 (10) | |
|---|---|---|---|---|---|---|---|---|---|---|---|
| I $ | U.S. = 1 | I $ | U.S. = 1 | I $ | U.S. = 1 | I $ | U.S. = 1 | I $ | U.S. = 1 | I $ | U.S. = 1 |
| 1,750 | 0.43 | 3,242 | 0.60 | 4,560 | 0.39 | 5,910 | 0.52 | 3,940 | 0.35 | 7,140 | 0.63 |
| 1,570 | 0.38 | 3,078 | 0.57 | 3,840 | 0.33 | 4,740 | 0.42 | 1,920 | 0.17 | 3,930 | 0.35 |
| n.a. | n.a. | 2,621 | 0.48 | n.a. | n.a. | 4,190 | 0.37 | 3,420[a] | 0.30 | 3,420 | 0.30 |
| 1,050 | 0.26 | 2,379 | 0.44 | 2,860 | 0.24 | 4,390[b] | 0.39 | 2,060 | 0.48 | 3,020 | 0.27 |
| 940 | 0.23 | 2,413 | 0.45 | 2,740 | 0.23 | 3,730[c] | 0.33 | 1,553 | 0.14 | 2,290 | 0.20 |
| 810 | 0.20 | 2,351 | 0.43 | 2,800 | 0.24 | — | — | 3,551 | 0.31 | 2,340 | 0.21 |
| 620 | 0.15 | 1,969 | 0.36 | 1,686 | 0.14 | 2,680 | 0.24 | 1,550 | 0.14 | 2,320 | 0.20 |
| | | | | 1,250 | 0.11 | — | | | | | |
| | | | | 900 | 0.08 | — | | | | | |
| | | | | 970 | 0.08 | — | | | | | |
| | | | | 450 | 0.04 | — | | | | | |
| | | | | 280 | 0.02 | — | | | | | |
| 2,060 | 0.50 | 3,269 | 0.60 | 5,840 | 0.50 | 10,230 | 0.90 | 10,230 | 0.90 | 10,230 | 0.90 |
| 2,380 | 0.58 | 4,026 | 0.74 | 7,550 | 0.65 | 12,180 | 1.07 | 12,180 | 1.07 | 12,180 | 1.07 |
| 2,700 | 0.66 | 3,937 | 0.73 | 7,320 | 0.63 | 12,950 | 1.14 | 12,950 | 1.14 | 12,950 | 1.14 |
| 2,130 | 0.52 | 3,852 | 0.71 | 5,800 | 0.50 | 9,720 | 0.86 | 9,720 | 0.86 | 9,720 | 0.86 |
| 2,140 | 0.52 | 3,502 | 0.65 | 5,750 | 0.49 | 11,730 | 1.03 | 11,730 | 1.03 | 11,720 | 1.03 |
| 2,520 | 0.61 | 3,924 | 0.73 | 7,360 | 0.63 | 13,590 | 1.20 | 13,590 | 1.20 | 13,590 | 1.20 |
| 800 | 0.20 | 2,157 | 0.40 | 2,580 | 0.26 | 4,520 | 0.23 | 4,520 | 0.23 | 4,520 | 0.23 |
| 1,570 | 0.38 | 2,858 | 0.53 | 3,090 | 0.26 | 4,880 | 0.43 | 4,880 | 0.43 | 4,880 | 0.43 |
| 1,480 | 0.36 | 2,845 | 0.53 | 4,300 | 0.37 | 6,480 | 0.57 | 6,480 | 0.57 | 6,480 | 0.57 |
| 1,930 | 0.47 | 3,638 | 0.67 | 5,070 | 0.43 | 9,890 | 0.87 | 9,890 | 0.87 | 9,890 | 0.87 |
| 2,720 | 0.66 | 4,010 | 0.74 | 6,300 | 0.54 | 11,470 | 1.01 | 11,470 | 1.01 | 11,470 | 1.01 |
| 2,600 | 0.63 | 3,932 | 0.73 | 6,770 | 0.58 | 12,650 | 1.11 | 12,620 | 1.11 | 12,650 | 1.11 |
| 750 | 0.18 | 1,886 | 0.35 | 1,800 | 0.15 | 2,350 | 0.21 | 2,350 | 0.212 | 2,350 | 0.21 |
| 1,090 | 0.26 | 2,463 | 0.46 | 3,280 | 0.28 | 5,350 | 0.47 | 5,350 | 0.47 | 5,350 | 0.47 |
| 3,470 | 0.85 | 4,585 | 0.85 | 8,600 | 0.74 | 13,520 | 1.19 | 13,520 | 1.19 | 13,520 | 1.19 |
| 2,650 | 0.65 | 4,000 | 0.74 | 6,510 | 0.56 | 16,440 | 1.45 | 16,440 | 1.45 | 16,440 | 1.45 |
| 280 | 0.07 | 880 | 0.16 | 900 | 0.08 | 1,460 | 0.13 | 1,460 | 0.13 | 1,460 | 0.13 |
| 2,690 | 0.66 | 3,853 | 0.71 | 6,540 | 0.56 | 7,920 | 0.70 | 7,920 | 0.70 | 7,920 | 0.70 |
| 4,100 | 1.00 | 5,410 | 1.00 | 11,700 | 1.00 | 11,360 | 1.00 | 11,360 | 1.00 | 11,360 | 1.00 |
| 690 | 0.17 | 1,755 | 0.32 | 2,170 | 0.19 | 2,620 | 0.23 | 2,620 | 0.23 | 2,620 | 0.23 |

The "Exchange rate based" spanning header covers columns (5), (6), (7), (8); "Prevailing exchange rates" covers columns (9) and (10).

Sources: Column 1: Kravis and others (1982); columns 2 and 5: Ehrlich and Pártos (1979, p. 99); column 3: Kravis and others (1982) for Hungary, Poland, and Romania and all market-type economies; data sources for other European centrally planned economies are shown in table 3-15; China: Kravis and others (1981c, p. 73); columns 4 and 7: Pártos (1982, pp. 12–13); column 6: United Nations/ECE (1980a, p. 61); column 8: centrally planned economies: table 3-18; column 7, market-type economy: *Atlas*, 1981; columns 9 and 10: table 3-18.

*Table 3-22. Comparison of Levels of per Capita Dollar GNP
of CPEs and Selected MTEs in 1973, on the Basis of the Physical
Indicators Method, ECE Version*
(United States = 100)

| CPE | | MTE | |
|---|---|---|---|
| Group A | | | |
| German Democratic | | Federal Republic of | |
| Republic | 0.60 | Germany | 0.73 |
| Czechoslovakia | 0.57 | United Kingdom | 0.71 |
| | | France | 0.65 |
| | | Austria | 0.60 |
| Group B | | | |
| U.S.S.R. | 0.48 | Italy | 0.53 |
| Poland | 0.45 | Ireland | 0.53 |
| Hungary | 0.44 | Spain | 0.46 |
| Bulgaria | 0.43 | | |
| Group C | | | |
| Romania | 0.36 | Greece | 0.40 |
| Portugal | 0.35 | | |
| Yugoslavia | 0.32 | | |
| Highlighted bilateral comparisons | | | |

$$\frac{\text{GDR}}{\text{FRG}} = 0.83 \qquad \frac{\text{Hungary}}{\text{Austria}} = 0.73 \qquad \frac{\text{Romania}}{\text{Yugoslavia}} = 1.12$$

*Note*: Group A has a high level of per capita GNP among the CPEs, Group B a medium
level, and Group C a low level.
*Source*: Table 3-21, column 6.


cratic Republic and the Federal Republic of Germany is highlighted for
the obvious reasons. The Hungary/Austria comparison is particularly
important because detailed computations were made of the relative development levels of the two countries in 1937 (they were joined in the
Austro-Hungarian monarchy until after World War I, so their statistical
practices were very similar), when Hungary's per capita GNP was found
to be 63 percent of Austria's (United Nations 1948). Romania is juxtaposed with Yugoslavia, the latter often considered—for geographic and
systemic reasons—to be the most appropriate non-CMEA reference country for Romania as well as for Bulgaria.

Because the Economic Commission for Europe employed the same
method to estimate the per capita dollar GNPs of the centrally planned
and market-type economies, its results may be considered one possible
set of reference points. We must, however, take into account that the
physical indicators method has an upward bias for the CPEs, as previously

noted. This bias probably explains the relatively high CPE/MTE ratio, most apparent in the bilateral comparisons between the three country pairs.


PURCHASING POWER PARITY, 1975. The basic bilateral CPE/MTE patterns are very similar to those found by the physical indicators method (see table 3-23). The most directly relevant bilateral comparisons, however, show the CPE/MTE ratios to be somewhat lower, in part probably reflecting the CPE bias in the method used by the Economic Commission for Europe. The PPP-based estimates themselves may of course have a CPE bias.


ERDI-ADJUSTED PURCHASING POWER PARITY, 1980. First it is important to note the big jump in the ratios of the developed market-type economies to the United States, which reflects primarily the rapid appreciation of many West European currencies against the dollar. The ratios (based on table 3-21, column 8) appear in table 3-24. Between 1975 and 1980, the


*Table 3-23. Comparison of Levels of per Capita Dollar GNP of CPEs and Selected MTEs in 1975, on the Basis of Purchasing Power Parity Convertors*
(United States = 1.00)

| CPE | | MTE | |
|---|---|---|---|
| Group A | | | |
| German Democratic Republic | 0.59 | Federal Republic of Germany | 0.83 |
| Czechoslovakia | 0.56 | France | 0.82 |
| | | Austria | 0.70 |
| | | United Kingdom | 0.64 |
| Group B | | | |
| U.S.S.R. | 0.50 | Spain | 0.56 |
| Hungary | 0.50 | Italy | 0.54 |
| Poland | 0.50 | Ireland | 0.43 |
| Group C | | | |
| Romania | 0.33 | Greece | n.a. |
| | | Portugal | n.a. |
| | | Yugoslavia | 0.36 |
| Highlighted bilateral comparisons | | | |
| $\frac{\text{GDR}}{\text{FRG}} = 0.71$ | | $\frac{\text{Hungary}}{\text{Austria}} = 0.71$ | $\frac{\text{Romania}}{\text{Yugoslavia}} = 0.92$ |

Note: n.a. = not available.
Source: Table 3-21, column 3.

*Table 3-24.  Comparison of Levels of per Capita Dollar GNP
of CPEs and Selected MTEs in 1980, on the Basis
of Adjusted PPP Convertors*
(United States = 1.00)

| CPE | | MTE | |
|---|---|---|---|
| *Group A* | | | |
| German Democratic Republic | 0.52 | Federal Republic of Germany | 1.20 |
| Czechoslovakia | 0.42 | France | 1.03 |
| | | Austria | 0.90 |
| | | United Kingdom | 0.70 |
| *Group B* | | | |
| U.S.S.R. | 0.37 | Italy | 0.57 |
| Hungary | 0.39 | Spain | 0.47 |
| Poland | 0.33 | Ireland | 0.43 |
| *Group C* | | | |
| Romania | 0.24 | Greece | 0.23 |
| | | Yugoslavia | 0.23 |
| | | Portugal | 0.21 |

*Highlighted bilateral comparisons*

$$\frac{\text{GDR}}{\text{FRG}} = 0.43 \qquad \frac{\text{Hungary}}{\text{Austria}} = 0.43 \qquad \frac{\text{Romania}}{\text{Yugoslavia}} = 1.04$$

*Source*: Table 3-21, column 8.

ratio between the Federal Republic of Germany and the United States jumped from 0.83 to 1.20, the ratio between France and the United States from 0.82 to 1.03, the ratio between Austria and the United States from 0.70 to 0.90, and so on. This is one important reason for the large decline in the bilateral ratios between centrally planned economies and West European market-type economies. If the ratio between the Federal Republic of Germany and the United States, and between Austria and the United States, had been the same in 1980 as in 1975, for example, the ratio between the German Democratic Republic and the Federal Republic of Germany would be 0.70 rather than 0.43, and the Hungary/Austria ratio would be 0.57, not 0.43.

Nevertheless, the CPE/MTE ratios are low, probably approaching the low end of what experts would consider to be still within a plausible range. The U.S.S.R.'s per capita income, for example, is less than two-fifths that of the United States, whereas Hungary's and Poland's per capita incomes are 68 percent and 58 percent, respectively, of that of Italy. We might argue, however, that the estimates are acceptable, in part because they are so strongly influenced by the exchange rate fluctuations of MTEs and in part because these CPEs' income levels are still significantly higher than, for example, those of Greece, Portugal, and Yugoslavia.

COMMERCIAL EXCHANGE RATES. Use of these official exchange rates yields the estimates shown in table 3-25, which cannot be considered plausible relative to those of MTEs.

Exchange rate conversion changes the ranking of the centrally planned economies, Bulgaria becoming the CMEA's second most highly developed country, its income level about twice as high as that of Czechoslovakia, Romania, or Poland. The results place the German Democratic Republic significantly below Italy, Spain, and Ireland, with Hungary and Czechoslovakia much below Greece, Yugoslavia, and Portugal. Exchange rate conversion yields a ratio between the German Democratic Republic and the Federal Republic of Germany of 0.29 and a Hungary/Austria ratio of 0.20, estimates that cannot be considered to fall within the plausible range, even if we take into account the possible overvaluation of many West European currencies.

*Table 3-25. Comparison of Levels of per Capita Dollar GNP of CPEs and Selected MTEs in 1980, on the Basis of Commercial Exchange Rate Convertors*
(United States = 1.00)

| CPE | | MTE | |
|---|---|---|---|
| | | *Group A* | |
| | | Federal Republic of Germany | 1.20 |
| | | France | 1.03 |
| | | Austria | 0.90 |
| | | United Kingdom | 0.70 |
| | | *Group B* | |
| German Democratic | | Italy | 0.57 |
| Republic | 0.35 | Spain | 0.43 |
| Bulgaria | 0.31 | Ireland | 0.43 |
| U.S.S.R. | 0.30 | | |
| | | *Group C* | |
| Hungary | 0.18 | Greece | 0.23 |
| Czechoslovakia | 0.17 | Yugoslavia | 0.23 |
| Poland | 0.14 | Portugal | 0.21 |
| Romania | 0.14 | | |
| | *Highlighted bilateral comparisons* | | |
| $\dfrac{\text{GDR}}{\text{FRG}} = 0.29$ | $\dfrac{\text{Hungary}}{\text{Austria}} = 0.20$ | | $\dfrac{\text{Romania}}{\text{Yugoslavia}} = 0.59$ |

*Source*: Table 3-21, column 9.

Table 3-26. *Comparison of Levels of per Capita Dollar GNP
of CPEs and Selected MTEs in 1980, on the Basis
of Tourist Exchange Rate Convertors*
(United States = 1.00)

| CPE | | MTE | |
|---|---|---|---|
| *Group A* | | | |
| German Democratic | | Federal Republic of | |
| Republic | 0.63 | Germany | 1.20 |
| | | France | 1.03 |
| | | Austria | 0.90 |
| | | United Kingdom | 0.70 |
| *Group B* | | | |
| Czechoslovakia | 0.35 | Italy | 0.57 |
| U.S.S.R. | 0.30 | Spain | 0.47 |
| Hungary | 0.27 | Ireland | 0.43 |
| *Group C* | | | |
| Bulgaria | 0.21 | Greece | 0.23 |
| Poland | 0.20 | Yugoslavia | 0.23 |
| Romania | 0.20 | Portugal | 0.21 |
| *Highlighted bilateral comparisons* | | | |
| $\frac{\text{GDR}}{\text{FRG}} = 0.53$ | $\frac{\text{Hungary}}{\text{Austria}} = 0.30$ | $\frac{\text{Romania}}{\text{Yugoslavia}} = 0.89$ | |

*Source*: Table 3-21, column 10.

TOURIST EXCHANGE RATES. Table 3-26 reveals the pattern when the
official tourist exchange rates of the centrally planned economies are
used as convertors.

Although this pattern is somewhat better than the preceding one, it is
important to note that Hungary and Poland both recently discarded their
separate tourist exchange rates and designated the commercial exchange
rate as the single, unified official exchange rate.

*Foreign Trade Participation Ratios Compared*

Table 3-27 presents the population, the alternative per capita GNPs,
and the implied trade participation ratios of seven CPEs and twenty-five
MTEs. Within each group, the countries are listed in order of increasing
size of population. TPRs (exports plus imports divided by GNP), which
have been found, other things being equal, to correlate positively with
the level of per capita GNP and negatively with country size (usually
measured by population), have been shown to be lower for CPEs than
for MTEs of approximately the same size and level of development, for
the systemic reasons summarized above.

The dollar value of a CPE's total exports and imports, which is independent of the exchange rates used, can be determined more readily than its GNP. Because the numerator of the trade participation ratio is held constant, the ratio will change if the estimated dollar value of GNP changes. A derived trade participation ratio cannot prove the accuracy of this or that convertor, but it may call into question the plausibility of a convertor if the resulting dollar per capita GNP yields a TPR significantly higher than those of comparable MTEs.

The trade participation ratios of individual CPEs and MTEs are juxtaposed below, the latter selected on the basis of comparability with respect to the size of a country, per capita GNP, and geographic location.

| *Bulgaria* | | *MTE* | |
|---|---|---|---|
| GNP at tourist exchange | | Portugal | 0.60 |
| rate | 0.95 | Yugoslavia | 0.38 |
| GNP at official | | Greece | 0.37 |
| exchange rate | 0.63 | | |

The per capita dollar GNP that results if the tourist exchange rate is used seems implausibly low, because it would imply that Bulgaria participates in foreign trade almost three times more intensively than Greece or Yugoslavia and more actively than all but two MTEs, Belgium and Ireland.

| *Hungary* | | *MTE* | |
|---|---|---|---|
| GNP at commercial | | Austria | 0.55 |
| exchange rate | 0.81 | Italy | 0.48 |
| GNP at tourist exchange | | Greece | 0.37 |
| rate | 0.55 | Spain | 0.27 |
| GNP at adjusted | | | |
| purchasing power | | | |
| parity | 0.38 | | |

The per capita dollar GNP that is obtained at the commercial exchange rate seems implausibly low because it would imply that Hungary participates in international trade three times more actively than Spain and much more intensively than Austria, Denmark, Switzerland, and all other West European countries except Belgium, the Netherlands, and Ireland.

| *Czechoslovakia* | | *MTE* | |
|---|---|---|---|
| GNP at foreign trade | | Netherlands | 0.93 |
| multiplier (estimated) | 1.02 | Austria | 0.55 |
| GNP at tourist exchange | | United Kingdom | 0.53 |
| rate | 0.50 | Italy | 0.48 |
| GNP at adjusted | | France | 0.39 |
| purchasing power | | | |
| parity | 0.41 | | |

*Table 3-27. Foreign Trade Participation Ratios,*
*Selected CPEs and MTEs, 1980*

| Country | Population (millions) (1) | Type of convertor (2) | Per capita GNP (current dollars) (3) | Implied TPR[a] (4) |
|---|---|---|---|---|
| *Centrally planned economies* | | | | |
| Bulgaria | 9.0 | official exchange rate | 3,551 | 0.63 |
| | | tourist exchange rate | 2,340 | 0.95 |
| Hungary | 10.8 | adjusted PPP[b] | 4,390 | 0.38 |
| | | commercial exchange rate | 2,060 | 0.81 |
| | | tourist exchange rate | 3,020 | 0.55 |
| Czechoslovakia | 15.3 | adjusted PPP | 4,740 | 0.41 |
| | | FTM | 1,920 | 1.02 |
| | | tourist exchange rate | 3,930 | 0.50 |
| German Democratic Republic | 16.9 | adjusted PPP | 5,910 | 0.36 |
| | | commercial exchange rate[c] | 3,940 | 0.55 |
| | | tourist exchange rate | 7,140 | 0.30 |
| Romania | 22.2 | adjusted PPP[b] | 2,680 | 0.43 |
| | | commercial exchange rate | 1,550 | 0.74 |
| | | tourist exchange rate | 2,320 | 0.49 |
| Poland | 35.8 | adjusted PPP[b] | 3,730 | 0.27 |
| | | commercial exchange rate | 1,553 | 0.65 |
| | | tourist exchange rate | 2,290 | 0.44 |
| U.S.S.R. | 165.5 | adjusted PPP | 4,190 | 0.13 |
| | | official exchange rate[d] | 3,420 | 0.18 |
| *Market-type economies* | | | | |
| Ireland | 3.3 | prevailing exchange rate | 4,880 | 1.22 |
| Israel | 3.9 | prevailing exchange rate | 4,500 | 0.75 |
| Norway | 4.1 | prevailing exchange rate | 12,650 | 0.68 |
| Finland | 4.9 | prevailing exchange rate | 9,720 | 0.62 |
| Denmark | 5.1 | prevailing exchange rate | 12,950 | 0.54 |
| Switzerland | 6.5 | prevailing exchange rate | 16,440 | 0.62 |
| Austria | 7.5 | prevailing exchange rate | 10,230 | 0.55 |
| Sweden | 8.3 | prevailing exchange rate | 13,520 | 0.57 |
| Greece | 9.6 | prevailing exchange rate | 4,380 | 0.37 |
| Portugal | 9.8 | prevailing exchange rate | 2,370 | 0.60 |
| Belgium | 9.8 | prevailing exchange rate | 12,180 | 1.13 |
| Chile | 11.1 | prevailing exchange rate | 2,150 | 0.44 |
| Iraq | 13.1 | prevailing exchange rate | 3,020 | 0.93 |
| Netherlands | 14.1 | prevailing exchange rate | 11,470 | 0.93 |
| Venezuela | 14.9 | prevailing exchange rate | 3,630 | 0.57 |
| Yugoslavia | 22.3 | prevailing exchange rate | 2,620 | 0.38 |
| Argentina | 27.7 | prevailing exchange rate | 2,390 | 0.28 |
| Spain | 37.4 | prevailing exchange rate | 5,400 | 0.27 |
| France | 53.5 | prevailing exchange rate | 11,730 | 0.39 |
| United Kingdom | 55.9 | prevailing exchange rate | 7,920 | 0.53 |

*Table 3-27   (continued)*

| Country | Population (millions) (1) | Type of convertor (2) | Per capita GNP (current dollars) (3) | Implied TPR[a] (4) |
|---|---|---|---|---|
| Italy | 56.9 | prevailing exchange rate | 6,480 | 0.48 |
| Federal Republic of Germany | 60.9 | prevailing exchange rate | 13,590 | 0.41 |
| Mexico | 69.8 | prevailing exchange rate | 2,090 | 0.24 |
| Brazil | 118.7 | prevailing exchange rate | 2,050 | 0.19 |
| United States | 227.7 | prevailing exchange rate | 11,360 | 0.18 |

a. Exports plus imports divided by GNP.
b. Based on ICP Phase III data.
c. Pro forma commercial exchange rate.
d. Same as the tourist exchange rate.
*Sources*: Column 1: World Bank (1982, table 1); columns 2 and 3, centrally planned economies: table 3-18; market-type economies: World Bank (1982, table 1); column 4: dollar value of exports and imports taken from World Bank (1982), table 8, divided by total GNP obtained by multiplying columns 1 and 3.

The juxtaposition suggests that the estimated foreign trade multiplier does not yield a plausible per capita dollar GNP estimate.

| German Democratic Republic | | MTE | |
|---|---|---|---|
| GNP at pro forma | | Austria | 0.55 |
| commercial rate | 0.55 | United Kingdom | 0.53 |
| GNP at adjusted purchasing | | Italy | 0.48 |
| power parity | 0.36 | Federal Republic | |
| GNP at tourist exchange rate | 0.30 | of Germany | 0.41 |

The trade participation ratio implied by the adjusted purchasing power parity is slightly lower than that of the Federal Republic of Germany. Because the German Democratic Republic is only one-third as large as the Federal Republic of Germany, a higher trade participation ratio would be expected. Because the German Democratic Republic is at a lower income level and is a centrally planned economy, however, a lower trade participation ratio would be more likely. None of the three convertors thus yields clearly implausible TPRs.

| Romania | | MTE | |
|---|---|---|---|
| GNP at commercial | | Portugal | 0.60 |
| exchange rate | 0.74 | Venezuela | 0.57 |
| GNP at adjusted purchasing | | Yugoslavia | 0.38 |
| power parity | 0.43 | Greece | 0.37 |
| GNP at tourist exchange rate | 0.49 | Argentina | 0.28 |

Because the dollar GNP obtained via the commercial exchange rate yields a trade participation ratio twice as high as that of Yugoslavia and Greece and higher than those of most of even the smaller West European countries, it does not appear to be plausible.

| Poland | | MTE | |
|---|---|---|---|
| GNP at commercial | | Sweden | 0.57 |
| exchange rate | 0.65 | Italy | 0.48 |
| GNP at tourist exchange | | Yugoslavia | 0.38 |
| rate | 0.44 | Argentina | 0.28 |
| GNP at adjusted | | Spain | 0.27 |
| purchasing power | | | |
| parity | 0.27 | | |

A comparison of trade participation ratios suggests that the use of the commercial exchange rate yields implausibly low per capita GNP estimates.

| U.S.S.R. | | MTE | |
|---|---|---|---|
| GNP at official | | Italy | 0.48 |
| exchange rate | 0.13 | Spain | 0.37 |
| GNP at adjusted | | Brazil | 0.19 |
| purchasing power | | United States | 0.18 |
| parity | 0.16 | | |

Although in comparison with the United States, the U.S.S.R. seems to have rather high trade participation ratios, neither one of the two estimates can be labeled clearly unrealistic.

The basic conclusion suggested by a comparison of trade participation ratios for CPEs and MTEs is that for the three CPEs for which commercial exchange rates might possibly be used—Hungary, Poland, and Romania—the resulting per capita dollar GNPs would appear to be exceedingly and perhaps implausibly low. The TPRs that result if the adjusted purchasing power parities were to be used as convertors appear to be relatively high—that is, the per capita dollar GNPs appear to be rather low—but still fall within plausible ranges.

### Levels of Energy Consumption per Capita Compared

A final check on the plausibility of alternative estimates is 1979 per capita energy consumption levels. Table 3-28 ranks fifty of the world's largest consumers of energy (excluding Saudi Arabia, Kuwait, and the United Arab Emirates) in terms of per capita energy consumption levels, expressed as kilograms of coal equivalents.

The German Democratic Republic and Czechoslovakia rank fifth and sixth, respectively, in the world, the U.S.S.R. and Poland twelfth and

*Table 3-28. Per Capita Energy Consumption, CPEs and MTEs, 1979*
(kilograms of coal equivalent)

| Country | Per capita energy consumption | Country | Per capita energy consumption |
|---|---|---|---|
| 1. Canada | 13,164 | 26. Israel | 3,513 |
| 2. Norway | 11,749 | 27. Italy | 3,312 |
| 3. United States | 11,681 | 28. Venezuela | 2,944 |
| 4. Sweden | 8,258 | 29. South Africa | 2,895 |
| 5. German Democratic | | 30. Dem. People's Rep. | |
| Republic | 7,136 | of Korea | 2,755 |
| 6. Czechoslovakia | 6,656 | 31. Spain | 2,698 |
| 7. Netherlands | 6,597 | 32. Yugoslavia | 2,415 |
| 8. Australia | 6,539 | 33. Libya | 2,254 |
| 9. Belgium | 6,513 | 34. Greece | 2,164 |
| 10. Federal Republic | | 35. Argentina | 1,965 |
| of Germany | 6,264 | 36. Mexico | 1,535 |
| 11. Finland | 6,001 | 37. Mongolia | 1,483 |
| 12. U.S.S.R. | 5,793 | 38. Hong Kong | 1,481 |
| 13. Singapore | 5,784 | 39. Rep. of Korea | 1,473 |
| 14. Poland | 5,752 | 40. Portugal | 1,443 |
| 15. Denmark | 5,726 | 41. Cuba | 1,358 |
| 16. Bulgaria | 5,487 | 42. Jamaica | 1,326 |
| 17. United Kingdom | 5,272 | 43. Uruguay | 1,219 |
| 18. Austria | 5,087 | 44. Chile | 1,153 |
| 19. Switzerland | 5,002 | 45. Iran | 1,141 |
| 20. France | 4,810 | 46. Albania | 1,118 |
| 21. New Zeland | 4,706 | 47. Lebanon | 1,028 |
| 22. Romania | 4,659 | 48. Brazil | 1,018 |
| 23. Japan | 4,048 | 49. Syria | 925 |
| 24. Hungary | 3,797 | 50. Colombia | 914 |
| 25. Ireland | 3,687 | | |

*Source*: World Bank (1982, table 7).

fourteenth, Bulgaria sixteenth, Romania twenty-second, Hungary twenty-fourth, and Cuba forty-first. The relatively low ranking of Hungary among the CMEA countries is probably explained, in part at least, by the fact that that country undertook an energy conservation program sooner and more intensively than the other CMEA countries. In 1960, Hungary ranked fourth among the CMEA countries in per capita energy consumption (see World Bank 1982, table 7). Even if we recognize that for structural and systemic reasons the CPEs tend to be relatively high and perhaps wasteful consumers of energy, it is still significant that, according to this indicator, all of the European CMEA countries rank on a par with the developed industrial countries.

## Conclusions

We have demonstrated that CPEs differ greatly in how they determine their various exchange rates. In none of them is the exchange rate market determined, nor could such a rate be estimated by adjusting one or another of their rates for distortions. Most CPEs have de facto multiple exchange rate systems, and their foreign trade transactions either are determined by direct quantitative allocations or take place at heavily taxed or subsidized rates. Therefore, for the group as a whole, it is not possible to use any of their exchange rates as a set of convertors to yield internationally comparable per capita dollar GNPs.

Our expert group found that the two most promising approaches to estimating per capita GNPs in dollars were the physical indicators method, whose great advantage is that it sidesteps currency conversion, and the use of purchasing power parity convertors. For the present project, the latter approach was recommended, principally because data for six of the eight CPEs were available for recent years, whereas physical-indicators-based GNP estimates ceased to be computed by international organizations as of 1973.

Once our group had decided to recommend the use of PPP-based convertors, we inadvertently became involved in a larger debate about the application of purchasing power parity versus exchange rate convertors to estimate dollar per capita GNP for *any* country, a debate that is a global issue not confined to CPEs. The outcome of the debate is of special significance for the developing countries, for which the alternative approaches may yield estimates that are several hundred percent apart. In brief, the basic problem is that, even for countries whose prevailing exchange rates are market determined and are applied uniformly to all foreign transactions, the prices of nontraded goods and services may bear little relationship to foreign prices even if there are no significant tariffs, quantitative restrictions, or transport expenses. This fact, the problem of large year-to-year fluctuations in prevailing exchange rates, and the fact that in many countries the prevailing exchange rate may be substantially different from the effective rate at which external transactions actually take place have prompted many experts generally to prefer PPP convertors for estimating internationally comparable dollar per capita GNPs.

To be sure, several theoretical and practical problems attend the computation and use of the PPP convertor. It, too, faces the usual index number problem, for example, even in the unlikely event that the actual average prices of all goods and services could be accurately determined and all produced items had exact equivalents in the other countries. Even under these ideal circumstances, the results of the comparisons would be influenced by the choice and weighting of the "international" prices. The most difficult general problem, however, is that, because PPP-converted GNPs are available only for selected countries, whereas exchange-rate-converted GNPs exist for practically all nations, it is not possible to discard the latter for operational purposes, however obvious their shortcomings for particular countries might be.

This conclusion—also the official position of the World Bank at this time (World Bank 1983, p. 27)—made it necessary for us to estimate proxy exchange rates for CPEs. In view of the many known problems of prevailing exchange rates and the major institutional differences between CPEs and MTEs, it is simply not possible to estimate accurately the correct exchange rate of a CPE. We believe, however, that *it is possible to use the systematic relationship between exchange rates and PPPs that has been found for market-type economies to adjust the PPPs of centrally planned economies so as to yield reasonable exchange-rate-type convertors for estimating their dollar per capita GNPs on an internationally comparable basis.*

There is no scientific test to assess the accuracy of a set of convertors for CPEs; accuracy is largely a matter of judgment. In this book, judgment is guided by the plausibility of the resulting per capita dollar GNP figures. According to each of the several plausibility criteria proposed, the set of convertors based on adjusted PPPs yields results that are more plausible than those obtained when employing other convertors.[17] It cannot be claimed, however, that the adjusted PPP method necessarily yields the most accurate estimates for each country. First, in the absence of an internationally agreed upon and universally applied method of PPP computations, fully accurate convertors are not available even for market-type economies. Using the prevailing exchange rates as convertors for market-type economies is itself a second-best solution, a compromise. Although there is a correlation between PPPs (as estimated by the ICP) and prevailing exchange rates (it appears to be a function largely of the level of per capita income), the theoretical and empirical determinants of the resulting ERDIs have not yet been fully resolved. Therefore, if we insist that for all centrally planned economies the only correct convertor is that derived by the adjusted PPP method, we may have to set a higher standard for these nations than the World Bank sets for market-type economies.

17. This statement does not take into account the per capita dollar GNP estimates obtained via the physical indicators method, because 1973 is the latest year for which estimates were available at this time (June 1983). Once the empirical results of the work done by Ehrlich and Pártos become available for a recent year, my statement may have to be modified.

## World Bank Decisions on Dollar GNP per Capita for CPEs

An extremely difficult problem arises when a CPE joins the World Bank and has a prevailing exchange rate substantially different from that derived via the adjusted PPP method, as was the case with Hungary in 1982. In deciding which convertor to accept for operational or *Atlas* purposes, a very important question would be whether the exchange rate of the CPE actually performs several of the basic *economic* functions that prevailing exchange rates perform in MTEs. Key considerations in this regard would be whether the country has a uniform or a multiple exchange rate system, whether and to what extent its prevailing exchange rates actually link foreign and domestic prices, whether enterprises have a significant degree of freedom in deciding where, what, and at what price to export and import, and if so, whether profit maximization at the firm level is an important basis for production and trade decisions. On the basis of these considerations, it can reasonably be argued that Hungary's prevailing and (since 1981) uniform exchange rate may be acceptable for operational purposes, even though the resulting dollar per capita GNP appears to be implausibly low (for a further discussion of this issue, see Hewett 1985). It is not unusual to find similar situations in the case of MTEs also.

In 1983, the World Bank estimated Hungary's per capita GNP in U.S. dollars for 1980 and 1981, using the official exchange rates as the conversion factors. The Bank included these estimates in its official publications (World Bank 1983, p. 22, and World Bank 1984, p. 144) with the following footnote:

> Several factors may influence both the level and comparability of this [the per capita dollar GNP] estimate with those of other countries, and the Bank is aware of other estimates that have been made in Hungary's case. These have used methodologies that attempt to take account, severally, of price and wage distortions, subsidies and taxes, and possible distortions introduced through the exchange rate, and have provided a range of alternative results.

Of the eight CPEs covered in this study, Romania is the only other CPE member of the World Bank and the International Monetary Fund. It joined these international organizations in 1972. For operational purposes, Romania's per capita dollar GNP is computed "by using adjusted official Romanian national accounts data and converting them to U.S. dollars at the effective exchange rate for foreign trade transactions in convertible currencies" (World Bank 1983, p. 22).

For all other CPEs included in this study as well as for Albania, the Democratic People's Republic of Korea, Mongolia, and Vietnam, no estimates are published because a "number of methodological issues concerning the estimation of per capita GNP for centrally planned economies remains unresolved. Until a broadly acceptable methodology is developed, GNP per capita estimates for non-member countries with centrally planned economies will not be shown" (World Bank 1983, p. 22).

In the next section I shall discuss the price systems and the role that prices and exchange rates play in CPEs, first in general and then in country-specific terms. Although the issue of price formation is the most relevant for growth rate calculations, the discussion will also shed light on some issues relating to the dollar conversion.

# Chapter 4

# *Prices*

Any economy, regardless of its economic or political system, that is concerned with the efficient use of resources should have economically meaningful prices, based on the principle and accurate measurement of the opportunity costs. This chapter presents factual and interpretative information on prices in CPEs with a view toward drawing some conclusions about the extent to which the prices of CPEs deviate from the opportunity cost standard as compared with deviations in other countries. I shall start with a general description of CPE price systems and price policies, focusing first on the construction of prices in traditional CPEs and the limited role they play there, then on the relationship between economic reforms and prices, concluding with a discussion on inflationary pressures and price policies in CPEs in recent years. I shall then summarize some of the key findings of the International Comparisons Project on the price structures of three CPEs (Hungary, Poland, and Romania), comparing them with the price structures of Yugoslavia, Austria, Italy, and Spain. A final section presents information on prices in individual CPEs, discussing, as available for each country:

- The basic principles of major postwar price reforms
- How prices are determined and what types of prices are (or were) in use during the most recent period for which this information could be found
- The extent of price flexibility
- Structure of prices, taxes, subsidies, and the role of the state budget
- Changes in the price level
- Conclusions regarding the extent of linkage between foreign and domestic prices.

The amount of information available varies a great deal by country. The sections on the U.S.S.R. and Hungary offer considerable detail; those on the other CPEs tend to be sketchy.

## General Description of CPE Price Systems and Price Policies

The price systems currently in place in CPEs have evolved from the price model of a traditional, Soviet-type CPE, whose basic features are summarized briefly. (Although the broad generalizations made in the following paragraphs are abstract statements about how the traditional CPE functions, they depict the essential features of such a system. The statements should not, however, be regarded as fully accurate descriptions of the operation of such systems.) Nearly all prices are set administratively at some level in the planning hierarchy and remain fixed for a long time. In the enterprise sector the lengthy time period between price adjustments facilitates plan construction and helps in the monitoring of plan implementation; in the consumer sector it also helps to avoid inflation.

Industrial wholesale prices are fixed on a branchwide cost-plus basis, making it possible for most branches and enterprises to earn sufficient revenue to cover current (but not necessarily also capital) costs and to show a small profit. Enterprises that cannot cover costs plus customary profit are subsidized; those with above average profits are taxed. Traditional CPEs are characterized by relatively low prices of energy, raw materials, and spare parts.

Agricultural procurement prices are fixed centrally and are typically set at low levels relative to the prices of most industrial inputs into agriculture and of finished industrial products. Direct controls, and sometimes coercion, are therefore needed to obtain the supplies, and so compulsory delivery quotas are assigned. The fixed quota system may be supplemented by a multiple-tier price incentive system to stimulate production and delivery to the state of quantities above the assigned quotas. Because this system provides insufficient stimulus for production even with the modest incentives (which take effect only after the large quotas have been met), compulsory deliveries in all countries were eventually replaced by a system of state purchases at contractual prices. This new system was introduced by Hungary and Romania in 1957, by the Soviet Union in 1958, by Bulgaria in 1959, by Czechoslovakia in 1960, by the German Democratic Republic in 1964, and by Poland in 1972. Subsequently many countries decided to pay higher prices for deliveries above the contracted amounts (Wädekin 1982) and to allow greater scope for farmers' markets, in which prices are free, or at least freer than in the official retail outlets. Since the early 1960s state purchase prices have been raised throughout the CMEA, in some countries rather substantially, partly as an incentive and partly to cover increased costs. Between 1970 and 1977 prices rose 83 percent in Poland, 28 percent in Hungary, 13 percent in the U.S.S.R., and 6 percent to 7 percent in Czechoslovakia and the German Democratic Republic (we have no information for Bulgaria and Romania) (Wädekin 1982, table 10.1), even though in all CPEs agricultural prices are still relatively low as compared with industrial prices. Because most retail food prices have remained by and large unchanged between 1964 and 1979, except in Hungary (even there the increases were modest), increasing price subsidies on basic food products (bread, dairy, meat) were required. By the late 1970s subsidy payments approached and in some cases exceeded 10 percent of NMP. In most countries relatively low farmgate prices exist side by side with subsidization of agricultural production in such forms as preferential prices for inputs (fertilizer, machinery and equipment, processed feed, and energy), lower taxes, preferential credits, and so on (Wädekin 1982). Such subsidization to the agricultural sector, however, must be evaluated in the light of the low purchase prices received by producers and the high prices charged for some industrial inputs and some consumer goods purchased by farmers. Moreover, it may be noted that agriculture is also subsidized in many MTEs.

Consumer prices are supposedly set at market-clearing levels for the economy as a whole; for example, the planned quantities of consumer goods and services valued at retail prices should correspond to the wage bill after taxes, plus net transfer payments, less savings. Actually the retail price level is frequently lower, resulting in queues and shortages. The state retail price is charged by state retail stores, consumer cooperative stores, and state and cooperative service establishments, such as restaurants and laundries. Relative prices often deviate substantially from the structure of costs; the two are kept apart by a plethora of turnover taxes and subsidies. Retail prices often do not reflect relative scarcities. The response of the consumer to prices is approximately the same as in a market-type economy, although consumer demand may not influence either the retail prices or the supply of available goods.

Services and sales on the collective farm market belong to the consumer sector, but each has its own principle of pricing. Educational and health services (their expansion is often cited as one of the impressive achievements of CPEs) are typically offered free or at highly subsidized prices. This phenomenon in turn is a factor in the relatively low wages and salaries typical in CPEs. At the same time, there has been a considerable lag in providing "communal" services, such as housing and urban transport, and "personal" services, such as repairs and cleaning. As a rule, no turnover taxes are levied on communal and everyday services, so their prices tend to be low and often require considerable subsidies.

Collective farm markets are places where farmers sell their produce after meeting state targets as well as the produce of private plots. Theoretically, prices are determined by demand and supply and are typically much higher than state retail prices. In practice, in some countries upper price limits may be prescribed by local authorities (Wädekin 1982). Such markets exist in all CPEs, but their relative importance is difficult to measure and is probably underestimated in the official statistics of many countries. Collective farm market sales appear to be relatively less important in Czechoslovakia and the German Democratic Republic and very important in Hungary and Poland. In 1978, collective farm markets accounted for about 9 percent of aggregate food sales in the U.S.S.R., according to official data (Gregory and Stuart 1981, p. 162).

CPEs conduct trade with non-CPEs approximately at world market prices and settle in convertible currency. The value of the transactions is published by the CPE in "devisa units"—that is, the actual Western currency value converted at the official exchange rate—except in Hungary, which since 1976 has used the commercial exchange rates. Trade flows valued in devisa units can thus be reconverted to actual dollars and so forth. In importing from MTEs, CPEs usually pay world market prices because international competition among MTEs for sales to CPEs ensures that prices do not rise higher. In exporting to MTEs, CPEs are generally able to obtain the current world price for energy and raw materials but typically receive less than the (West-West) world market price of similar (but not necessarily fully identical) products in exporting agricultural goods, semimanufactures, machinery, and industrial consumer products. At any given time the discount varies by country and product, generally rising with the degree of processing, and reflects three sets of factors. One is the poorer quality, on the average, of CPE nonagricultural products. The second is systemic shortcomings of CPE export pricing: exporting on the basis of plan directives, which impedes the flexibility required to obtain the best price; barter and compensation deals inconvenient for the Western partner and costly to reexport, so that large discounts are typically charged; and the fact that CPEs have not yet learned to compete effectively on the international market with nonprice variables, such as marketing, advertising, service, quick adjustment to the buyer's style and assortment specifications, flexible financing, and so on, so that much of the burden of competition falls on the price. The third factor is Western discrimination—both tariff and nontariff—which often forces the CPE seller to accept a lower export price than would a competitor from a market-type economy. Discrimination may be implicit, as when CPEs do not receive preferential access to EEC markets granted to the Common Market's members, to associate members, and to many developing countries, or explicit, as when a CPE is denied most-favored-nation tariff treatment or faces restrictive import quotas.

In trade with other CPEs, transactions are priced predominantly at average world market prices of an agreed-upon earlier period—currently a moving average of the preceding five years—and are settled bilaterally in so-called transferable rubles, an artificial currency unit. The TR price is the agreed-upon world market price in dollars converted to TR at the official TR/dollar rate. (The rate of the TR has been slightly different from that of the Soviet domestic ruble since Western currencies began floating, because the currency basket and the weights are different for the two types of rubles.) As in the case of trade with the West, intra-CMEA trade flows valued in devisa units can be reconverted to dollar (and other currency) values. Western world market prices are used because each CMEA country sets its domestic prices differently and in some respects arbitrarily, so that no trade partner is willing to accept the domestic prices of others for valuing export and imports. Intra-CMEA prices can be determined relatively easily for energy, raw materials, and other primary products because these are mostly standardized commodities traded on world markets at published prices. Between 1973 and 1982, world prices of energy and many raw materials had risen sharply; CMEA prices, because of the price rule, had risen more slowly. Thus as a net exporter of energy and raw materials, the U.S.S.R. had obtained for these goods prices lower than current world market prices; the difference may be called an implicit Soviet price subsidy. For most manufactured goods, there is only a world market price range for similar but in most cases not identical products. The very little accurate information available on intra-CMEA prices of manufactured goods suggests that prices were relatively high during the 1960s (Marer 1972). To what extent they remained high in 1980 and thereafter is difficult to say because during the 1970s world market prices may have risen faster than intra-CMEA prices; within the CMEA adjustments are made much less frequently.

More generally, application of the CMEA price formula in recent years has meant that intra-CMEA prices have lagged—in some years considerably—behind world market prices. One consequence is that intra-CMEA trade flows have tended to understate the real value of transactions as compared with valuation based on current world prices. The extent of the bias changes significantly from one year to the next and is impossible to quantify because statistical information on intra-CMEA trade and credit transactions is incomplete. Moreover, trade in manufactures at possibly higher than world prices may represent at least a partial offset to the undervaluation of intra-CMEA trade in primary products. If world market prices stabilize, the intra-CMEA price bias will be reduced. If world market prices of energy and other key products were to decline substantially and on a sustained basis, intra-CMEA trade flows could once again be biased upward as compared to valuation at current world prices.

A significant recent development is that a growing share of intra-CMEA trade is valued at current world market prices and is settled in convertible currency. Payments in convertible currency usually involve goods in strong demand in the CMEA that have ready markets in Western countries, which a CPE agrees to export to another CPE in quantities above those specified in the five-year trade agreements or under special protocol that parallels the transferable ruble protocol agreements. Thus a certain portion of Soviet oil and raw materials is sold to the East European countries at current world market prices and is paid for in dollars, just as a portion of Soviet imports from Eastern Europe, for example, agricultural commodities, is priced and settled in the same way. No systematic information is available on the size and balance of this trade within the CMEA. Trade with China, and with Yugoslavia and possibly other non-CMEA centrally planned economies also, is valued at current world prices and is settled in convertible currency.

In traditional CPEs, the state has a foreign trade monopoly, which means that the Ministry of Foreign Trade has sole authority to determine the commodity and country composition of exports and imports. It also means that producing enterprises are not allowed to deal directly with foreign exporters and importers but must operate through specialized foreign trade organizations, each with a monopoly in a designated group of products. The monopoly position of the ministry is reinforced by the inconvertibility of national currency units and by prohibitions that prevent organizations or individuals from holding or dealing in foreign currencies. Exchange rates do not effectively link foreign and domestic prices and are generally arbitrary. Imports resold by the FTOs to domestic users are priced the same as domestically produced goods and are settled in domestic currency; exports delivered by domestic enterprises to the FTO are paid for at the fixed domestic price in domestic currency. In exports the FTO thus spends national currency units and earns foreign currency; in imports it spends foreign currency and earns national currency units. Any difference between trade valued in foreign and domestic prices is settled automatically with the state budget and appears as part of the "special earnings on foreign trade" in the national income accounts, as explained in chapter 2. Traditional CPEs thus have two layers of insulation between foreign and domestic prices. One is the "foreign trade price equalization" method just indicated; the other is the system of variable turnover taxes and subsidies that are used to insulate cost of production and wholesale prices from retail prices.

Money and credit in the enterprise sector are "passive" in the sense that the flow of funds to enterprises is adjusted by taxes, subsidies, and credits to implement the allocation of resources and goods previously made essentially in physical terms. Credit is used mainly to provide enterprises with the financial resources necessary to carry planned inventories and to finance the collection gap. The main objective of monetary policy is to provide sufficient liquidity to enterprises to enable them to fulfill the plan. In the private sector, however, the purchases of consumers and the activities of small-scale producers and traders will be influenced significantly by their access to money.

The state budget functions to collect that portion of the income of enterprises, collectives, cooperatives, and the population that the planners decide to centralize and redistribute to finance investments, productive activities of enterprises, and public consumption. In a centrally planned economy, a larger share of the GNP flows through the state budget than in a market-type economy because most investment is financed directly from the state budget and because communal consumption is a larger share of total consumption. Details on state budget revenues and expenditures provide information on the nature of the economic and price system of a country.

Enterprise management's duty is to execute the plan instructions. The reward and penalty system is designed to motivate managers to try to overfulfill the plan. The typical manager will be cautious not to overfulfill it by too large a margin because the production level achieved in one period will be the basis for setting the targets for the next period. Even under a most centralized system, however, plan implementation requires some flexibility of decisionmaking at the enterprise level. Enterprise profitability is calculated but is usually not a basis for action by the planning authorities, whose directives and rationing decisions often override the price signals. Enterprise managers, however, try to concentrate on producing the more profitable items to fulfill profitability targets and to obtain the largest possible allocations to the bonus fund. The traditional CPE system leads to predictable kinds of behavior by enterprise managers: focus on increasing the quantity of output but insufficient attention to controlling cost and improving productivity; attempts to hoard capital, material, and labor; the hiding of some reserve capacity from superiors; and the exertion of maximum pressure to obtain additional investment.

### Price Reforms

Traditional centrally planned economies eventually introduce a series of economic reforms. The reforms can be of various types and usually involve some decentralization of decisionmaking. There are two main alternative models of decentralization: administrative and economic (Bornstein 1977). "Administrative decentralization" is the partial devolution of authority over selected decisions from higher to middle or to lower tiers in the hierarchy; enterprise activities continue to be coordinated vertically, through an administrative command chain. "Economic decentralization," by contrast, assigns a greater role to market forces in determining the allocation of resources, the composition of inputs and outputs, and to some extent the distribution of income; firm activities are coordinated principally through horizontal market links. Whether a centrally planned economy retains the essential contours of a traditional centrally planned economy or whether it introduces one or another type of decentralization, periodically it will have price reforms, price revisions, and price changes. Price reform refers to a basic change in the way prices are constructed, altering significantly their level and structure. Price revision does not change the basic principles of price formation but modifies the price level and structure in some sectors. Price changes refer to less significant price alterations.

Basic changes in methods of price formation must be distinguished from changes in the role of prices. Centrally planned economies begin to reform their price system when they realize that scarce resources are not free, so that cost tags must be attached to them and so that costs, including imports, must be calculated more realistically. One issue that economists in CPEs consider very important is the formula for allocating Marx's "surplus value." According to Marx, the value of a commodity is composed of current labor (measured by employee compensation), labor embodied in materials and in machinery and equipment (the latter measured by depreciation), and surplus value (which goes to the employer in a market-type economy). The various price formation models proposed by economists for a planned economy that does not permit prices to be determined by market forces differ mainly in their methods of allocating "surplus value" (called "surplus product" in CPEs):

1. In proportion to wages ("value prices")
2. In proportion to the sum of material costs and wages ("cost value prices")
3. In proportion to the amount of fixed and working capital ("production prices")
4. A combination of points 1 and 3 ("two channel prices").

Because none of these models will generate prices coinciding with relative scarcities, Western economists believe that they cannot be optimum guides to resource allocation. Nevertheless, approach 3 is the economically most meaningful method of profit calculation.

Regarding the role of prices, distinctions between center and enterprise and between current production and investments are useful. Better prices most likely result in better decisions by the *center* because improved prices promote more rational calculations. The impact of better prices on enterprise decisions will depend on their economic, financial, and political environments. Regarding current decisions, the key question is: will higher relative prices cause enterprises to economize on higher-priced inputs and to expand activities that as a result of changing relative prices become more profitable (and vice versa), or will there be no such impact and possibly even a perverse impact? In a traditional centrally planned economy, enterprises follow cost-plus pricing methods, under which a "perverse" reaction to changed relative prices is the rule, not the exception. Regarding investment decisions, the key questions are: is there differentiation in the profitability (defined as return on capital) of branches? If yes, does that differentiation reasonably reflect the country's international comparative advantage? If yes, is there a mechanism for expanding (constricting) the production capacity of the relatively more (less) profitable sectors? In a traditional centrally planned economy, the answers are generally negative.

The structure and function of prices in CPEs after reforms have been introduced depend on each country's domestic politics, economic system, economic policy objectives, level of development, and size and resource endowment and on the importance of foreign trade. Today the price systems of CPEs have common as well as distinctive features, some of which have already been noted. As a further example, every CPE has officially fixed, regulated, and unregulated prices, but their sphere of operation and relative importance vary by country. Other differences between them include how the profit markup is computed and how long producer prices remain fixed. During the 1950s and 1960s prices used to remain unchanged for a long time, at a minimum for the duration of the five-year plans. In recent years, prices may be changed more often, owing in part to accelerated price changes on the world market that affect not only East-West prices but intra-CMEA prices also. The closer a CPE's economic system remains to the traditional model, the less frequent will be its price reforms and revisions, fundamentally because in such economies prices play a less important role.

### Do CPEs Have Inflation?

Even traditional CPEs are subject to inflationary pressures, both the cost push and demand pull kind. Paradoxically, costs and therefore prices tend to rise when a CPE moves toward a fuller, economically more meaningful definition of costs, which usually entails increasing depreciation charges, introducing an interest charge on capital and rent, and valuing imports more realistically. As agriculture becomes a bottleneck sector, purchase prices will be increased to stimulate output. The costs of extracting domestically produced energy and raw materials tend to increase over time, as does the cost of imported energy and raw materials. As a rule, CPEs have not yet learned to contain external inflation by exchange rate appreciation. The deterioration in the terms of trade that the East European countries have suffered since 1973 is an inflation factor that in any event cannot be contained by exchange rate appreciation. In many CPEs, average wages have been increasing to provide work incentive; the rate of wage increases is also inflationary if it exceeds the rate of productivity improvements. New expenses for geological prospecting and environmental protection push up costs in addition. In recent years, large interest payments on external debt and inability to obtain further credits meant that domestic utilization had to be kept below domestic production, exerting an upward pressure on consumer prices. CPEs also tend to be characterized by strong excess demand on their factor and product markets, the result of taut planning, which is another source of inflationary pressure, even though it may not be reflected in the financial accounts.

The sources and extent of inflationary pressure have differed among the CPEs, as have the policies they use to cope with the problem. In some countries price reforms have altered only the structure of costs and prices; in others price levels have also risen. One of the unique features of a CPE is that it need not maintain a close link between producer (wholesale) and consumer (retail) prices, because taxes and subsidies can be manipulated to bridge the gap. Producer and consumer prices are bridged by turnover taxes and subsidies, usually set as specific amounts, in some cases as a percentage of the wholesale or the retail price. In most CPEs, the prices of basic consumer necessities changed little until 1979, so that the state budget had to allocate an increasing share of turnover tax revenues to finance growing consumer price subsidies, just as increasing net subsidies were required by enterprises in the East European CPEs because deteriorating terms of trade were not reflected fully in the prices of the relatively higher-priced import items.

Excessive reliance on these insulation systems has real social costs because it reduces the efficiency of production as well as consumption. The sum of the price equalization taxes and subsidies is a measure of price distortions. If net subsidies increase and state budget revenues cannot be raised from other sources, this will preempt resources that would otherwise be available to finance investment and public consumption. In most CPEs, artificially low prices on many consumer goods and services have been contributing to a growing excess demand and insufficient increases in supply, leading to increasing shortages of many consumer items. Beginning in 1979, however, five of the seven CMEA countries had considerably and repeatedly raised the prices of many consumer goods and services sold in the state retail sector. Hungary and Bulgaria did so sharply, Romania, Czechoslovakia, and Poland more modestly (although, in 1982, the Polish authorities raised consumer prices very sharply). The U.S.S.R. and the German Democratic Republic increased consumer prices very little. The main reasons for the fundamental change in the consumer price policies of the five countries were the need to reduce the growing imbalance between supply and demand and the need to reduce consumer demand to free resources for exports to finance deteriorating terms of trade and external debt service.

The CPEs differ more in their consumer price policies than in their producer price policies. During the 1970s some open inflation was allowed in Hungary and Poland, although at rates much below those registered by the MTEs. Some modest inflation can be measured in Bulgaria, Czechoslovakia, and Romania, whereas retail prices changed little in the U.S.S.R. and the German Democratic Republic, as shown in their official consumer price indexes (Csikós-Nagy and Rácz 1982):

| | |
|---|---|
| Hungary | 158.4 |
| Poland | 156.6 |
| Bulgaria | 126.4 |
| Czechoslovakia | 117.8 |
| Romania | 109.7 |
| U.S.S.R. | 103.0 |
| German Democratic Republic | 101.4 |

The figures given here represent 1980 consumer price level as a percentage of 1967 price level.

It is important to note, however, that since 1968 Hungary's method of measuring consumer price changes in the official indexes has significantly differed from those of the other countries. In several other CPEs the consumer price index does not include the free market prices of agricultural products, omits the prices of services, and measures price changes only when the price of an item on the price list is changed. Not only is the coverage of the Hungarian price index more comprehensive and based on actual price observations, but it also reflects changes in weights arising from forced substitutions or from the replacement of a product of poorer quality with one of better quality (Csikós-Nagy and Rácz 1982, p. 31). In other words, in six of the seven countries the actual inflation has been greater than that measured by their official price indexes. Even so, the Hungarian authorities apparently rely on open inflation much more than on increased shortages to cope with inflationary pressures.

# Price Structures of Hungary, Poland, and Romania as Revealed by the ICP

Table 4-1 shows the relation of the price structure of Hungary, Poland, Romania, and selected MTEs to the structure of international prices. For each country, the figures represent the ratio of the share of expenditure of a given GNP component in national prices to the same share in international prices. The value for GNP as a whole is one; a value greater than one indicates that, relative to the relationship of the country's prices to international prices for its GNP as a whole, the country's price for that particular component is priced high; a figure less than one shows that the component is relatively low priced (Kravis et al. 1982, p. 17). The goods and services that compose GNP are partitioned three alternative ways: first by the major final expenditure categories of consumption, capital formation, and government; next by commodities and services; and then by tradables and nontradables. Regarding final expenditure categories, it should be noted that the ICP classifies public expenditures on education, health, and recreation as part of consumption, whereas the system of national accounts includes these under government. Services are defined as nonstorable goods, which include the services rendered by household employees, teachers, and government employees; repairs of various kinds; rents; public transport and communication; public entertainment; hotels and restaurants; and household services. All other items are regarded as commodities. Tradables consist of all commodities except construction; nontradables are all services plus construction.

*Table 4-1. Relationship of the National Price Structure to the International Price Structure of Selected CPEs and Non-CPEs, 1975*

| GDP | CPE | | | | MIE | | |
|---|---|---|---|---|---|---|---|
| Component | Hungary | Poland | Romania | Yugoslavia | Austria | Italy | Spain |
| Consumption[a] | 0.94 | 0.96 | 0.91 | 0.91 | 0.93 | 1.01 | 0.98 |
| Capital formation | 1.16 | 1.11 | 1.19 | 1.25 | 1.11 | 0.89 | 1.03 |
| Government[a] | 0.96 | 0.87 | 0.85 | 1.01 | 1.30 | 1.12 | 1.48 |
| Commodities | 1.14 | 1.14 | 1.17 | 1.11 | 0.97 | 0.98 | 1.01 |
| Services | 0.68 | 0.66 | 0.61 | 0.76 | 1.07 | 1.04 | 0.97 |
| Tradables | 1.14 | 1.17 | 1.26 | 1.04 | 0.90 | 1.01 | 1.01 |
| Nontradables | 0.85 | 0.81 | 0.73 | 0.94 | 1.14 | 0.99 | 0.98 |
| GDP | 1.00 | 1.00 | 1.00 | 1.00 | 1.00 | 1.00 | 1.00 |

a. Public expenditures on education, health, and recreation (which SNA includes under government) are classified as part of consumption.
*Source:* Kravis and others (1982, tables 1-8 and 6-11).

For each of the three breakdowns, the basic patterns found are similar for the three CPEs. A comparison of relative prices by main expenditure categories reveals that investment is relatively expensive in CPEs as well as in Yugoslavia. In this respect the pattern among centrally planned economies is the same as that among developing countries and the opposite of that in industrial Western countries, where investment is relatively low priced (Austria is the only high-income country where investment is significantly more expensive than GDP as a whole).

The International Comparison Project confirms that services are extremely low priced in the CPEs; only the poorest of all countries included in the project (such as India, Kenya, Pakistan, and Thailand) have services that are priced relatively as low as in the CPEs, in part because in CPEs more services are provided free. Even though the International Comparison Project assigns values to free services by pricing the inputs, the availability of free services makes wages less at the same real income, which in turn produces relatively lower prices for labor-intensive items such as services (Kravis et al. 1982, p. 193). When services are relatively low priced, nontradables will be relatively low priced, too, since nontradables are defined as services plus construction.[1]

## Prices by Country

### U.S.S.R.

Since the introduction of the traditional CPE system during the first five-year plan (1928–32), the U.S.S.R. has had four successive price reforms, in 1936, 1949, 1955, and 1966–67, each increasing the producer price level somewhat. The price system of the U.S.S.R. conforms to that described above in connection with the "traditional CPE system," because the U.S.S.R. was the birthplace of that system. The key changes introduced during the 1966–67 reforms were (Bornstein 1976):

1. The introduction of a capital charge in the form of a tax on the average annual value of the enterprise's undepreciated fixed and working capital, valued at cost
2. The introduction of a differential rent payment for some enterprises in the extractive industry, payable out of profits

---

1. Further details on relative prices may be obtained from the binary comparisons between each of the CPEs and the two reference countries, the United States and Austria, respectively, which show purchasing power parities by twenty-six consumption, seven capital formation, and two government categories, plus some subaggregations (Kravis and others 1982, app. 7).

3. The increase of wholesale prices by about 10 percent to enable them to cover cost as newly defined plus an average of about 15 percent profit on the value of fixed and working capital, differentiating the profit rate by industrial branch. Part of this profit was to be used to pay the capital charge at a basic rate of 6 percent, another part to form three enterprise funds, one for paying bonuses, one for covering social-cultural expenditures, and one for financing small, enterprise-initiated investments.

In industry, cost includes direct and indirect labor, materials, depreciation allowances, and overhead. Interest and rental charges are not normally included in costs but are paid from gross profits. Depreciation does not include charges for obsolescence. Because cost figures are averages for low- and high-cost producers, many enterprises will be producing at a loss and will have to be subsidized. As a rule, this subsidization will not affect their survival and operations or even their chances for continued expansion of capacity.

Although since the 1966–67 reform profitability has been calculated in relation to assets by branch, this method cannot be used to determine the prices of individual products because the amount of assets involved in the production of each item is impossible to ascertain. The prices of individual products are therefore formed by adding a profit markup to costs. The sum of profits so derived yields the desired branch profitability rate. The markup percentage is determined in several steps. First, the target rate of profitability is applied to the branch's capital to obtain the planned amount of profit to be realized on sales. Second, this profit amount is divided by the estimated total cost of output to find the standard branch rate of profit in relation to cost. Third, this standard rate is added to the planned costs of individual products to obtain a tentative price. Fourth, the tentative price may be increased or lowered to yield above- or below-average profitability to encourage or discourage production (Bornstein 1976, p. 22).

In all the CMEA countries, except in Hungary since 1980, the producer (ex factory) price of industrial products is typically formed on a cost-plus basis. Although the definition of cost and the basis on which the profit markup is computed may be different (see above), the basic approach of calculating the "plus" in the cost-plus formula is probably comparable to the method just described for the U.S.S.R.

In the U.S.S.R., the term "industrial producer prices" (sometimes referred to as "industrial wholesale prices") encompasses the prices of producer goods, including raw materials, semimanufactures, and machinery as well as consumer manufactures. It excludes prices at which procurement agencies obtain agricultural products from farms but includes the prices at which they are subsequently sold to state enterprises for processing or to trade organizations for retail sale without further processing. It also excludes prices at which export and import transactions are settled abroad but includes prices at which exports are bought from and imports are resold to domestic enterprises (Bornstein 1976, p. 20).

In the U.S.S.R., there are three kinds of producer prices: (1) the factory producer (wholesale) price, at which the producer sells its output; (2) the industrial wholesale price, which is paid by the state enterprise buyer and includes also transport expenses borne by the seller, sales markup, and turnover tax, if any (which in the mid-1970s averaged about 8 percent on heavy industry products); and (3) the "settlement" or "accounting" price, used in some branches, such as mining, where production costs may diverge greatly, so that individual or groups of enterprises may receive different settlement prices. The branch sales organization resells at the uniform industry wholesale price, however.

Profits calculated as rates of return on fixed and working capital are distributed very unevenly among the sectors, so that profits are not reliable indicators of the contribution of capital to production (*U.S.S.R.* 1982, table 7).

|  | *Profits as percentage of fixed and working capital, 1972* |
|---|---|
| Electric power | 10.2 |
| Oil extraction | 26.0 |
| Oil refining | 21.8 |
| Gas | 46.0 |
| Coal | 6.3 |
| Ferrous metals | 16.0 |
| Chemicals | 19.8 |
| Machinery | 20.2 |
| Wood, pulp, paper | 17.7 |
| Construction materials | 11.8 |
| Light industry | 27.0 |
| Food industry | 24.5 |
| Sugar | 5.5 |
| Meat | 59.3 |
| Transport | 12.7 |
| River transport | 12.2 |
| Automobile transport | 31.5 |
| Communications | 13.9 |
| All industry | 19.3 |

In the nonmaterial service sectors there is no charge for the use of capital and no profit markup because enterprises are financed from the state budget. These are further reasons why the prices of services, computed on the basis of cost, are low.

Some turnover taxes are levied on interindustry sales (especially on fuels), but they originate mainly on consumer products, as shown by the relative importance of this levy in light industry and the food industry (*U.S.S.R.* 1982, table 5; see table 4-2). Within each sector, turnover tax rates vary a great deal with the product. All of the turnover tax revenue shown for the machinery sector, for example, arises from taxing its consumer products, such as the automobile, radio, and television. Within the food industry, no taxes are levied on fish, meat, dairy products, flour, fruits, and vegetables, whereas the tax represents 30 percent of the gross output of the sugar industry and 56 percent of the gross output of "other foods," which include the manufacture of alcoholic beverages. Subsidies are paid mainly on such agricultural products as dairy and meat, on which procurement prices have increased while retail prices have changed little. In 1980, agricultural subsidies amounted to 37 billion rubles, which compares with net value added in agriculture of 69 billion rubles, according to official statistics. Housing also continues to be heavily subsidized, unlike housing in the East European countries, where there has been a move to raise the absurdly low rents (Campbell 1985).

The tax structure has changed in recent years, with the turnover tax declining and deductions from profit increasing in relative importance in the state budget (Gregory and Stuart 1981, p. 144; see table 4-3). A similar trend is observable also in the countries of Eastern Europe.

Most prices are administered centrally and remain fixed for extended periods, except for prices on the free farm market (and of course on the illegal markets). The official wholesale and retail price indexes show only a very modest inflation. Both indexes suffer from deficiencies that introduce a downward bias (see the discussion of inflation, above). Western computations show somewhat higher rates of inflation.

*Table 4-2.  U.S.S.R.: Turnover Taxes, by Industry Sectors, 1972*

| Sector | Rubles (billions) | Percentage of gross output |
|---|---|---|
| Metals | 0.1 | 0.2 |
| Fuels | 5.9 | 15.1 |
| Electric power | 0.6 | 4.1 |
| Machinery | 4.3 | 3.7 |
| Chemicals | 1.1 | 3.7 |
| Wood, pulp, paper | 0.2 | 0.9 |
| Construction materials | 0.4 | 1.4 |
| Light industry | 15.7 | 18.0 |
| Food industry | 26.2 | 20.8 |
| Other industry | 1.0 | 7.6 |

*Source: U.S.S.R.* (1982, table 5).

*Table 4-3. U.S.S.R.: Tax Structure*
(percent)

| Budget revenue structure | 1950 | 1960 | 1970 | 1978 |
|---|---|---|---|---|
| Turnover tax | 56 | 41 | 32 | 32 |
| Deductions from profit | 10 | 24 | 35 | 30 |
| Social insurance | 5 | 5 | 5 | 5 |
| Taxes on population | 9 | 7 | 8 | 8 |
| Other revenues | 20 | 23 | 20 | 25 |
| Total | 100 | 100 | 100 | 100 |

*Source:* Gregory and Stuart (1981, p. 144).

In broad outlines, pricing in the foreign trade sector adheres to the system described at the beginning of this chapter. The conclusion that, in a traditional CPE, foreign and domestic prices are not linked by the exchange rate is valid for the U.S.S.R. even today. The domestic prices of exports and imports are formed differently from those of nontraded products, however, as described in Treml and Kostinsky (1982).

Because export products must undergo certain modifications and improvements to make them competitive abroad, producers of exports are often compensated by a higher price, either in the form of special price supplements (for example, on machinery, on some chemicals, and on consumer appliances) or in the form of specially posted export prices (for example, on petroleum products, lumber, and woodworking products). It has been estimated that special export price supplements add between 30 percent and 40 percent to the domestic price of comparable machinery produced for the domestic market. Because a similar system may be employed in some of the other CMEA countries also, this could be an important reason for the high foreign trade multipliers—and the commercial exchange rates based on them—in centrally planned economies.

The domestic prices of imports in actual practice may not be fully independent from the actual price of imports, although the linkage is not automatic. In the case of machinery for which domestically produced analogues are not available, predetermined conversion coefficients may be applied to the actual import price to set the domestic price. That is, the import price originally denominated in dollars or in TRs is first converted to devisa rubles at the official exchange rate, then multiplied by one of the special conversion coefficients to obtain the domestic price (Treml and Kostinsky 1982, p. 21).

In order to promote exports and to motivate firms to meet delivery schedules and quality requirements, Soviet enterprises producing for export may retain small amounts (about 5 percent) of the foreign exchange earned on sales of their products, which they are free to spend on imports.

Comparable foreign exchange retention schemes are in effect in most CPEs.

## Bulgaria

Very little information is available; in broad outlines, Bulgarian price determination and price policy are probably quite similar to those in the U.S.S.R., except for the somewhat greater influence of foreign prices on domestic prices, owing to the country's much greater dependence on foreign trade. The structure of producer prices has been reformed every five to ten years, for example, in 1962, in 1971, and in 1980–82. An experimental price reform was enacted in January 1980, taking into account "average international prices," and a full price reform in 1982 (Singh and Park 1985).

Domestic prices of imported goods are determined as follows (Singh and Park 1985):

Raw materials: foreign price converted at the official exchange rate plus or minus turnover taxes or subsidies. Domestic prices are fixed as a five-year moving average; any difference between the actual price and the fixed domestic price is taxed or subsidized.

Producer goods: foreign price converted at the official rate plus customs duties plus transport costs plus profit margin.

Consumer goods: foreign price converted at the official rate plus customs duties plus indirect taxes if domestic goods of the same type are also taxed plus additional taxes based on social policy.

In sum, there appears to be some limited linkage between domestic and foreign prices, especially for producer goods. Economic reforms introduced in 1979 and modified in 1982 have given Bulgarian enterprises a little more flexibility than is usually found in a traditional CPE: the number and detail of compulsory plan targets have been reduced, and Bulgarian firms have the right to decide what to produce and where to market output above the quantities specified in the plan in physical units. In some cases, foreign trade organizations form partnerships with producing enterprises to reduce the isolation of domestic producers from the foreign market. Some limited flexibility has also been introduced into price formation: although most prices remain centrally determined and are fixed for extended periods, in some cases only the maximum price is set; in others, prices can be determined freely by contract (Szombathelyi 1982). It is unlikely that so-called "free" prices can be determined more freely than in Hungary. (See the discussion of "free" prices in Hungary, below, under "Price Flexibility.")

A retail price reform in November 1979 increased many retail prices to an extent unprecedented since the CPE system was introduced in Bulgaria, raising the prices of basic food products by 30 percent to 40 percent, energy by 60 percent to 100 percent, construction materials by 50 percent, and so forth. These changes were linked to average wage increases of 25–30 percent (Szombathelyi 1982).

### Czechoslovakia

After the aborted reform attempts of 1966–68, Czechoslovakia returned to an economic system whose basic features appear to be close to those characteristic of traditional centrally planned economies.

The method of determining the profit markup to obtain industrial producer (wholesale) prices has been changed several times. Until 1967 the markup was added on a cost-plus basis; between 1967 and 1977 the "two channel prices" method was in use: profit is allocated proportionately to the value of fixed capital and working capital. The wholesale price level was lowered somewhat in both the 1967 and 1977 price reforms, in the latter case by 4.2 percent (Havlik and Levcik 1985).

The consumer pays what is called "final realization price," which is the wholesale price plus the turnover tax (or minus subsidies) on the product. The tax (subsidy) is accounted for in the branch in which the commodities are produced, even though the turnover tax is levied at the retail level only and is paid by the consumer. Intraenterprise sales are not generally subject to any kind of turnover tax (Havlik and Levcik 1985). In the state budget, net turnover tax revenues have declined over time, whereas remittances from profits have increased. In 1977, retail prices exceeded wholesale prices by about 26 percent (in 1973 by 23 percent); until 1967 about 80 percent of the difference was collected in the form of turnover taxes; a considerably smaller share after 1967 (Havlik and Levcik 1985).

The description of price measures being introduced during the current seventh (1981–85) five-year plan gives some insight into the price system that was in effect through 1980. According to an article published in the December 1981 issue of a leading Czechoslovak journal (Sysakova 1981), four main measures have been taken.

Domestic and foreign prices are gradually being linked, not only in the export sector, where to some extent they have already been linked, but also in sectors that supply firms that export "because they also influence the ability of the exporters to compete on foreign markets" (Sysakova 1981, p. 77). Before I cite the new measures outlined in the article, I should note that Czechoslovakia apparently has a system in which all enterprises except those manufacturing industrial exports (to all or to convertible currency destinations only?) pay the fixed domestic price for imports; exporting firms pay the actual cost of imports converted to Kcs at the appropriate foreign trade multiplier and receive the actual export proceeds similarly converted. Taxes and subsidies probably cover gains and losses more or less automatically, although probably with some type of incentive to increase export earnings and to reduce import costs. The new regulations appear to introduce only a slight change. Prices of "important" energy and raw material imports used in manufacturing will remain fixed except those purchased by firms that are manufacturing exports, where energy and raw materials prices—"together with the prices of less important imported inputs used by *any* manufacturer"— will be "planned and calculated in current prices" (Sysakova 1981, p. 83). The use of "current prices" probably means that, instead of the fixed domestic price, the actual import price converted via a current foreign trade multiplier will be used. In brief, the change appears to be an extension of the system of "current pricing" of imports to subcontractors of exporting firms and, with respect to imports of marginal importance only, to all other industrial firms.

Another slight change involves the computation of the foreign trade multipliers. Although their values are classified information (!), for quite some time they have apparently been calculated separately in ruble and nonruble trade, by industrial branches, groups of trade partner countries, and exports and imports. The practice until 1980 was to fix the foreign trade multipliers by forecasting the average ratio of internal to foreign prices for the coming five-year plan and to keep them for five years, disregarding changes in domestic and export prices (Sysakova 1981). The new system, "in preparation" in 1981 and described somewhat cryptically, was to fix the foreign trade multipliers "on the basis of the ratio of 1982 domestic prices to average foreign prices forecast for 1981 and 1982 for both socialist and capitalist countries. In subsequent years these rates will be changed insofar as required by the necessity of revising the basic relation of domestic and foreign price levels set in the plan" (Sysakova 1981, p. 83).

The third change is the continued but now more systematic increase of the domestic wholesale prices of energy. The central regulation of the prices of imported basic raw materials, however, will be maintained; the only change is "a more flexible adjustment of these prices in line with the real price trends on the markets" (Sysakova 1981, p. 78).

"Finally, special incentives are being provided for exports: In special cases, a price incentive and disincentive system will be introduced . . . by means of additions to and deductions from the commercial [*sic*] prices"

(Sysakova 1981, p. 80). In exports the system appears similar to that currently in use in the U.S.S.R. (see above), probably with the additional feature to penalize/reward the using/saving of imported energy and raw materials. Another new measure to provide export incentives is that

> earnings from foreign trade will be separated from the other activities of the enterprise, and profits from it will not be included in the [overall] profit balance so that foreign trade earnings will not be subject to taxation in the form of payments to the state budget but could be retained by the enterprise, to form special funds providing material incentives tied to export work. This will remedy the present unsatisfactory situation whereby out of every 100 Kcs from foreign trade, the enterprise really received no more than 10 Kcs [Sysakova 1981, p. 84].

(The last sentence probably refers to profits, not revenues, from foreign trade; otherwise the system was not accurately described above.) These new measures are supplemented with foreign exchange retention schemes for enterprises exporting for convertible currency, which average 0.5– 6.0 percent of (convertible-currency?) earnings.

The article cited concludes that the main difference between the Czechoslovak and the Soviet system of pricing is the greater stability of wholesale prices in the U.S.S.R. over the period of the five-year plan. The Czechoslovak system of adjusting the wholesale prices of key materials annually and providing greater flexibility in the pricing of some traded commodities is justified by the greater importance of trade in that country. The conclusion reached here, however, is that apparently there is still no uniform exchange rate and that the linkage between foreign and domestic producer prices is only a partial one even for the goods actually traded.

### German Democratic Republic

Prices set in 1944 remained basically unchanged until 1964.[2] Important basic materials were priced considerably below cost and required large subsidies; prices of consumer goods were set much higher than costs except for the prices of the heavily subsidized basics. As a result of these price distortions, there was a wasteful use of materials, little incentive for modernization, and distorted investment calculations. In 1962 fixed

---

2. This paragraph and the three below are based on Bundesministerium (1979), translated and summarized at the author's request by John Garland, whose contribution is gratefully acknowledged.

capital was revalued and more realistic depreciation rates were established. During 1964–67 a series of price reforms was implemented in
stages. Industry prices were revised on the basis of estimated costs to
reduce price distortions and subsidization. Prices of most raw materials
and capital goods rose by 40 percent to 70 percent, but consumer prices
remained largely unchanged. A 6 percent interest charge on capital was
introduced in 1967. Between 1968 and 1970 a series of price reforms
was planned and partly introduced. One innovation was a new method
of calculating the profit markup as a variable percentage not of actual
but of the hypothetically necessary fixed and working capital, to be added
to average branch prime costs. In 1971 a general price freeze was ordered.
It did not, however, extend to new or improved products, for which
extremely complex bureaucratic price-determining procedures were devised.

Since 1971, three methods of price formation have been employed. For
a large share of products, prices established during the 1964–67 reforms
still prevail. For a second group of products, the so-called asset-related
(or "production") prices devised during the late 1960s are used. For new
or improved products, a series of complex and periodically changed price
formation rules apply. One such change, in effect since 1976, is that the
producer is able to reap a guaranteed price advantage for several years.
This price advantage is based in part on the "additional utility" that new
materials or products provide to the user. The determination of "additional utility" must to some extent be subjective and subject to considerable
bargaining.

The German Democratic Republic's basic method of industrial price
formation can be summarized schematically (the terminology employed
by the country expert [Collier 1985], if different, appears in parentheses):

*Prime* costs

*plus* gross profits (including the "additional utility" share on new
   products)

*equals* factory (producer) price

*plus* turnover (product specific) taxes

*equals* delivery (purchase) price

*plus* wholesale margin

*equals* wholesale delivery price

*plus* retail margin

*equals* retail price.

The method of calculating prime costs appears to have some features
unique to the German Democratic Republic—essentially, that the clas-

sification of prime cost components corresponds to the basic factory departments, as described in Collier (1985). The 6 percent capital charge is paid from the gross profit margin and accounts for about 50 percent of gross profit. From the remaining net profits after taxes, prescribed ᴖmounts must be placed into separate funds for bonuses, firm-financed investments, acquisition of working capital, loan repayment, and insurance. Any excess over planned profits is split fifty-fifty between the state and the enterprise (Collier 1985). The structure of state budget revenues and subsidy payments changed between 1970 and 1981, as shown in table 4-4; additional details can be found in Collier (1985).

The energy price explosion after 1973 presented a major dilemma to the authorities. Even though there is basically no direct link between foreign and domestic prices, increased subsidies would have unduly burdened the budget and would not have stimulated conservation. On the other hand, an immediate and full adjustment achieved by increasing the prices of imports so soon after the 1976–80 plan was prepared and put into effect using the existing prices would have presented considerable difficulties for monitoring plan fulfillment and performance. Therefore it was decided to introduce price adjustments gradually. Beginning in 1976, energy and raw material prices were raised. As of 1977 mainly the prices of semimanufactures were increased; as of 1978, finished product prices were increased. Consumer prices, however, have remained practically unchanged, most probably for political reasons.

*Table 4-4. The German Democratic Republic: State Budget Revenues and Subsidy Payments, 1970–81*
(billion marks)

| Item | 1970 | 1975 | 1980 | 1981 |
|---|---|---|---|---|
| Receipts from socialist enterprises | 38.0 | 70.3 | 97.6 | 99.6 |
|    Capital charge | 5.9 | 13.3 | 18.2 | 19.8 |
|    Net profit tax | 12.7 | 26.7 | 40.1 | 42.1 |
|    Turnover and other taxes | 19.4 | 30.3 | 39.3 | 37.7 |
| Receipts from all sources | 32.6 | 44.4 | 63.1 | 67.9 |
|    Total budget receipts | 70.6 | 114.7 | 160.7 | 167.5 |
| Subsidies | 14.5 | 27.3 | 416.7 | 53.1 |
|    To socialist enterprises | 3.6 | 5.0 | 7.1 | 7.6 |
|    To agriculture | 1.2 | 3.0 | 8.5 | 8.6 |
|    On food | 4.8 | 7.2 | 7.8 | 11.2 |
|    On other consumer goods and services | 2.5 | 4.2 | 9.1 | 9.1 |
|    On housing | 2.4 | 7.9 | 14.2 | 16.6 |

*Source:* Collier (1985, tables 2 and 3).

*Table 4-5.  Hungary: Average Annual Price Changes, 1947–81*
(percent)

| Period | Industry | Construction | Agriculture | Consumer |
|--------|----------|--------------|-------------|----------|
| 1947–49 | 6.9 | n.a. | 15.5 | 15.0 |
| 1950–52 | 12.6 | 1.5 | 8.0 | 20.4 |
| 1953–57 | 0.6 | 3.1 | 17.8 | −0.8 |
| 1958–59 | 15.4 | 30.5 | −3.5 | −1.0 |
| 1960–65 | −1.4 | −1.2 | 2.9 | 0.7 |
| 1966–68 | 2.1 | 4.4 | 7.1 | 0.8 |
| 1969–78 | 2.9 | 3.8 | 3.5 | 2.8 |
| 1979–81 | 9.0 | 3.0 | 5.7 | 7.5 |
| 1982 | 4.5 | 6.2 | −0.3 | 6.9 |

*Sources:* Csikós-Nagy and Rácz (1982, table 1); 1982: *Heti világgazdaság* (Budapest), February 12, 1983, p. 7.


## Hungary

EVOLUTION OF THE PRICE SYSTEM. Table 4-5 presents the average annual industrial, construction, agricultural, and retail price changes by subperiods. When the traditional CPE system was introduced in 1950, retail prices were increased considerably and producer prices much less. The more than 60 percent difference between the average of the two price levels was mopped up by turnover taxes, which (together with a substantial decline in real wages and in the standard of living) helped finance rapid industrialization. All prices were fixed by the authorities, who alone could change them. Industrial wholesale prices were based on narrowly defined branchwide average costs: wages, materials, and depreciation (at an unrealistically low rate), plus taxes. Capital and natural resources were free. Firms producing at a loss were subsidized; those with above-average profits were taxed. Between 1953 and 1969 consumer prices changed hardly at all, although producer prices increased moderately in most years (table 4-5).

Systemic and price reforms began in 1957 in agriculture, where compulsory deliveries were replaced with voluntary contracts. State purchase prices were raised regularly to stimulate production. The economywide movement to measure production costs more accurately began in 1959: depreciation rates were raised, a wage tax was introduced, and the prices of most imports were set at more realistic levels by using foreign trade multipliers, not the official exchange rates. These measures led to large cost increases. Reductions in industrial turnover taxes enabled enterprises to absorb some cost increases, although in 1959 industrial producer prices still rose 15 percent and construction prices 31 percent (table 4-5). In

1964 a 5 percent charge on fixed and working capital was introduced.

The New Economic Mechanism, introduced in 1968, abolished the compulsory plan targets of enterprises. Domestic prices of energy and raw materials (except imported feed and inputs for the production of synthetic materials) were set at actual import costs (averaging the import prices from the West and the CMEA). The prices of industrial products were fixed at essentially cost plus. The capital stock was revalued and more realistic depreciation charges were established. Rent was introduced as a cost element, at 5 percent of property value. A new basis for computing the profit markup was fixed as an industrywide average of 6.5 percent of the sum of fixed and working capital, the markup differentiated by sector. The actual rate of profit, however, was 45 percent greater because enterprises predicted higher production costs during the preparation of the New Economic Mechanism in order to provide "reserves."

As a result of the price revisions and reforms of 1957, 1959, 1964, and 1968, costs were more fully taken into account, and imports were valued more realistically, although most prices and the exchange rate were to remain fixed for long periods. The intention was that lasting changes in world market prices would eventually be mirrored in domestic prices, whereas temporary price fluctuations would be buffered, but the rules for distinguishing between the two were not clarified. In any event, for several years after the 1973 world price explosion, much of the increase in import prices was neutralized by subsidies on imports and taxes on exports. Until 1979, rapidly rising external prices and deteriorating terms of trade were allowed to have only a limited impact on domestic prices.

A fundamentally new price system was introduced on January 1, 1980. Four main categories of rules were established for setting and adjusting domestic prices: (1) import based; (2) export based; (3) proportional; and (4) cost plus. The relative importance of the three types of prices in the main state sectors in 1980 was that shown in table 4-6.

1. Import-based prices: for designated raw materials constituting approximately 80 percent of industrial material inputs to industry (excluding food processing), domestic prices are set on the basis of the actual or potential convertible-currency (that is, the world market) import price that prevails for at least one quarter, converted at the prevailing commercial exchange rate, plus commercial and transport costs. The same price applies to domestically produced materials and to those imported from the CMEA; a producer's differential turnover tax is levied if their forint price is lower than the world market price. For domestically manufactured products sold on the domestic market, the actual or potential convertible-currency import price is supposed to set the upper limit,

Table 4-6. *Hungary: Three Types of Prices*
*in the Main State Sectors, 1980*
(percent)

| | Price | | |
|---|---|---|---|
| Sector | Competitive[a] | Proportional | Cost-plus |
| Industry | 65 | 15 | 20 |
| Construction | — | — | 100 |
| Agriculture | — | ————100[b] ———— | |
| Transport, communications | — | 100 | — |
| Other | — | 30 | 70 |
| Total in the economy | 35 | 35 | 30 |

*Note:* Dashes indicate not applicable.

a. The sum of import-based and export-based prices.

b. The profit markup is based on the "principle of proportionality," designed to bring a demand element into relative farm prices; the basic price reflects average cost of production. Retail farm markets are excluded because they are not part of the state sector.

*Source:* Csikós-Nagy (1980, table 30).

regardless of which system of price determination applies. Because actual import competition is limited, however, and the hypothetical world market price for Hungarian manufactures is difficult to establish, domestic prices of manufactures are de facto determined by one of the subsequent price rules.

2. Export-based prices: to manufacturers exporting to the convertible-currency area at least 5 percent of their total sales, and for all metallurgical and aluminum products, different rules apply on convertible-currency exports and on domestic sales. On convertible-currency exports, the producer receives the forint value of the actual foreign price, calculated at the prevailing exchange rate, minus commercial costs, plus a 10 percent turnover tax rebate (the percentage is reduced in subsequent years), plus the subsidy (if any), which may be granted in various ways ranging from direct payments (mainly on processed food) to "modernization" grants to credits granted on concessionary terms for the sake of promoting exports. On domestic sales, a series of rules apply. The first rule is that prices are to be set by the producer on the basis of domestic cost plus a profit margin, the latter linked to the actual profit margin on exports to the convertible-currency area. Since 1968 all exporting enterprises have had to calculate routinely the ratio of the forint cost of earning a unit of foreign exchange (that is, the firm's own foreign trade multiplier). When this ratio for a firm adjusted by the 10 percent tax rebate is the same as the exchange rate, the firm can apply a profit margin of 6 percent; the profit can rise to 12 percent for firms that have a forint/dollar ratio

one-fourth lower than the exchange rate; the profit margin declines to zero for firms with a forint/dollar rate one-third higher than the exchange rate (Balassa 1982). The second rule is an additional one that domestic prices can be increased only proportionately with changes in export prices in forints. This is intended to substitute for competition, which in Hungary is still meager, to hold down price increases by monopolistic or oligopolistic producers. The third rule stipulates that the domestic price must be the lower of that produced by the first rule or the second. If export-related costs rise by more than domestic costs, or if export prices fall because products become outdated, an enterprise must therefore lower its domestic prices. A fourth rule was introduced in mid-1981 to stimulate exports: enterprises that raise their exports in forint terms by a set percentage (established by regulation) are partially exempt from the second rule in that it remains in force only for upward changes in world prices and not for downward changes.

The enumerated rules apply to an enterprise's total operations and to its average domestic prices. Within that average, it can set the prices of individual products to respond to market forces. The rules thus aim to control enterprise profits, not prices directly. The philosophy of the new, "competitive" price system is to simulate foreign competition. In industry, real competition is limited among domestic firms because of the small size of the country, because of a highly concentrated industrial structure, and because bankruptcy has been only a remote threat until now; it is limited between domestic and foreign firms because of severe import restrictions that have to do with the balance of payments. Simulating foreign competition, however, is very difficult and results in a great deal of bargaining between the enterprises and the authorities about the implementation of the complex cost and pricing rules.

3. Prices set proportionately: for about 15 percent of industrial production and for most of agriculture, transport, and communications, prices are linked to the prices of comparable products determined on some other basis. In industry, in other words, the prices of many products are set in proportion to import-based or export-based prices and must follow changes therein. In practice, many firms that do not export significant quantities must follow the price policies of specific larger firms with similar product profiles.

4. Cost-plus and other methods: typically, prices are set to cover costs and an allowed profit markup. In construction, for example, the authorities fix not prices but norms for the cost of labor, materials, and profit margins for particular categories of work.

PRICE FLEXIBILITY. A significant innovation of the New Economic Mechanism was the introduction of limited price flexibility. It was the first time that a CPE had allowed some prices in the state sector to respond to market forces. A three-tiered system was established, involving fixed, limited (prices fluctuating between upper and lower limits), and free prices. In reality, prices in the first two categories can be considered fixed, and the flexibility of "free" prices is very limited. Between 1968 and 1980 the share of nominally free prices increased from 25 percent to 55 percent in the consumer sector, from 60 percent to 82 percent in the industrial sector (producer prices), and from 5 percent to 37 percent in agriculture (International Monetary Fund 1982, chart 4 and p. 12). Prices of products on which enterprises must follow the pricing rules described in (1) and (2) above are classified as "free" prices, together with products for which prices are truly determined by domestic supply and demand, so that "free" prices do not mean the same as in market-type economies. Free prices are not entirely free to respond to demand and supply because the authorities rightly fear that excess demand and the highly concentrated industrial structure would result in serious inflation if controls were removed. In a centrally planned economy consumer prices have to be kept in check for political and ideological reasons, although the extent of this restraint varies with time and between countries. Until about 1968 the thinking in Hungary was that inflation should not exceed 1–2 percent. In fact, the constraint was even more confining: the prices of 50 percent of the basket of goods and services purchased by the average income earner had to remain unchanged. This restriction froze the prices of about 70 percent of the "basic necessities" basket (Csikós-Nagy 1980, p. 27). During the first half of the 1970s the politically acceptable inflation target was between 2.5 percent and 3.5 percent; by 1976 it was about 5 percent. Since 1979—temporarily, it is hoped—planners have had to accept rates as high as 9 percent. Much of the inflation in the various price indexes shown in table 4-5 is the result of price actions taken by the authorities (including decisions on when and how much changes in world prices will be allowed to impact on domestic prices), not the unchecked outcome of demand and supply forces. Thus, although since 1968 a significant and growing share of prices is nominally free, most prices are subject to indirect controls through the continued regulation of wages, rules pertaining to the calculation of costs and profit margins, penalties attached to "unfair" profits, and the requirement of prior notification of the Material and Price Office of any price increases, which it may deny.

PRICE STRUCTURES. A very important feature of the Hungarian price system is that the price levels of services, agricultural commodities, and consumer goods are relatively low and industrial products are relatively high. Whereas during the 1950s the Hungarian price structure was the traditional CPE type in that net turnover taxes levied on agricultural and

Table 4-7. *Hungary: State Budgets, 1970–81*
(billions of forints)

| Item | 1970 | 1975 | 1976 | 1977 | 1978 | 1979 | 1980 | 1981 |
|---|---|---|---|---|---|---|---|---|
| *Revenues* | | | | | | | | |
| Direct taxes | | | | | | | | |
|   Wage taxes and social security contributions | 25.0 | 37.4 | 48.9 | 54.1 | 59.4 | 60.8 | 53.7 | 63.7 |
|   Profits and income taxes | 52.0 | 99.3 | 82.7 | 88.5 | 97.0 | 99.2 | 102.6 | 121.1 |
|   Production taxes and rents | 11.8 | 25.9 | 44.7 | 51.8 | 57.3 | 60.7 | 21.9 | 20.6 |
|   Taxes on capital | 25.2 | 25.0 | 24.9 | 26.6 | 28.8 | 30.9 | 2.4 | 1.1 |
|   Total direct taxes | 114.0 | 187.6 | 201.2 | 221.0 | 242.5 | 251.6 | 180.6 | 206.5 |
| Indirect taxes | | | | | | | | |
|   Turnover taxes | 23.9 | 30.0 | 27.6 | 28.3 | 30.6 | 52.0 | 60.9 | n.a. |
|   Tariffs and import sales taxes | 13.1 | 21.9 | 27.6 | 29.9 | 32.8 | 31.3 | 22.0 | 23.7 |
|   Differential producers' sales taxes | — | — | — | — | — | — | 71.0 | n.a. |
|   Total indirect taxes | 37.0 | 51.9 | 55.2 | 58.2 | 63.4 | 83.3 | 153.9 | 176.4 |
| Other revenues | 20.9 | 73.8 | 64.0 | 82.1 | 77.0 | 76.7 | 88.5 | 89.7 |
|   Total revenues | 171.9 | 313.3 | 320.4 | 361.3 | 382.9 | 411.6 | 423.0 | 472.6 |
| *Expenditure* | | | | | | | | |
| Investment | 37.4 | 65.0 | 68.3 | 79.6 | 77.3 | 81.9 | 69.6 | 59.7 |
| Price and production support | 50.0 | 103.4 | 100.6 | 121.7 | 126.5 | 135.4 | 131.8 | 144.5 |
| Social security | 22.2 | 43.0 | 49.4 | 49.5 | 53.6 | 62.2 | 77.7 | 90.4 |
| Health, education, culture | 21.2 | 34.8 | 37.1 | 40.1 | 46.1 | 49.6 | 56.0 | 67.6 |
| Defense and internal security | 14.8 | 19.2 | 19.3 | 20.9 | 24.2 | 25.5 | 27.8 | 30.9 |
| Other | 30.1 | 50.8 | 48.2 | 53.0 | 58.7 | 60.6 | 64.6 | 89.0 |
|   Total expenditure | 175.7 | 316.2 | 322.9 | 364.8 | 386.4 | 415.2 | 427.5 | 482.1 |
| *Budget deficit* | 3.8 | 3.0 | 2.5 | 3.5 | 3.5 | 3.6 | 4.5 | 9.5 |

*Note:* n.a. = not available. Dashes indicate years for which there was no such tax category.
*Sources:* Hungary, Ministry of Finance (1982, pp. 34–35); International Monetary Fund (1982, table 23).

industrial consumer goods before they reached the consumer provided much of the revenue for the state budget, since 1968 much of the state budget income is generated by the various direct and indirect levies paid by industrial producers, as shown in table 4-7, which presents the revenue and expenditure structure of the state budget. Levies on producers of course raise the industrial wholesale price, whereas increases in subsidies hold down consumer prices, creating the anomaly of nearly identical producer and consumer price levels (Csikós-Nagy and Rácz 1982).

|  | Consumer versus producer price levels (percentage difference) |
|---|---|
| 1949 | +18 |
| 1952 | +63 |
| 1959 | +18 |
| 1968 | +5 |
| 1972 | +3 |
| 1975 | 0 |
| 1976 | −3 |
| 1978 | −4 |
| 1980 (Jan. 1) | +3 |
| 1980 | +1 |
| 1981 | +0.5 |

Thus we see that in 1968 the consumer price level exceeded the producer price level by only 5 percent. In 1975 the two were identical. In subsequent years one of the two price levels became higher by a few percentage points until 1980. Since then consumer prices have exceeded producer prices by small margins. Behind this average relationship we find that consumer prices generally exceed producer prices for industrial goods and remain below producer prices for foodstuffs, transport, communications, and a number of services, which continue to be subsidized through the state budget (table 4-7). Computations carried out just before the New Economic Mechanism was introduced revealed that there were unusually large and economically unjustified differences between the structure of consumer prices and the structure of costs of producing those goods. Only about 10 percent of the consumer basket was priced near the cost of producing the items; 30 percent of the basket was priced to yield very high turnover tax revenues, whereas 60 percent was sold at a loss or at prices yielding significantly less than average operating surplus margins. Basic foods were subsidized 20 percent to 40 percent; heating fuel and passenger transport 45 percent to 55 percent; other services, first and foremost rent, by 165 percent. The relative prices of even close substitutes often deviated from their cost ratios. International comparisons revealed that the other CPEs did not have equally large and widespread discrepancies between retail prices and costs (Csikós-Nagy 1980, pp. 20–31). Although the consumer price increases introduced since 1976 have improved the situation somewhat, the system of taxation and consumer price formation remains unconventional.

LINKAGE OF FOREIGN AND DOMESTIC PRICES. The forint/dollar exchange rate introduced in 1968 (called the foreign trade multiplier until 1976) was based on the average domestic cost of earning a dollar in convertible-currency exports.[3] Although the comparison was made only for *traded* goods, the peculiar feature of the practical identity of the producer and consumer price *levels* conceptually means that, in effect, consumer prices, not producer prices, were used to value the numerator of the foreign trade multiplier.[4] One of the key findings in chapter 3 was the large discrepancy between Hungary's FTM-based exchange rate and purchasing power parity (table 3-6). If the FTM were computed to approximate the purchasing power parity of exports, the appropriate analogue in the denominator would be Hungary's export basket valued at Western *retail* prices. In fact, the prices actually used in the denominator of the foreign trade multiplier are several layers lower:

> Western retail prices of Hungary's exports
> *less* retail markup and taxes on consumption
> *equals* Western wholesale prices
> *less* wholesale markup and taxes
> *equals* the Western importer's domestic price
> *less* tariffs, other border charges, and importer's markup
> *equals* price at border of importing country
> *less* CPE price differential (difference between the price a CPE exporter and a non-CPE exporter receive for comparable products)
> *equals* Hungary's export price.
> *less* direct and indirect costs of Hungary's foreign trade operations (subtracted when computing the foreign trade multiplier)
> *equals* price in the denominator of the foreign trade multiplier.

Thus it is not surprising to find a very large discrepancy between Hungary's FTM-based exchange rate and purchasing power parity even for traded

---

3. Important implications for ascertaining correctly the actual foreign trade prices at which Hungary trades with CMEA and Western countries are noted in chapter 3, n. 9, and related text.

4. Since production for convertible-currency export involves extra cost, it is possible that the average price in the numerator was even significantly higher than retail prices.

goods; the purchasing power parity for all tradables and nontradables (GNP) would of course be even lower because services are relatively low priced in Hungary, as in the other CPEs, as was documented in table 4-1.

Between 1968 and 1981 the basic principle of Hungary's exchange rate policy was to adjust the rate to moderate the influence of foreign inflation on domestic producer prices. According to calculations made by the International Monetary Fund, Hungary's effective exchange rate index (exchange rate adjusted for inflation in Hungary and the weighted average inflation in its main Western trade partner countries) showed no particular trend between 1970 and 1981, with periods of depreciation (1970–74 and 1977–79) alternating with periods of appreciation (1975–76 and 1980–81; International Monetary Fund 1982). Thus in 1980 Hungary's prevailing commercial exchange rate still reflected approximately the relationship that had been expressed by the foreign trade multiplier in 1968.

To what extent does the exchange rate link world prices and Hungary's domestic prices? As far as the domestic producer price of convertible currency imports and exports is concerned, the link was direct and substantial between 1968 and 1972 and has once again been so since 1980; between 1973 and 1979 the linkage was partial. Since 1980 Hungary has practiced marginal cost pricing for energy and raw materials; that is, the user pays the current world market price, regardless of the (typically lower) production or import cost from other sources. Price change of basic materials will also have a direct impact on producer prices. The prices of most domestically sold industrial manufactures and those of most consumer goods are linked to world market prices only indirectly in that the direction (and perhaps the extent) of price adjustments is influenced by changes in world market prices (that is, by the prices of Hungary's exports and imports). Improvements during the last several years notwithstanding, however, the structure of Hungarian prices—especially those of consumer goods—is still very different from the structure of world market prices. The pricing of agricultural and food industry products is largely independent of world market prices, which of course is a situation not unique to Hungary or even to CPEs.

In sum, there appears to be a stronger and more direct link between foreign and domestic prices in Hungary than in other CPEs. The major difference between Hungary and market-type economies is that there appears to be only a weak link between the foreign and domestic prices of tradables other than for the goods actually traded. To be sure, in this respect Hungary may not be very different from many developing countries.

Since 1968 most Hungarian enterprises have a degree of freedom to decide the composition, the direction, and the price of their output, exports, and imports. Profit maximization has been *a* (if not always *the*) motive prompting these decisions. Although the freedom of Hungarian enterprises to make production and trade decisions is significantly greater than that of firms in other CPEs, the Hungarian firms' freedom of choice is constrained—for example, by their dependence on the authorities for much of new investment and by the need to fulfill the state's long-term contractual obligations with the other CMEA countries.

*Poland*

A major price reform, introduced on January 1, 1971, was followed by a new economic and financial system in 1973, which, however, had only a limited immediate impact on prices. During 1976–78 a major price revision was undertaken in three annual steps, and another major price revision/reform took effect on January 1, 1982. Little information is available on the substantive changes, if any, that were made in the price system beyond the fact that many prices were increased considerably. The descriptions below refer to the price system operating through 1980.

In industry, costs are determined as the average cost of producing a product in all (most) enterprises. The 1971 price reform changed the profit calculation, shifting from a simple percentage markup to the formula (Fallenbuchl 1985):

$$S = \frac{a + b + c}{k}100$$

where:

S = profit margin to be applied as a percentage of the average cost of production of a product
a = 3 percent of the gross fixed capital stock
b = 5 percent of the net fixed capital stock
c = 3 percent of the total cost of gross material output
k = total cost of the commodity.

The profit margin so computed is adjusted to take into consideration (1) the firm's or association's need to finance expansion of capacity or other large, approved, nonstandard outlays and (2) the prices of close substitutes.

Six types of prices are distinguished (Fallenbuchl 1985).

1. Factory (producer) prices at which producers in the socialist sector sell their output.

2. Realized prices at which socialist production and trade organizations obtain producer goods from other enterprises in the socialist sector. (Real-

ized prices differ from factory prices by the amount of turnover taxes/ subsidies and price equalization taxes/subsidies; see above.)

3. Wholesale prices at which retail outlets obtain goods destined for consumption or resale for production purposes to the private sector (agriculture, construction, handicrafts, and service establishments). The price includes the wholesale operating margin.

4. Retail prices at which consumers obtain goods and services in state and cooperative retail establishments. The price includes the retail operating margin.

5. Agricultural procurement prices.

6. Market prices, determined by demand and supply, at which the population buys consumption goods, mainly agricultural produce from farmers.

Turnover and price equalization taxes and subsidies are similar in nature and perform many of the same functions. The major difference between them is that turnover tax/subsidy rates tend to remain fixed for longer periods, whereas price equalization taxes/subsidies vary as needed to bridge any gap between the factory price and the realized price that remains after the payment of turnover taxes/subsidies. The sum of turnover and price equalization taxes and subsidies is one measure of the extent to which prices are distorted; the sum divided by NMP yields an "index of the degree of price distortion," which during the 1970–80 period had the following values, expressed as percentages (Fallenbuchl 1985, table III-9):

| | |
|------|------|
| 1970 | 49.4 |
| 1971 | 28.2 |
| 1972 | 29.1 |
| 1973 | 29.2 |
| 1974 | 36.7 |
| 1975 | 39.9 |
| 1976 | 46.9 |
| 1977 | 46.3 |
| 1978 | 46.2 |
| 1979 | 51.8 |
| 1980 | 65.7 |

Total financial accumulation in the socialist sector is equal to the sum of turnover plus price equalization taxes minus subsidies, plus enterprise profits minus losses. The annual amounts of the various kinds of tax and subsidy transactions between 1970 and 1980 are presented in Fallenbuchl (1985, table III-9). The tabulation reveals that, although during the ten-year period turnover taxes rose by 160 percent, price equalization taxes by 240 percent, and net profits by only 30 percent, subsidies grew almost fivefold. The country expert is able to show taxes and subsidies by the economy's main sectors for 1970, 1975, 1979, and 1980, revealing that in most years industry provided close to 100 percent, in some years more than 100 percent, of total financial accumulation in the socialist sector (Fallenbuchl 1985, table III-10). The consumption of food products has been heavily subsidized, but this fact may not necessarily imply that the agricultural sector has been comparatively inefficient.

The official price indexes, available for 1970–80, show a significant price increase, as can be seen from data presented in table 4-8. In socialist industry, large price increases occurred, especially during the first year of the 1976–78 price revisions (8.5 percent); during 1976–80, prices increased by more than 25 percent. Consumer prices increased regularly beginning in 1973, with the largest increases occurring in 1974 (7.1 percent) and 1978–80 (8–9 percent per annum). The most rapid increases were registered in the free market prices of food and in such services as education and telecommunications, although for the services the index reflects in part the low initial price base. Agricultural procurement prices also rose by 83 percent between 1970 and 1977 (latest year available), the fastest increase seen in any country in the CMEA.

*Table 4-8. Poland: Changes in Official Price Indexes, 1970–80*
(percent)

| | Price change | |
|---|---|---|
| Price index | 1970–80 (total) | 1976–80 (average annual) |
| Socialist industry | n.a. | 4.7 |
| Goods and material services for consumption | 57.1 | 6.8 |
| Food | 61.5 | 8.0 |
| Meat and poultry | | |
| State retail | 33.9 | 6.4 |
| Free market | 189.6 | 17.8 |
| Vegetables, fruit | | |
| State retail | 150.0 | 13.7 |
| Free market | 244.2 | 19.3 |
| Potatoes | | |
| State retail | 196.0 | 24.4 |
| Free market | 286.0 | 20.0 |
| Services | 44.8 | 5.4 |
| Goods and services sold to private sector not for consumption | 64.1 | 8.0 |
| Nonmaterial services | | |
| Education | 137.0 | 10.1 |
| Post and telecommunications | 142.7 | 10.0 |

*Note:* n.a. = not available.
*Source:* Fallenbuchl (1985, tables III-2, III-3, III-4, III-5).

The official price indexes are believed to understate considerably the extent of inflation in Poland—in the socialist sector mainly because of the pervasive introducion of spurious "new" products (Fallenbuchl 1985, p. 36), in the consumer sector because the index measures price movements of a basket that is not properly representative or weighted. Consumer price increases since 1980 have become greater owing in part to accelerating inflationary pressures during 1981 as the economy was collapsing and in part to the drastic increases in official prices as of 1982, as the authorities were attempting to move toward an equilibrium between the population's purchasing power (which increased rapidly after the mid-1970s) and the reduced availability of consumer supplies. There is no reliable estimate of the inflation rate since 1980.

The price indexes available through 1980 reveal the following about price policy in Poland: (1) planners seem to prefer to make large price adjustments infrequently rather than to implement more gradual increases over time, probably for reasons of administrative convenience, even though the planners' approach is politically less palatable; and (2) there was a tendency to increase components of the price index at different times to reduce the total impact of price changes in any one year (Fallenbuchl 1985, p. 38).

Concerning the linkage between foreign and domestic prices, during the eleven years between the 1971 and the 1982 reforms, the following system operated. For key imported raw materials and intermediate goods, the *realized prices* were calculated as the average of prices actually paid during the preceding two years, converted to national currency units at "conversion coefficients" established separately for intra-CMEA and extra-CMEA transactions (see below). The domestic prices of all other imports were computed at prices actually paid, converted by the same coefficients. The domestic prices of exported energy, raw materials, and agricultural products were those fixed by the authorities for sale on the domestic market (that is, the "traditional CPE" system); the prices of exported manufactures were obtained from prices actually received abroad, converted by the coefficients.

The conversion coefficients used in trade with non-CMEA countries were those shown in table 3-7, column 3, where they are called "commercial exchange rates" to describe the function they performed and because they officially became commercial exchange rates effective January 1, 1982. The rates were reportedly based on, but were not identical to, the foreign trade multiplier; their actual zloty/dollar value was considered to be a state secret until 1980. The rates were to be calculated as the foreign trade multiplier plus a fixed markup, which in 1980 was reportedly 30 percent (Fallenbuchl 1985, p. 50). The data in table 3-7 seem to confirm this point for 1980: the FTM was 34.82 zloty/dollar, and a 30 percent markup yields 45.27 zloty/dollar, which is very close to the zloty/ dollar rate of 45. As of July 1, 1982, the FTM was 80, when it became the single, unified exchange rate of the country, although its value continued to depreciate as the authorities tried to deal with the country's immense balance-of-payment problems. In calculating the new domestic prices introduced on January 1, 1982, a zloty/dollar rate of 50 was reportedly used to value imports. Since 1982 all foreign trade transactions except those involving the most important raw materials and intermediate goods have been converted at the new uniform exchange rate of 80 (Fallenbuchl 1985, p. 50); there is no information on the domestic pricing of the other kinds of trade transactions, but presumably their zloty prices are those set by the authorities for domestic transactions.

## Romania

There is less detailed information on Romanian prices than on prices of most other CPEs. Producer price reforms have taken place during 1963–65 and 1972–76 and as of January 1, 1981, but we know little of the resulting changes in the level and structure of prices except that industrial prices continue to be relatively high and agricultural and service prices relatively low, a pattern similar to that seen in the other CMEA countries. Some additional light is thrown on prices by a brief study by one of the principal investigators of the International Comparison Project, who compared the 1975 price structure of Romania with that of Hungary, Poland, and groups of market-type economies (Heston 1982). A summary of the study (Jackson 1985, table 9 and pp. 20–22) stresses that in 1975 Romanian prices were less similar in structure and had greater variability than those of the price structures of the reference countries, which may have reflected the outmoded character of Romania's basic price structure dating from 1963.

Detailed information is presented on the structure of costs and "accumulation" (depreciation, taxes, and profits) in state industry during 1951–80, by the five main industrial sectors for 1965, 1970, and 1975 and in even greater sectoral detail for 1975 and 1980 (Jackson 1985, tables 13 through 15b). In the absence of intraregional or international comparisons of cost structures, however, few conclusions can be drawn about the structure of prices or the system of taxation and subsidization.

During 1963–73 the profit markup was simply proportional to costs. During 1974–77 a new tax on fixed and working capital was introduced. It was replaced in 1977 with a higher tax on profits. In 1979 a new levy on the value of net production was assessed, which resembles a value-added tax (Jackson 1985). The information on taxes, subsidies, and the state budget is very sketchy. Although a breakdown of state budget revenues is available yearly for 1970–80 (Jackson 1985, table 19), little explanation or analysis accompanies it, perhaps because the economic contents of many items are defined only vaguely. It is evident that during the 1970s Romania experimented with alternative ways of taxing the activities of enterprises, gradually relying less on turnover and other taxes on goods and more on taxes on enterprise profits. In this respect, too, Romania conforms to trends observed in the other CMEA countries. There is practically no information on subsidies except that very large amounts (in 1980 amounting to about 10 percent of NMP) were connected with the low prices of imported petroleum (Jackson 1985, p. 20). We may speculate that much of this huge subsidy went to the domestic industry extracting crude oil at significantly higher cost than the pre-1973 prices still in effect in 1980. Much of this large subsidy was scheduled to disappear in 1981 as a result of reforms in prices and exchange rates.

There was no major reform in the retail price system until 1982, although the prices of some goods and services were increased after 1978, notably those of gasoline and fares on urban transport. According to the official "socialist" retail price index (disregarding transactions on the free market), prices increased less than 1 percent per annum until 1978 and only about 2 percent per annum between 1978 and 1981 (Jackson 1985, table 10). A comprehensively revised set of retail prices was to be introduced in 1982, increasing the consumer price level by a planned 11 percent.

Prior to 1981, foreign and domestic prices were kept apart for all except capital goods transactions by the traditional foreign trade price equalization mechanism. The domestic prices of exports are higher than those of goods sold at home because of "special export costs, packaging, and transport to the Romanian border" (Jackson 1985, p. 49). In exports (all of them? or in manufactures only?) 5 percent of the difference— favorable or unfavorable—between the domestic price adjusted for export costs and the actual foreign price converted at the commercial exchange rate (that is, the price equalization subsidy or tax) remained with the producer as an incentive. To what extent the mode of settlement on capital goods transactions differed fundamentally from the one just described is not clear, but we may speculate that exporters were given greater incentives to sell abroad and to obtain a good price.

The January 1, 1981, producer price reform brought relative prices into closer conformity with those on the world market. The commercial exchange rate was also changed from eighteen to fifteen leu/dollar, moving it closer to the average foreign trade multiplier (table 3-10). The new settlement system that was introduced gradually moved away from automatic foreign trade price equalization. There was established a system of multiple but discrete numbers of exchange rates—reportedly somewhat fewer than thirty—that are applied to specific types of export transactions. Multiple exchange rates are reportedly used more in exports. In imports there are special rates only on the purchase of crude oil and on some other basic inputs; for all other imports the user reportedly pays the actual price multiplied by the prevailing commercial exchange rate. One advantage of the new system is that external price changes during the year are supposed to have an impact on the costs, revenues, and therefore profitability of Romanian exporters and importers. Another benefit is that the dispersion of the conversion coefficients around the commercial exchange rate, if it is now smaller than under the system of automatic price equalization, should improve the general efficiency of resource allocation, provided that automatic taxes and subsidies in some other form do not replace automatic price equalization. The Romanian authorities intend to reduce the number of multiple exchange rates each year and eventually to achieve a unified exchange rate.

## Cuba

The Cuban price system is a mixture of a simple version of the traditional CPE price system in the state and agricultural sectors and a nonconventional, multilayer system in the consumer sector.[5] Enterprise (producer) prices are based on the cost of production plus a profit markup (probably a simple percentage addition); wholesale prices include turnover taxes/subsidies plus a wholesale markup; retail prices incorporate an additional markup or subsidy. Enterprises pay social security and turnover taxes and a levy on profit.

About 30 percent of consumer goods (by value) are rationed, including the most important foodstuffs and beverages, tobacco, shoes, and essential clothing. Many of these items are sold at subsidized prices. The prices of rationed consumer goods remained practically unchanged from March 1962 (when rationing began) until December 1981 (when retail prices were increased). Inasmuch as wages, salaries, and other monetary payments to the population had in the meantime increased much faster than the supply of rationed consumer goods, the excess money holdings of the population fueled a large black market, in existence since 1962, on which prices are from five to fifteen times higher. To combat the black market, to reduce the large monetary overhang of the population, and to be able to provide monetary incentives to workers, the state in 1973 inaugurated

5. My discussion is based on Mesa-Lago and Perez-Lopez (1985, section 3) unless otherwise noted.

an official "parallel market" where additional supplies of rationed goods and other commodities are sold at prices three to eight times higher. The prices are fixed and are periodically adjusted by the state, taking into account supply and demand pressures. (Scarce consumer durables are also sold—in effect rationed—through the workplace at rather high prices.) Because the black market has continued to flourish and the "monetary overhang" of the population increased after 1975, in 1980 "free farm markets" were permitted to come into existence at which farmers can sell their agricultural surplus after they have met compulsory delivery obligations to the state at the fixed, low procurement prices. Thus in agriculture Cuba has a system that was discontinued in the European CMEA countries during the late 1950s or early 1960s, as we have seen. Prices on the free farm market are higher than those of rationed goods but lower than those on the black market.

In view of the continued generous increases in monetary payments to the population, the scarce supply of consumer goods and services, and lack of opportunities to spend money (housing, education, health care, and other basic services are free or are very low priced, and there are practically no opportunities for foreign travel, for purchase of a home, or for investment in business ventures), inflationary pressures have continued to grow. This was the main reason for the December 1981 retail price reform, which increased the prices of 1,510 consumer items, including those of basic goods, from 7 percent to 525 percent. The overall average price increase was 65 percent. For the 1962–82 period as a whole, no official consumer price index has been published. Lack of reliable and comprehensive time-series information on prices and expenditure patterns on each of the four markets that exist side by side precludes the possibility of constructing a meaningful consumer price index, although the country authors show that, during 1961–81, inflation in producer and consumer prices was not insubstantial.

Domestic and external prices are not linked in any way. Cuba almost certainly relies on the traditional CPE mechanism of foreign trade price equalization to insulate domestic from foreign prices. Most of Cuba's trade is with the CMEA countries, denominated and settled in transferable rubles. Many of the key commodities traded, such as sugar exports and oil imports, are priced by its trade partners so as to provide huge subsidies to Cuba (Theriot and Matheson 1979).

## Conclusions

The current price systems of CPEs have evolved from the price model of a traditional, Soviet-type CPE where

- Nearly all prices are set administratively and remain unchanged for years.
- Industrial wholesale prices are set by branchwide costs, narrowly defined, so that most firms can earn revenue to cover current costs plus a standard profit.
- Firms that cannot cover costs are subsidized; those with above-average profits are taxed.
- Agricultural procurement prices are set very low.
- Consumer prices are supposed to be set to clear markets, but the prices of many consumer goods are lower than the market-clearing level, as indicated by frequent shortages and queuing.
- Turnover taxes and subsidies, set at different rates on products, keep apart the level and structure of producer and consumer prices.
- Foreign trade prices in transactions with the West are based on current world market prices and, in trade with the CMEA, on past world market prices.
- Domestic prices of traded goods are determined according to the same principles as the fixed domestic prices of nontraded goods.
- Exchange rates can be completely arbitrary and do not link foreign and domestic prices.
- Prices play only a marginal role in resource allocation.

By comparison with the structure of prices prevailing in MTEs at the same level of development as the CMEA countries, investment goods are relatively expensive, whereas agricultural products and services are relatively cheap. Consumer prices, on the average, are relatively inexpensive (one reason why wages are also low), with basic necessities priced extremely low and all other consumer goods high. This basic pattern has not been altered by repeated price reforms and revisions.

CPEs have undertaken a series of price reforms and revisions that have common and distinctive features. Similarities include fuller and thus more realistic definitions of costs; increased agricultural procurement prices as production incentives; more frequent revisions in the East European countries of producer prices of basic materials to reflect rapid increases in their world market prices; and strong inflationary pressures generated by these and other measures, which are typically allowed to affect producer prices more than consumer prices. Main differences among the countries include the frequency with which prices are adjusted; the degree of price flexibility; the extent to which foreign and domestic prices are linked; and, most important, the role of prices in economic decisions. Reasons for the differences can be found in historical traditions, domestic politics, basic changes in economic system, the size of the country, and the importance of foreign trade. Generally speaking, the smaller the role of ideology in economic decisions, the greater the tradition of economic analysis, and the more dependent a country is on trade, the greater the role of prices and the linkage between the domestic economy and prices in the foreign sector.

The linkage between domestic and foreign prices in CPEs is summarized in table 4-9. It shows that CPEs have a variety of systems and that the systems are periodically changed. There appears to be no direct link in the U.S.S.R., the German Democratic Republic, and Cuba, suggesting that these countries' price (and perhaps economic) systems have remained the closest to the traditional model; some linkage in Bulgaria, Czechoslovakia, Poland, and (since 1981) Romania; and substantial linkage since 1980 in Hungary. Two important aspects of the linkage are whether a unified or a multiple exchange rate system operates, indicated in the last column of table 4-9, and whether taxes and subsidies equalize more or less automatically the differences between domestic and foreign prices, which cannot be determined without an in-depth analysis of how an economy operates. Multiple exchange rates and tax/subsidy schemes are interchangeable. Hungary's system most resembles that of a market-type economy; one major difference is that Hungary's foreign and domestic prices of nontraded goods are apparently only weakly linked. Another is that the structure of Hungarian prices differs greatly from the structure of world market prices.

Differences among the CPEs in the type of conversion coefficients used when linking foreign and domestic prices are a significant finding. Bulgaria, Hungary, and since 1982 Poland rely on their commercial or their unified exchange rates but differ significantly in the automatic granting of subsidies and levying of taxes on trade transactions. The basis for Bulgaria's exchange rate is unknown. Hungary's exchange rate is based on its export foreign trade multiplier, and Poland's on the export FTM plus a large markup (that is, currency depreciation). The U.S.S.R. relies on its official exchange rate adjusted by a series of internal exchange rates. Its exchange rate was set in 1961, reportedly on the basis of purchasing power parity, but the adjustments made since then do not reflect relative price movements in the U.S.S.R. and trade partner countries. Czechoslovakia and Romania employ multiple export foreign trade multipliers, but we know neither how many are used nor their transaction-specific values, which are considered state secrets.

Analysis of CPE price systems helps explain the large differences found earlier between exchange rates and purchasing power parities, with Hungary being an important case in point. Hungary's commercial exchange rate

*Table 4-9. Linkage between Foreign and Domestic Prices in CPEs*

| Country | Extent of linkage, if any, between foreign and domestic prices | If linked, type of conversion coefficient used and basis for its determination |
|---|---|---|
| U.S.S.R. | Basically no linkage except for imported machinery without domestic analogues | Official exchange rate + IER-type coefficient[a] |
| Bulgaria | For manufacturing producers' goods only (domestic prices adjusted more frequently, partly according to world market prices) | Official exchange rate (basis unknown) |
| Czechoslovakia | Since 1981: Firms exporting manufactures and their subcontractors (exports and imports); most firms importing "less important items" (domestic prices of basic materials adjusted more frequently, partly on the basis of world market prices) | Series of FTMs[a] periodically adjusted |
| German Democratic Republic | Apparently none except through more frequent adjustment of prices of imported basic products, partly on the basis of world market prices | — |
| Hungary | Since 1980: Users of energy and raw materials required to pay current world market price regardless of source. Importers generally and exporters of | Official exchange rate (FTM-based) |

| | | |
|---|---|---|
| | manufacturers pay/receive actual foreign prices (prices of a significant portion of nontraded manufactures indirectly tied to export or import prices) | |
| Poland | 1971–81:<br>Imported raw materials and intermediate production: average prices of previous two years; all other imports: prices actually paid; applicable to exporters of manufactures (imports and exports)<br>Since 1982:<br>All transactions except those involving most important basic inputs | Conversion coefficient ($FTM^a$ + 30 percent markup)<br><br>Official exchange rate ($FTM$ + large markup) |
| Romania | Through 1980:<br>No linkage except for some export incentive<br>Since 1981:<br>  1. Import of crude oil and some other basic materials<br>  2. All other imports<br>  3. Exports | —<br><br>Special rates:[a]<br>Commercial exchange rate ($FTM$-based)<br>About 30 $FTM^a$ |
| Cuba | Apparently no linkage | — |

a. Actual values are a state secret.

*Source:* Compiled by the author.

163

(the uniform rate since 1981) was set in 1968 on the basis of the domestic cost of earning a dollar in convertible-currency exports. Since then the rate has been adjusted approximately for inflation at home and in trade partner countries (as previously described), so that it should still approximate the domestic cost of earning a dollar. An important feature of the Hungarian price system is that producer prices are relatively high and consumer prices relatively low; producer and consumer price levels are practically identical, a characteristic explained by the Hungarian system of taxation and subsidization. The practical significance of this fact is that the numerator of the foreign trade multiplier is effectively the same as it would be if Hungarian retail prices were used. In fact, it is probably significantly higher.[6] Therefore the appropriate analogue to the numerator for purchasing power parity computations would be Hungary's export basket valued at Western retail prices, whereas in the foreign trade multiplier the prices used are very much—possibly several hundred percent—lower because there are five layers of markups between the prices Hungary receives for exports and retail prices in Western countries. As a result we see a large difference between Hungary's FTM-based exchange rate and purchasing power parity even for traded goods; the purchasing power parity for GNP (tradables plus nontradables) would be even lower because services are relatively low priced.

6. The prices of goods of industrial origin, which make up 80 percent to 90 percent of Hungary's convertible-currency exports, are higher in Hungary than in any other CMEA country. Moreover, the domestic prices of convertible-currency exports are typically higher in CPEs than the domestic prices of nontraded goods.

# Chapter 5

# *Growth Rates*

This chapter begins with a general discussion of the official growth rate computations of CPEs, focusing on whether these computations are comparable with the aggregate growth rate statistics available for MTEs. Three main problem areas are identified: theoretical problems in the measurement and interpretation of official growth statistics in light of the distorted nature of prices and exchange rates in CPEs; questions of statistical accuracy and methodology; and differences in coverage between official net material product and independently computed GNP growth rates. The main conclusion is that the kinds of systematic price distortions in CPEs that were documented in chapter 4 of this report introduce a significant bias into the official growth rates of CPEs, although there are very important differences among the countries.

A second section examines alternative approaches to correcting for price distortions and other methodological problems, concluding that the so-called adjusted factor cost method is the main feasible alternative to official growth computations based on prevailing prices. There follows a description of the AFC method in general terms and with specific attention to its application to the U.S.S.R. and to the countries of Eastern Europe. A summary comparison of the growth rates of the official net material product and AFC-based gross national product is also provided. Finally, I examine selected issues relating to growth rate computations in country-specific detail, highlighting the main findings of the country authors.

## What Is Wrong with Official Growth Rates?

Although there are very important differences among the CPEs in their methods of growth rate computation, it is still valid to generalize that the official growth rates of most centrally planned economies cannot be compared meaningfully with the GNP growth rates of market-type economies owing to three sets of problems: theoretical uncertainty as to what is being measured by official CPE growth statistics, methodological shortcomings, and differences in coverage.

## Theoretical Problems

The theoretical problems of measurement stem from the artificial nature of CPE exchange rates and prices, documented in chapters 3 and 4. Economic theory suggests that GNP growth rates measure either an economy's production potential or the welfare of its population. To measure production potential, before prices can be considered to be proper weights in aggregating output, it is theoretically necessary for the relative prices of goods to equal their relative marginal costs and for the rate of return to each factor of production to be equal in all of its uses (the so-called factor cost standard). To measure the growth of welfare, the principal theoretical requirement is that prices be market determined, reflecting consumer preferences (welfare standard; Bergson 1961). Although these requirements are not fulfilled perfectly in MTEs, the deviations of their prices from these theoretical standards are not so substantial as to introduce major systematic distortions into the growth rates of most countries. In CPEs, however, deviations of prevailing prices from either standard are typically very substantial, as was documented in chapter 4. Prices differ from factor costs (1) because of the often large and arbitrary taxes and subsidies on products; (2) because of the absence of realistic interest and rent charges on assets; and (3) because of the widely varying profit rates on fixed and working capital by sectors and branches. Prices in CPEs deviate from the welfare standard because of disequilibria in the market for consumer goods and absence of a mechanism by which the population can express its preferences regarding the allocation of resources between consumption and other final uses of output (Campbell 1966, p. 24).

Whether or not the distortions in measured growth rates caused by the methods of price formation are serious depends largely on how wide the differences in sectoral growth rates are. If the dispersion is small, that is, if the economy is not undergoing major structural transformation, the distortions in NMP or GNP growth rates will be small, regardless of how large the price distortions are. Even if a country is undergoing major structural transformation, the price distortions that affect the weights of the component indexes may offset each other. Thus prices will distort NMP or GNP growth indexes only if the component volume indexes are widely dispersed and there is a correlation between the extent of price distortion and the relative growth of the volume indexes.

Gross output is typically valued at "market" prices in MTEs and at "prevailing" (also called "established"), or "realized," prices in CPEs. In both cases these are the prices paid by the last purchaser of a product or service. The different types of prices used are a potentially very important source of difference between official and independently computed growth indexes because the weights between sectors will be different from those within sectors. This difference can be termed the "weighting-induced gap." Most important is the overstatement in the official indexes of value added in industry (in some countries also construction) because prices in these sectors incorporate high net taxes, whereas in agriculture prices are much lower relative to costs. Because industry and construction in most CPEs have been growing much more rapidly than other sectors, the relatively high weights assigned to these sectors will result in higher growth rates than would be the case with prices corrected for these distortions.

Differences in price weights could also have a significant impact on the sectoral indexes themselves because prices are used to weight component products or branches in industry and to determine the composition of sales in the trade sector, but to the best of my knowledge this topic has not yet been investigated.

## Problems of Statistical Accuracy and Methods

The methodology for computing the official growth rates of NMP is the so-called *double-deflation* method. Two series, the current value of gross output and the current value of material inputs, are each deflated by the relevant price index; the difference between the two deflated series yields value added in constant prices, the basis for computing real NMP growth rates. The same method is employed to calculate the real growth by sector and subsector. Although this is a perfectly acceptable procedure, its practical application tends to yield growth rates that are upward biased, partly for systemic reasons and partly because of the statistical procedure followed in many CPEs.

The system-induced bias is especially pronounced in traditional CPEs, where the main criterion by which enterprise managers and officials at all levels in the administrative hierarchy are judged and rewarded is whether or not they are increasing production, as measured by gross or net output. Thus nearly everyone has a material interest in reporting high production figures. Statistical reporting agencies have to work with data provided by the enterprises and the administrative hierarchy. A further system-related problem is that in most CPEs the statistical agencies are not independent and thus may be subject to pressures to use methods in computing growth rates that place the performance of particular sectors, or that of the economy, in maximum favorable light. There are very important differences among the CPEs regarding these matters, however. It was the consensus at the workshops that Hungary's data are much less affected by these systemic problems. Under the economic reforms introduced in 1968, enterprises are no longer rewarded on the basis of incremental gross or net output but largely on the basis of profit. Also significant is the fact that by the 1960s the country had reestablished the independence of its statistical reporting agencies. Moreover, the country expert concludes, "at least in recent years, the Hungarian government has not followed the practice [of some other CPEs] of withholding important data series because the facts are unpleasant" (Hewett 1985, p. 17).

Turning to questions of methodology (which can be influenced by the economic and political system), for most CPEs a very important source of bias is that the price deflators used in the double-deflation method are downward biased. The chief reason is the methods employed to introduce new products. Enterprises are instructed to value their output in "constant prices." In view of the pressure to report growth, however, a manager might make the same amount of output look bigger on paper in any of several ways. He might, for example, redesign some of his products slightly so that they can be labeled new products. In CPEs there is not even theoretical, much less practical, agreement on the definition of a new product. For "new" products there are no constant prices because they were not being produced in the base year. Although the rules vary with the country, the constant price of a new product is often the temporary price set for it in the first period of its production. The manager will typically show excessively high cost estimates, and on this basis a high price will be set. As a result, the manager can turn out the same number of essentially identical products as in the past year, committing about the same amount of labor and raw materials to production but showing a higher value in "constant" prices than he did for the old products (Campbell 1966, p. 116). The price deflators actually used for the spurious new products thus do not reflect the artificial price increases and are downward biased. Such problems are not entirely absent from MTEs. The main difference, however, is that firms in MTEs are not subject to the pressures to fulfill production quotas that producers face in traditional CPEs.

The method used by the statistical offices to account for new products in constructing the sectoral price indexes may also be problematic. Part of the problem is that faced by price statisticians in all countries: often there are no consistent guidelines or information between sectors (or countries) about the best treatment of quality changes. For this reason and others, growth rates may not be fully comparable even between MTEs. Some problems, however, are likely to be especially significant for CPEs.

Spurious new products, for example, are difficult to screen out adequately when a chained index is used, because it is in the interest of the producer reporting the original data to hide the fact that some alleged new products are not really new; in so doing, the producer facilitates plan fulfillment. A perhaps more important problem is that new products tend to be priced at high introductory-prototype prices rather than at lower serial production prices (Cohn 1972, p. 132), even if the cost calculations are accurate.

Very important also is the "index number" problem. As a general proposition, for an economy undergoing rapid structural transformation, as the CPEs did during the postwar period, growth rates will tend to be higher the earlier the year whose prices are used as weights. This is called *index number relativity*, or the "Gerschenkron effect," after the economist who analyzed it in his study of Soviet industrial production (Gerschenkron 1947). An intuitive explanation of the problem would be as follows. During the course of rapid industrialization and structural transformation, there will tend to be a negative correlation between the rates of growth of a sector's output and the rates of growth of the sector's prices. Prices in the fastest-growing sectors (machinery, chemicals, and electronics) will show a tendency to decline *relative* to prices of the more slowly growing sectors (light industries and food industries in the case of most CPEs) as advanced technology is introduced and as economies of scale are achieved. Thus the earlier the year whose prices are used as weights, the larger the relative weights of the more rapidly growing sectors, and the other sectors will therefore be assigned relatively smaller weights. This tendency is generally valid for most CPEs, although their prices often remain fixed for many years and their methods of price formation have many unusual features. This tendency is also an important reason why there is no single "true" growth rate but a whole series of growth rates, one for each set of price weights. To reach a statistically acceptable compromise for a single growth rate, it would be reasonable to revise price weights periodically, at least once every ten years, and to employ price weights of approximately a midyear in the period for which the growth rate is computed. Several CPEs systematically employ early year price weights and thus show a higher growth rate than they would if more standard statistical methods had been applied. The extent to which this difference is a problem varies from country to country and by historical periods, as indicated in the discussion of growth rates by country.

*Differences in Coverage*

The official measures of growth published in CPEs refer to net material product, which includes only the value added in the production of goods and a few services. The value added in the rest of the service sector and depreciation—about one-fourth of the resources used to produce the GNP—are excluded.

Whether or not the exclusion of "nonmaterial" services introduces any bias will depend on whether NMP or the service sector is growing faster, which in turn will in part depend on how the contribution of services is measured. Because in CPEs about three-quarters of the "output" in nonmaterial services is not marketed (examples include public administration, health care, and education), output can be estimated only on the basis of input, that is, on the basis of employment. Hungary is the only CPE that officially computes net material product as well as gross national product and the respective growth rates. Following the practice of some market-type economies, the Hungarian central statistical office assumes an annual 1.5 percent increase in labor productivity in this sector. Incidentally, the productivity assumption applied by Western countries is far from uniform. Although most countries make no adjustment to the growth of the service sector on the basis of employment trends—that is, they tacitly assume that productivity remains unchanged in this sector—some countries assume an annual productivity increase of 1 percent, 1.5 percent, or 2 percent; others allow for the same productivity gain that is achieved, on the average, in sectors whose output can be marketed (Drechsler 1982).

In the case of Hungary, the official net material product and gross national product growth rates are about the same. In fact, between 1970 and 1980 GNP was growing slightly faster (Hewett 1985, table 2). This, however, results, first, from the fact that NMP itself does not grow unusually rapidly (less than 5 percent per annum) and, second, from the assumption of a 1.5 percent per annum increase in labor productivity in the nonmaterial service sectors. In CPEs in which net material product is growing more rapidly than labor input in the nonmaterial services, the exclusion of this sector from net material product and its inclusion in GNP is likely to be a significant source of the discrepancy that explains the faster growth of net material product, especially if, in the independent estimates of the GNP of a CPE, the growth rates in the service sector are based on employment, unadjusted for productivity, as they usually are.

It is not immediately obvious whether any systematic bias results from GNP's inclusion and NMP's exclusion of depreciation; the consequences would have to be determined for each country in terms of the distribution of fixed assets and depreciation rates between sectors (Alton 1981, p. 361).

I might observe, furthermore, that NMP is computed by subtracting from the gross output of material sectors only material costs and not the costs of inputs purchased from the excluded "nonmaterial" service sectors. Although the total of such purchases is typically small—2 percent to 5 percent (see table 2-1)—if the relatively rapidly growing sectors, such as industry, were to account for a disproportionate or growing share of the total of such purchases, then NMP growth rates would be upward biased (Alton 1981, p. 361). It has not been demonstrated, however, that dissimilar treatment causes any systematic bias in the NMP index.

## Alternatives to Official Growth Indexes

The previous section asked what was wrong with the official indexes of typical CPEs. The discussion enumerated several problems but suggested that the arbitrary nature of prices is *the* most important factor, or one of the most important, because the way prices are distorted tends to give relatively large weights to the relatively fastest-growing sectors and because the growth of output is also overstated through the relatively high prices assigned to "new" products.

Can prices be corrected to eliminate or reduce distortions? Four main alternative price standards have been suggested in the literature.

### World Market Prices

World market prices might be acceptable were there not immense practical difficulties in obtaining meaningful ones on a timely basis for all goods and services produced in a country. Although world market prices might be used in such areas as project evaluation, they do not represent a practical alternative to realized prices.

### International Prices

International prices computed by the ICP, and expressed in international dollars, theoretically offer as their main advantage the avoidance of disparities in growth rates resulting from shifts in the composition of output. A main disadvantage is that such prices effectively represent the price structures of the rich countries. Independent of the questions that have been raised regarding the ICP methodology and results, there are large costs and practical difficulties in including the centrally planned economies in ICP-type studies.

### Approximate Basic Value Prices

Approximate basic value prices are market or prevailing prices cleansed of net indirect taxes—that is, calculated by subtracting indirect taxes and adding subsidies. The system of national accounts calls this method of valuation "approximate basic values"; the material product system calls it "prices excluding turnover taxes": in Hungarian practice, measurement at "prices excluding commodity taxes." In the view of a leading Hungarian expert, whether this mode of price determination is better than prevailing prices depends on why subsidies/taxes were granted/levied in the first place. If a consumer good is subsidized for social reasons, for example, the higher price excluding the subsidies is probably a better measure of the product's relative importance than prevailing prices. If, however, a subsidy is granted to the producer to cover his losses, the relative importance of the product would be better indicated by the judgment of the market, that is, without adjustment for the subsidy. In still other cases the operating surplus of a producer might be taxed or enlarged via subsidies in order to correct for an opposite kind of intervention at an earlier stage of production. Relatively high commodity (turnover) taxes, for example, may be levied on machinery products precisely because taxation was relatively low, say, in metallurgy (Drechsler 1982).[1] In any event, because approximate basic value prices are not available systematically for the CPEs, as a practical matter they cannot be relied on for systematic adjustment.

### Adjusted Factor Cost

AFC appears to be a practically feasible alternative to prevailing prices in CPEs. In brief, the adjustment involves eliminating the turnover tax, subsidies, and profits that are components of various aggregates when valued at prevailing prices and adding notional amounts for returns to fixed and working capital and land. AFC prices, and GNP growth rate computations based on them, are available and will continue to be available for seven centrally planned economies and possibly eventually also for an eighth, Cuba (a project was under way in 1983 at Wharton Econometric Forecasting Associates to compute growth rates for Cuba by applying the AFC method). Theory tells us that valuing production accord-

1. In Hungarian practice, many of the data published are at prices that exclude commodity taxes. Even with calculations that express some national income aggregates at realized prices, the production of individual branches is computed at prices excluding commodity taxes, to which the balance of turnover taxes and subsidies is then added as a single item. One problem with this method is that changes in the balance of turnover taxes and subsidies are not easy to interpret because of the frequent changes in methods of price formation, subsidization, and taxation. A further difficulty in Hungary is that some publications designate as producer prices values that exclude commodity taxes, which is confusing because, in international practice, producer prices are usually juxtaposed with retail prices. Thus producer prices too can be realized prices.

ing to a factor cost standard makes it possible to put a "production potential" interpretation on the aggregates and their components. For these reasons, but also because the intrasectoral and intersectoral weights this method provides for growth rate computations are comparable to those employed in computing the growth statistics of MTEs, the adjusted factor cost method represents an alternative to official growth rates that must be considered. In the next section I shall describe and critique the AFC method. I shall also examine the way in which it is applied to the Soviet Union and to the six countries of Eastern Europe. A subsequent section will compare the official and the AFC-based growth rates. Finally, I shall make a few observations concerning the growth rates derived from the physical indicators method for MTEs and CPEs, comparing them with the official index numbers.

## The Adjusted Factor Cost Approach to Growth Rate Calculations

Prompted by the problems with the official growth rates of CPEs described above, scholars in the West for more than a generation have devoted a great deal of time and effort to computing alternative estimates of the economic growth of centrally planned economies, using official CPE data but replicating as much as possible the standards of valuation and the construction of national income accounts that were developed by the U.S. Department of Commerce and the Organisation for Economic Co-operation and Development. Although the most important difference between the method used by the national central statistical offices and the approach taken by the independent estimates concerns the valuation—and therefore the weighting—of products, branches, and sectors, the independent estimates also follow a basically different approach to constructing indexes of growth. Whereas the CPEs typically use the double-deflation method described earlier, the independent estimates made in the West rely on indexes constructed from samples of officially published physical production data to construct an index of GNP by sector of origin and on samples of officially published consumption, investment, and government activity data to construct an index of GNP by end use. The discussion here focuses only on GNP indexes by sector of origin, but the sources cited almost always publish indexes of GNP by end use also.

The indexes of the growth of GNP and its major components are computed as weighted averages of subcomponent indexes. To construct an index of industrial production, for example, a large product sample (usually several hundred) is collected and grouped into eight, twelve, or more industrial branches, weighted as appropriately as possible with domestic prices and value added by subsectors. The branch indexes are aggregated into an overall industrial production index by value-added weights. The index of agricultural production is computed similarly, combining output data (adjusted for own consumption) for several dozen types of crops and livestock products. For the service sectors except housing, the indexes are based largely on employment; for housing, on official measures of the housing stock. The index of GNP by sector of origin is formed by combining the indexes of industrial and agricultural production with similar indexes for the remaining production sectors.

The valuation in these independent estimates is adjusted factor cost, which is the reason for the designation "adjusted factor cost approach" that was pioneered by Bergson. (See Bergson 1961 and the large body of literature cited in *U.S.S.R.* 1982, p. 11.) Broadly speaking, the AFC approach ensures that prices are equal to average costs and that factor prices are equal between markets and proportional to factor productivities. The AFC approach requires or assumes the following (*U.S.S.R.* 1982, p. 37):

- All product prices must resolve into charges for primary inputs: labor, capital, and land.
- Differences in wage rates among sectors represent differences in labor productivity and workers' disutility.
- Rent is charged for the use of superior land and other natural resources.
- The capital charge comprises depreciation and interest payment based on the same rate of interest throughout the economy, corresponding to the average level of capital productivity in the country.

Although the ways in which these principles are applied may differ slightly, there is a consensus regarding the basic validity of the approach and nearly a generation of cumulative experience in applying it to compute the growth rates of the Soviet Union (*U.S.S.R.* 1982) and of the six countries of Eastern Europe by the Research Project on National Income in East Central Europe.[2]

2. There is, for example, a difference of opinion as to whether the capital stock should be valued gross or net of depreciation. The AFC method applied to the U.S.S.R. uses capital stock data before depreciation (*U.S.S.R.* 1982, p. 37); as applied to the six countries of Eastern Europe, net of depreciation (Alton 1981, p. 358). Another difference is in the method of calculating the uniform rate of interest that is to be applied.

The production weights of GNP sectors are derived within the material production sphere by taking as an overall constraint the NMP produced in a selected base year. This control value is then attributed to (1) labor, comprising wage and wagelike payments plus social security contributions, sector by sector, and (2) nonlabor factors of production (estimated as the difference between the control total and the total cost of labor), which is distributed to production sectors largely on the basis of their percentage shares in the total values of fixed and working capital. GNP is reached by adding depreciation and by estimating value added in the service sectors excluded from the net material product (Alton 1981, p. 358).

The most important criticism by far of the AFC approach is that it does not adequately measure quality improvements and the introduction of new products, and so the resulting indexes of growth are likely to be downward biased. The reason is that the sectoral indexes are based on the output of products reported mostly in physical units. The product sample is likely to be biased toward traditional items (for example, tons of steel) rather than toward modern products (for example, computers), especially in the case of countries (such as the German Democratic Republic) where there has been a steep decline in the amount of economic information published.

Such criticism is answered by the observation that some of the items included in the samples are themselves value aggregates, especially for countries for which the physical product sample size is small. These value indexes presumably incorporate quality improvements and in fact may contain a significant upward bias. It has been argued in defense of the AFC method that because the biases in official and physical data are offsetting, their use in combination should provide a reasonable measure of real growth (U.S.S.R. 1982, p. vii). Although in principle this is correct, the consensus of the workshop participants was that the growth rate estimates for each country for each subperiod must be judged case by case. It was also suggested that the Research Project on National Income could usefully publish the importance of the value series in the sample for each country in approximately the same way that this information is available for the Soviet indexes in U.S.S.R. (1982, p. 183 and appendix table A). In further defense of the AFC method, it has also been noted that, in the case of Romania (and possibly in other countries?), the published physical series themselves incorporate product changes by using technical coefficients that are similar to constant prices. Electrical motors, for example, will be assigned coefficients indicating how many "standard" electrical motors they represent; such coefficients may have a bias in either direction (Jackson 1985, p. 58). The problem of insufficient measurement of quality improvements affects first and foremost the industrial production indexes, because in agriculture, construction, and other sectors there is a much lower rate of introduction of new products or quality changes in the traditional products.

Poor sample size for some countries in some years has been noted as a serious problem, affecting not the method, of course, but the possibility of application. To be sure, the sectoral indexes constructed in the West, reflecting physical output data, are always based on as large a sample as possible, in view of the data published in CPE official sources. Irrespective of sample size, however, it is possible, though by no means certain, that some of the discrepancy between the independent Western and the official CPE sectoral indexes reflects the poorer data available to outsiders if their sample is biased toward commodities that grow more slowly in quantity or quality (Hewett 1985, p. 16). In the case of the indexes prepared by the Research Project on National Income, the sample size varies greatly from country to country, from sector to sector, and from year to year. The sample size is quite good for Hungary, for example, where in industry alone the index is based on approximately 500 commodities. Still, this is only about one-tenth of the number of commodities with which the Hungarian central statistical office works in constructing its industrial production index. The sample for other countries used by the Research Project on National Income tends to be much poorer. It was recommended at both workshops that the Research Project could very valuably make available a list of the products—by country, by year, and by sector—on which its sectoral indexes are based, following a format similar to that available for the Soviet Union in *U.S.S.R.* (1982, pp. 179–244). Several additional issues were raised during the first workshop regarding the application of the AFC method to the countries of Eastern Europe by the Research Project.

1. In making factor cost calculations, the Research Project takes essentially the total nonlabor income of the material sector as a return to capital, redistributing that income among different sectors in accordance with the capital stock used in the sectors. Total nonlabor income is a rather artificial figure from an economic standpoint because it has little to do with the productivity of the capital in the countries concerned and instead reflects the fiscal needs of their governments. If countries happen to be investing more, spending more on defense, and so forth, they must generate more profit and taxes from the public sector. Thus something that in the Research Project's method is recorded as a return to capital (which affects the weights) will change just because the government's fiscal needs have changed, making it hard to know how to interpret such

calculations. To be sure, the rate of return in different countries is not so very different from what might be considered reasonable. Instead, it was suggested at the workshop, why not begin with an assumed but economically meaningful rate of return on capital?[3]

2. The Research Project has imputed a rate of return to the housing sector that is equal to the average rate of return in each country's other sectors. For purposes of comparing the growth rates of CPEs and non-CPEs, however, it should be noted that housing is typically undervalued in the West because it does not earn a rate of return comparable to other sectors. That the rates of return on housing are low in non-CPEs may be due to price controls or to the fact that people invest in housing partly for capital gains, which do not appear in national accounts calculations. Be that as it may, the Research Project's weights for housing are typically high by MTE standards, with the share of income in the housing sector as a percentage of NMP ranging from 4 percent for Romania to almost 9 percent for Hungary, whereas the comparable number, say, for Italy would be 3 percent, for the United Kingdom 2 percent, for Norway 1 percent, and for France 0.8 percent, calculated on the basis of Denison's figures computed for the early 1960s. For purposes of comparability, Bergson suggested, it might be appropriate to impute half of the normal return to housing. Although this allowance is arbitrary, it may be a fairer way to compile data for the CPEs than is giving their housing sectors a full rate of return.

3. The Research Project obtains agricultural rent essentially by arbitrarily doubling the fixed capital employed in that sector. The weight for agriculture thus reflects the return to the resultant aggregate plus labor earnings. To determine how realistic these assumptions are, Bergson took the share of GNP originating in agriculture and divided it by the share of agriculture in total employment, obtaining a ratio of income originating to the worker, that is, the relative productivity of a worker in agriculture. The figure runs from 0.62 for Romania to 1.1 for the German Democratic Republic, statistics that are relatively high compared with those for Western countries. According to OECD data, the U.S. figure is a high 0.77, but France's is 0.49, West Germany's 0.44, Italy's 0.8, and so on. If we

3. In applying the method to the U.S.S.R., a sophisticated procedure is used: first, turnover taxes and subsidies on final goods and services are eliminated, and the effect is traced on production cost in all sectors by using the official input-output table. Next a repricing algorithm is applied to determine the interest rate so that the rate of return on each sector's fixed and working capital is equalized. The capital stock series are based on official data, gross of depreciation (*U.S.S.R.* 1982, pp. 37, 40).

had comparable figures for the developing countries, the figures computed by the Research Project for the East European countries probably would look even higher. Although the official data certainly tend to overweight industry by any standard, it is possible that the Research Project's method may have gone somewhat in the other direction regarding the high share of agriculture.

Taking these suggestions into account, after the first workshop the Research Project recomputed the growth rates of the six East European CPEs by assigning alternative AFC weights, allowing a uniform 12 percent rate of return on capital in all sectors, except agriculture and housing, where the adjusted rate was 6 percent, thus reducing the relative weights of agriculture and housing and raising those of industry and other sectors. These new computations can be found in Alton (1982), where it is concluded that the consequences of using alternative weights for GNP growth rates are small.

Further research on several important problems was recommended during the workshops. It would be useful to survey the methods employed by MTEs, including the developing countries, to construct their indexes of growth and the ways in which those methods are applied in practice, for example, with respect to the introduction of new products. There is certainly nothing inherently wrong with using the double-deflation method (it is the approach reportedly recommended by the United Nations) to determine real value added by sector; the problem is the shortcoming in the way that CPEs are applying it.

A related task of research, especially useful for the World Bank and for projects on CPEs, would be to compare the differences, if any, in the growth rates that result from the application of the double-deflation method versus the aggregation of physical series method for a group of MTEs, including developing countries. In this case it would be important to examine carefully how individual countries treat quality changes in compiling various price or quantity indexes. Because for MTEs the valuation problem would certainly be much less important, systematic differences, if they were to be found between the growth rates provided by the two types of estimates, could be the basis for estimating the presumed bias in the AFC method applied to CPEs. (A pilot research project along these lines is reportedly under way at the Research Project.)

It would also be instructive to investigate empirically the specific reasons for differences in CPE growth rates calculated by the double-deflation and adjusted factor cost methods. Specifically, what is the comparative importance of the differences in weighting between major sectors and within the sectors?

## Official Growth Rates versus AFC-Based Growth Rates

The official and the AFC-based computations can be compared by focusing on net material product, both the total and the sector amounts. In a sector-of-origin approach, NMP essentially comprises five sectors: industry, agriculture, construction, transport and communications, and trade.[4] Table 5-1 compares the structure of NMP (that is, the relative weights of the five sectors) at established prices and at alternative AFC prices, the latter representing the revised estimates of the Research Project explained above. For the East European countries, the AFC and adjusted AFC weights refer to various benchmark years during 1975–77. The structure at established prices is calculated for each country for the same year or for a nearby year, in current or constant prices.[5] For the U.S.S.R., the valuations are for 1970 in both sets of prices.

The key question for growth rate computations is the shares of industry and agriculture because their combined shares account for between two-thirds and three-quarters of NMP and in most countries industry has been growing much faster than agriculture. The share of the trade sector can be very different at alternative prices because in some countries value added in this sector reflects taxes and subsidies on consumption and, in some cases, also foreign trade price equalization (see Alton 1981, table 4, which shows how the share of this sector fluctuates at alternative sets of established prices).

Table 5-1 shows at a glance the impact of the first workshop's recommendations to the Research Project for computing the AFC weights for

4. For the sake of comparability, the small "other" sector was omitted in calculating the structure in established prices because this sector has no precise counterpart in adjusted factor cost computations. The official sectoral indexes and the AFC-based sectoral indexes are not fully comparable because the official indexes exclude depreciation while including nonmaterial service inputs, whereas the AFC-based indexes include depreciation and exclude nonmaterial service inputs. Sectoral boundaries may also not be fully identical. Bulgaria and Romania have now joined the majority of CPEs in adding passenger transport and communications serving nonmaterial sectors to material production, for example, and Czechoslovakia and the U.S.S.R. are the only two European CMEA countries that have still not done so.

5. Ideally, the structure in established prices should be the base year used in constructing the official indexes of each country, but for several CPEs the base year cannot be identified or was changed during 1970–80. In table 5-1, for Poland the AFC benchmark year is 1977, whereas the established price refers to 1978 production and structure valued in constant prices as of January 1, 1977. The structure of NMP calculated in established prices may change between two time periods if the price structure is altered by sectors growing at different rates or by reforms.

Table 5-1. The Seven CMEA Countries: Structure of NMP at Established Prices and at Adjusted Factor Cost Prices, Base Years, 1975–78

| Sector | U.S.S.R. | | Bulgaria | | | Czechoslovakia | | | German Democratic Republic | | |
|---|---|---|---|---|---|---|---|---|---|---|---|
| | EP 1970 | AFC 1970 | EP 1977ᵃ | AFC 1975 | AAFC 1975 | EP 1978ᵇ | AFC 1977 | AAFC 1977 | EP 1975ᶜ | AFC 1975 | AAFC 1975 |
| Industry | 52.9 | 41.4 | 52.8 | 41.3 | 43.8 | 60.1 | 47.6 | 50.8 | 60.8 | 53.9 | 56.6 |
| Agriculture | 23.7 | 27.3 | 18.8 | 32.6 | 28.8 | 9.1 | 20.8 | 15.8 | 11.4 | 18.4 | 14.1 |
| Construction | 8.5 | 9.4 | 9.1 | 7.9 | 8.2 | 11.3 | 11.0 | 11.9 | 7.6 | 6.6 | 7.2 |
| Transport and communications | 9.4 | 12.4 | 8.9 | 9.6 | 10.1 | 4.5ᵈ | 9.7 | 10.1 | 5.1 | 10.3 | 10.9 |
| Trade | 5.5 | 9.4 | 10.4 | 8.5 | 9.0 | 15.0 | 10.9 | 11.3 | 15.0 | 10.7 | 11.3 |
| Total | 100.0 | 100.0 | 100.0 | 100.0 | 100.0 | 100.0 | 100.0 | 100.0 | 100.0 | 100.0 | 100.0 |

| Sector | Hungary | | | Poland | | | Romania | | |
|---|---|---|---|---|---|---|---|---|---|
| | EP 1975[c] | AFC 1976 | AAFC 1976 | EP 1978[e] | AFC 1977 | AAFC 1977 | EP 1978[b] | AFC 1977 | AAFC 1977 |
| Industry | 59.7 | 40.0 | 43.5 | 53.7 | 41.6 | 44.6 | 57.9 | 43.8 | 46.2 |
| Agriculture | 16.6 | 31.7[f] | 25.5 | 15.8 | 32.2 | 27.1 | 15.3 | 32.1 | 28.4 |
| Construction | 11.0 | 9.3 | 10.4 | 11.9 | 8.9 | 10.0 | 10.2 | 8.3 | 8.8 |
| Transport and communications | 4.8 | 10.2 | 11.1 | 8.0 | 9.7 | 10.4 | 5.9 | 7.2 | 7.6 |
| Trade | 7.9 | 8.7 | 9.3 | 10.7 | 7.6 | 7.8 | 10.7[g] | 8.6 | 9.0 |
| Total | 100.0 | 100.0 | 100.0 | 100.0 | 100.0 | 100.0 | 100.0 | 100.0 | 100.0 |

*Note:* EP = established prices. AAFC = alternative adjusted factor cost.

a. 1977 output in current prices.
b. 1978 output in current prices.
c. 1975 output in current prices.
d. Excludes passenger transport and communications.
e. 1978 output in constant prices of January 1, 1977.
f. 1978 output in constant prices (2.2 percent of NMP).
g. Includes water management (2.2 percent of NMP).
h. Includes miscellaneous other material sectors.

*Sources:* U.S.S.R.: *U.S.S.R.* (1982, pt. 1, table 11); East Europe at EP: Alton (1981, table 4); at AFC: Alton (1982, tables 1–6); at AAFC: Alton (1982, table 18).

the East European countries. According to the AFC as it was initially computed, for example, in Bulgaria in 1976 industry represented 41.3 percent and agriculture 32.6 percent of NMP; after adjusting the assumptions underlying the AFC method, the shares changed to 43.8 percent for industry and 28.8 percent for agriculture, that is, the structure becomes more similar to that shown by the official statistics, as expected. The pattern is similar for each East European country. For the U.S.S.R., the AFC structure has been calculated according to methods that compare with the revised AFC structure for Eastern Europe. Because the revised AFC shares are believed to be more realistic, only they will be compared with structures at established prices.

I shall focus first on industry. A comparison of the sector's share in established prices with its share in (adjusted) AFC prices suggests the extent to which the prices prevailing in a CPE overweight this sector (assuming that the year indicated is the base year for the official index).

|  | Share of industry at EPs ÷ share of industry at AFC |
|---|---|
| Hungary, 1975–76 | 1.37 |
| U.S.S.R., 1970 | 1.28 |
| Romania, 1977–78 | 1.25 |
| Bulgaria, 1975–77 | 1.21 |
| Poland, 1977–78 | 1.20 |
| Czechoslovakia, 1977–78 | 1.18 |
| German Democratic Republic, 1975 | 1.07 |

The tabulation confirms that industrial prices are relatively high in all CPEs but are relatively the highest in Hungary. This finding supports— and in part is explained by—the peculiar features of the price system of Hungary that I described earlier: since 1968 much of the state budget revenue has been generated by a series of steep levies on industrial producers, which has raised industrial producer prices and has created the anomaly of producer and consumer price levels that are about the same (see chapter 4). One consequence will be relatively high foreign trade multipliers on products originating in the industrial sector. During 1975–81, industry provided from 80 percent to 90 percent of Hungary's exports to MTEs (total exports to nonsocialist countries less raw and basic materials of agricultural origin, agricultural products, and livestock; products of the food industry are considered industrial). The implications of this finding for Hungary's FTM-based exchange rates are obvious.

Turning to agriculture, we may make a comparison similar to that made for industry, thereby confirming that this sector is underpriced in all CPEs:

|  | Share of agriculture at EPs ÷ share of agriculture at AFC |
|---|---|
| Romania, 1977–78 | 0.54 |
| Poland, 1977–78 | 0.58 |
| Czechoslovakia, 1977–78 | 0.58 |
| Hungary, 1975–76 | 0.65 |
| Bulgaria, 1975–77 | 0.65 |
| German Democratic Republic, 1975 | 0.81 |
| U.S.S.R., 1970 | 0.87 |

Table 5-2 compares 1970–80 official and AFC-based "synthetic" growth indexes in constant prices. The synthetic measure of net material product is derived from the GNP accounts as a weighted average of the growth rates of the five sectors that approximately compose net material product, using the AFC weights shown in table 5-1.

Conceptually, the difference between the synthetic and the official NMP indexes may be decomposed into the "intersectoral weighting-induced gap," that is, the gap due to differences in the weights assigned to the sectors, and to the "sector-index-induced gap," that is, the gap explained by differences in the sectoral indexes themselves. As a practical matter, the problems mentioned in note 2 may also be responsible for discrepancies between the synthetic and official indexes. (If official NMP and synthetic GNP indexes were compared, a third factor would be the "coverage-induced gap," that is, the gap due to the omission of services and depreciation in the indexes of the centrally planned economies.) The information readily available to me is insufficient to permit a comprehensive analysis of the kind indicated. Some relevant facts and interpretations, however, will be presented by country in the next section; the analysis here is confined to a few general observations.

Table 5-3 shows the pattern revealed by the ratios of the official to the synthetic indexes of growth for NMP and for four of the sectors, trade excluded, ranking the countries from largest to smallest differences in NMP growth indexes. We must be very cautious in drawing conclusions about the accuracy of any particular index in either set of computations. If, for example, for a given country in a given sector the number of physical sample items is small, the AFC index must be based largely on the official value series, so the two series will be close by definition and should not be interpreted as confirming each other's accuracy.

Table 5-2. Seven CPEs: Index of NMP Growth by Sectors, Synthetic and Official Indexes, 1970–80
(1970 = 100)

| Country and index | Industry | Agriculture | Construction | Transport and communications | Trade | NMP | Average NMP growth rate 1970–80[a] | Ratio (official/synthetic) |
|---|---|---|---|---|---|---|---|---|
| U.S.S.R. | | | | | | | | |
| Synthetic | 158 | 90 | 148 | 165 | 145 | 138 | 3.3 | 1.5 |
| Official | 178 | n.a. | n.a. | n.a. | n.a. | 162 | 4.9 | |
| Bulgaria | | | | | | | | |
| Synthetic | 158 | 94 | 145 | 173 | 155 | 140 | 3.4 | 2.1 |
| Official | 216 | 85 | 170 | 221 | 562[b] | 196 | 7.0 | |
| Czechoslovakia | | | | | | | | |
| Synthetic | 138 | 117 | 128 | 140 | 140 | 134 | 3.0 | 1.6 |
| Official | 159 | 110 | 159 | 178 | 206 | 158 | 4.7 | |
| German Democratic Republic | | | | | | | | |
| Synthetic | 137 | 120 | 145 | 146 | 142 | 137 | 3.2 | 1.5 |
| Official | 168 | 116 | 146 | 143 | 160 | 159 | 4.7 | |
| Hungary | | | | | | | | |
| Synthetic | 128 | 131 | 121 | 143 | 151 | 132 | 2.8 | 1.7 |
| Official | 176 | 124 | 157 | n.a. | n.a. | 159 | 4.7 | |

184

| | | | | | | | | |
|---|---|---|---|---|---|---|---|---|
| Poland | | | | | | | | |
| Synthetic | 149 | 97 | 172 | 220 | 163 | 146 | 3.9 | 1.4 |
| Official | 165 | 124 | 142 | 221 | 198 | 169 | 5.4 | |
| Romania[c] | | | | | | | | |
| Synthetic | 193 | 152 | 139 | 189 | 205[d] | 177 | 5.9 | 1.6 |
| Official | 279 | 144 | 195 | 221 | n.a. | 242 | 9.2 | |

*Note:* n.a. = not available.

a. Compound growth from end-point index numbers: $I_n = I_0(1 + r)^n$".

b. Between 1979 and 1980 the index more than doubled, and there are large fluctuations in other years also, which suggests that the index probably incorporates foreign trade price equalization gains and losses.

c. Housing is assumed to be valued at "effective prices"; how much subsidy is involved is not known. Moreover, no adjustments are made to the official figures for (1) net exports of services, (2) travel expenses of employees, and (3) losses.

d. A similar problem to that indicated for Bulgaria in *b* was present in the Romanian index from 1965 to 1972. The index fell, for example, from 100 in 1965 to less than 30 in 1977, when its publication was discontinued. Since 1975, Romania appears to have followed a different method.

*Sources:* U.S.S.R.: *U.S.S.R.* (1982, chap. 1, table A-5; chap. 2, table 10) and Campbell (1985, p. 34); East European countries, synthetic indexes: based on Alton (1982, tables 1–6 and 18); official indexes, Bulgaria: Singh and Park (1985, table 2); Czechoslovakia: Havlik and Levcik (1985, p. 24) and the statistical yearbook of Czechoslovakia, 1982, p. 149; German Democratic Republic: 1970–78: Alton (1981, table 16); 1979–80: Deutsches Institut für Wirtschaftsforschung (Berlin), *Wochenberichte*, various issues; Hungary: Központi Statisztikai Hivatal, *Statisztikai évkönyv*, 1980; Poland: Fallenbuchl (1985, table V-1); Romania: 1970–78: Alton (1981, table 16); 1979–80: Wharton Econometric Forecasting Associates, *Romanian Crisis or Turning Point* (Washington, D.C., 1981).

*Table 5-3. Seven CPEs: Ratios of Official to Synthetic Indexes of Growth for NMP and for Four Sectors*

| Country | NMP | Industry | Agriculture | Construction | Transport and communication |
|---|---|---|---|---|---|
| Bulgaria | 1.40 | 1.36 | 0.90 | 1.17 | 1.28 |
| Romania | 1.37 | 1.45 | 0.95 | 1.40 | 1.17 |
| Hungary | 1.20 | 1.38 | 0.89 | 1.30 | n.a. |
| Czechoslovakia | 1.18 | 1.15 | 0.94 | 1.24 | 1.27 |
| U.S.S.R. | 1.17 | 1.13 | n.a. | n.a. | n.a. |
| Poland | 1.16 | 1.11 | 1.28 | 0.83 | 1.00 |
| German Democratic Republic | 1.16 | 1.23 | 0.97 | 1.01 | 0.98 |

*Note:* n.a. = not available.
*Source:* Table 5-2.

The comparison reveals, as expected, that much of the difference arises in industry. In every case the official index shows a higher rate of growth than the recomputed index. The record also confirms that, with the possible exception of Hungary, industry has grown considerably faster during the 1970s than agriculture. This is also the pattern in Hungary, according to the official index (which shows industry increasing by 76 percent and agriculture by only 17 percent), whereas, according to the Research Project's calculations, the two sectors grew at about the same 30 percent rate.

It is quite surprising to find, however, that the largest differences between the official and the recomputed industrial production indexes are in Hungary and in Romania—these two being the highest in the CMEA. It is the place of Hungary that is surprising because, in the view of this project's country expert and the expert from the Hungarian central statistical office who participated in the second workshop, the Hungarian indexes are quite good; in the view of the country expert and several other workshop participants, they are arguably the best in Eastern Europe. In contrast, the country expert on Romania gives several reasons for supposing that the official industrial production index of that country is upward biased (Jackson 1985).

The two sets of indexes for agriculture are much closer; in fact, in some instances the official index shows a somewhat slower rate of growth than the recomputed index. Poland is apparently the single exception; in Poland the official indexes of agricultural production exceed the recomputed one by a much larger margin than in industry, a finding that again is unexpected and requires an explanation.

## Growth Rates Derived by the Physical Indicators Method

As I noted in discussing the physical indicators method, one of its advantages is that it can yield internationally comparable growth rates provided that adjustments are made for changes over time in (1) the value of the dollar in which the original GDPs are expressed; (2) the relationship between the dollar and other national currencies; and (3) the relationship between the per capita dollar GDPs and the different physical indicators in the various benchmark years. The ECE's version of the physical indicators method has computed "implied" growth rates for market-type economies and for the seven European CMEA countries and Yugoslavia for 1950–73 and subperiods (United Nations/ECE 1980*a*). Inasmuch as these implied growth rates are available only until 1973, the results are of mainly historical interest. They are principally significant for this project as they call attention to the fact that the differences between the official and the implied growth rates are much larger for CPEs than for MTEs, underscoring the problems with CPEs' growth rates that I discussed previously.

The relationship between the official growth rates and those implied by the physical indicators method differs from country to country. To facilitate meaningful international comparisons, the ECE made a notable innovation: it employed an "adjusted" index as a scale of reference. "The adjusted index was estimated in such a way as to indicate what the rate of growth of the per capita GDP in the U.S. would have been had the relationship between the official index to the index implied in the [physical indicators] estimates corresponded to the 'typical' relationship in the other countries during the given period" (United Nations/ECE 1980*a*). The indexes so obtained, converted into average annual growth rates, were then compared with the official indexes, whether those were calculated for the per capita growth rate of GDP or GNP by the market-type economies or for the per capita growth rate of NMP by the centrally planned economies and Yugoslavia. Table 5-4 summarizes the results.

It is striking to find that, whereas for most market-type economies the differences between the official and implied growth rates were generally small (for the MTE group as a whole the official growth rates exceeded the implied growth rates by only 0.1 percent per annum during the 1951–73 period), the differences for centrally planned economies as a group were much larger, the official growth rates exceeding the implied growth rates by 1.7 percent per annum during the same period. The ECE concludes:

> Among the eight countries subscribing to the material product concept [the CMEA countries and Yugoslavia], particularly large discrepancies are to be found in the German Democratic Republic (−3.2 percentage

*Table 5-4. Selected MTEs and CPEs: Average Annual Growth Rates of per Capita GDP: Physical Indicators Estimates and Official Growth Rates, 1951–73*
(percent)

| Country | Physical indicators estimates (1) | Official growth rates (2) | (1) − (2) |
|---|---|---|---|
| MTEs and Yugoslavia | | | |
| Australia | 2.3 | 2.8 | − 0.5 |
| Austria | 4.4 | 5.0 | − 0.6 |
| Belgium | 3.2 | 3.5 | − 0.3 |
| Canada | 2.7 | 2.8 | − 0.1 |
| Denmark | 3.4 | 3.4 | 0.0 |
| Finland | 4.7 | 4.4 | 0.3 |
| France | 3.9 | 4.3 | − 0.4 |
| Germany, Federal Republic of | 4.2 | 5.2 | − 1.0 |
| Greece | 6.3 | 6.1 | 0.2 |
| Ireland | 3.8 | 3.0 | 0.8 |
| Italy | 4.6 | 5.2 | − 0.6 |
| Japan | 6.6 | 8.5 | − 1.9 |
| Netherlands | 3.6 | 3.6 | 0.0 |
| New Zealand | 2.1 | 1.8 | 0.3 |
| Norway | 3.6 | 3.3 | 0.3 |
| Portugal | 4.6 | 5.3 | − 0.7 |
| Spain | 5.2 | 5.2 | 0.0 |
| Sweden | 3.0 | 2.8 | 0.2 |
| Switzerland | 3.3 | 2.7 | 0.6 |
| Turkey | 4.6 | 3.0 | 1.6 |
| United Kingdom | 2.6 | 2.5 | 0.1 |
| United States | 2.4 | 2.4 | 0.0 |
| Yugoslavia | 5.3 | 5.6 | − 0.3 |
| MTEs, average | — | — | − 0.1 |
| | | | |
| CPEs | | | |
| Bulgaria | 6.6 | 7.6 | − 1.0 |
| Czechoslovakia | 3.9 | 5.0 | − 1.1 |
| German Democratic Republic | 4.0 | 7.2 | − 3.2 |
| Hungary | 4.8 | 5.3 | − 0.5 |
| Poland | 4.5 | 5.9 | − 1.4 |
| Romania | 5.9 | 8.5 | − 2.6 |
| U.S.S.R. | 4.8 | 6.7 | − 1.9 |
| CPEs, average | — | — | − 1.7 |

*Source:* United Nations/ECE (1980a, table III-7).

points), and Romania ($-2.6$ percentage points). The discrepancy is also relatively large in the Soviet Union ($-1.9$ percentage points) and varies between $-1.4$ and $-1.0$ percentage points in Bulgaria, Czechoslovakia and Poland. It falls to 0.5 percentage points in Hungary and Yugoslavia or even less, but it remains negative there also [United Nations/ECE 1980a, p. 27].

## Country-Specific Findings

### U.S.S.R.

Much more research has been done to evaluate the validity of Soviet production indexes than to assess the indexes of all other CPEs combined. The studies have always concluded that the Soviet NMP index is biased upward. Table 5-5 shows the values computed in *U.S.S.R.* (1982, p. 25).

During the 1970s the "coverage-induced gap" between official NMP and Western GNP indexes disappeared because there is little difference between the synthetic index that strips GNP to cover only material production and the full GNP growth rate index (Campbell 1985). Much of the difference between the two indexes is attributable to the "sector-index-induced gap" in industry and is explained by the problems of new product pricing and by related problems that exaggerate gross output and understate the price deflators (Campbell 1985, p. 32). One major study concluded:

> The Soviet incentive system used to determine the size of bonuses for enterprise managers results in inflationary pressure in the Soviet industrial sector. The primary mechanism for releasing this pressure is the overpricing of new products. This mechanism is employed because of

*Table 5-5. U.S.S.R.: Official and Synthetic Indexes of Net Material Product, 1951–80*
(percent per annum)

| Years | Official NMP (1) | Synthetic NMP (2) | (1) ÷ (2) |
|-------|------------------|-------------------|-----------|
| 1951–55 | 11.1 | 7.6 | 1.46 |
| 1956–60 | 9.1 | 7.1 | 1.28 |
| 1961–65 | 6.5 | 5.1 | 1.27 |
| 1966–70 | 7.7 | 5.6 | 1.37 |
| 1971–75 | 5.7 | 3.7 | 1.54 |
| 1976–80 | 4.2 | 2.6 | 1.61 |

Source: U.S.S.R. (1982, p. 25).

the upward rigidity of Soviet established prices for older products. The inflation inherent in the overpricing of new products is disguised in that it is not reflected in Soviet price indices. Unlike Western price indices, Soviet price indices do not use splicing techniques to incorporate new products and their prices. The official Soviet price index for industrial product increased by less than 10% over the 1960–75 period. For the same period a Western-style index of Soviet prices increased by roughly 25% or at an average annual rate of about 1.5%. The official Soviet price index for machine-building and metalworking products declined by almost 25% over the 1960–75 period. For the same period a Western-style price index increased by roughly 40%, or at an average annual rate of 2.25% [Steiner 1982, pp. 278–79].

The incidence of overpricing has been discussed extensively in the Soviet literature. For example, N. Glushkov, the chairman of the U.S.S.R. State Committee for Prices, stated in 1980: "Of the 7,000 industrial enterprises checked out by price-forming organs in 1979, practically every second enterprise was found to have violations of wholesale prices" (quoted in Steiner 1982, p. 280).

A very detailed description is available of the methodology of the recomputed net industrial and agricultural production indexes; descriptions of the real output indexes for the other NMP sectors are much sketchier, but they generally follow comparable procedures (Campbell 1985, p. 33).

The independently constructed industrial production index (*U.S.S.R.* 1982, pt. 2) uses a five-tier stratification of industry: individual products (for example, iron ore); input-output sectors (ferrous ores); branches (ferrous metals); major industry groups (industrial materials); and total industry. Product data are aggregated into sector indexes using 1967 producer prices as weights. Branch indexes are calculated from sector indexes using value-added weights derived from the 1972 input-output table valued in producer prices. The aggregations from branches to industry groups and finally to total industry employ the independently derived value-added weights based on AFC prices rather than on established prices.

The basic sample comprises 312 products measured in one of three ways: (1) physical quantities (tons, square meters, or number); in some cases the raw product data are adjusted by indexes of quality change over time in the standard product; (2) official ruble value series (for example, the value of production of agricultural machinery), which, however, are likely to incorporate concealed inflation; and (3) official gross-value-of-output indexes for various product groups (mineral chemicals, machinery repair), which are also subject to the kinds of limitations noted for official value series. Physical output series account for 94 percent of the number of statistical series in the index. By value, the percentage composition of the sample is:

| | |
|---|---|
| Physical units | 73.3 |
| Ruble value | 10.7 |
| Gross-value-of-output index | 8.0 |
| Unrepresented | 8.0 |
| Total | 100.0 |

Because both the ruble and the gross-value-of-output index are value based, somewhat less than one-fifth of the industrial production index is value based.

In evaluating the reasonableness of the index, those responsible for constructing it conclude that the most serious problems are in the machinery branch, where evidence suggests that the quantity series may bias the growth rate for selected machinery products downward by as much as 1 percent per year because of failure to account for improvements in quality and changes in product mix; the bias in the quantity series for the other branches is probably smaller. This bias is offset by the disguised inflation in the value series in the machinery sample, which may be as much as three percentage points per year:

As for the net effect of these biases, if all the differences in growth rates between the value and physical series in the producer durables sector, where the problems of bias are the worst, were actually attributable to inflation, the [reconstructed] index would overstate machinery growth by a maximum of 1.2 percentage points per year and overall industrial growth by 0.3 percentage points. But the machinery inflation bias is probably much less because the quantity series, by understating growth, partially offset the upward biases of the value series [U.S.S.R. 1982, p. 178].

The seventy-three-page description of the construction of the industrial production series fully documents the method and calculations and provides the full list of the samples used.

A similarly detailed explanation and evaluation is also available for the index of agricultural production (U.S.S.R. 1982, pt. 3) which is based on the output of twenty-eight individual crops, ten livestock products, and four items of livestock inventory, covering about 80 percent of crop and 95 percent of livestock production. Official statistics are corrected for well-documented measurement errors. The physical production data are aggregated for the most part with average prices received by all producers for products sold in 1970, in some cases procurement prices, into two subsector indexes, one for crops and one for livestock.

Important problems in constructing the index include, first, the uncertain estimates for own consumption, especially seed and feed, that must be subtracted from gross output to derive net output and, second, the paucity and unreliability of published agricultural statistics. Outright falsification of data—at lower levels regarding output and own consumption and at higher levels by reporting some output series without correction for the large waste—is also a problem. As long as the extent of falsification changes little over time, however, it should have no major impact on the index. When the index is compared with three independently computed indexes of Soviet agricultural output for the 1960s and 1970s, the growth rates differ by less than 0.5 percent per annum, even though the indexes themselves vary widely in coverage and weighting (U.S.S.R. 1982, pp. 250–51).

Before I discuss the individual East European countries, a few general observations are in order about the independent estimates for these countries that have been constructed and published for nearly two decades by the Research Project on National Income. The work of the Research Project is based entirely on data that are found in the publicly available official sources of the centrally planned economies and in the publications of international organizations that use data submitted by the CPEs. The same is true also for the U.S.S.R. The effort made by the Research Project to construct GNP accounts and growth indexes has been very considerably smaller for the six East European countries combined than the attempt made by others in the West to assess the U.S.S.R. The Research Project generally employs methodologies that are comparable in broad outlines to those for the U.S.S.R. even though in specific areas there are some differences.

There are very important differences between the East European countries in the volume, detail, accuracy, and documentation of the methodology of the data they make available. These differences of course affect all work on independent assessment. The Research Project, for example, demonstrates that, in constructing agricultural production indexes, the statistical information available is best for Hungary and Poland and better for Czechoslovakia and the German Democratic Republic than for Bulgaria or Romania. In the case of Romania, the Research Project has had to depend on fragmentary information (RPNI 1982, p. 9). The situation is similar in other areas of economic activity, although the ranking of the countries is not the same for each and every set of statistics.

The Research Project constructs GNP accounts and growth indexes simultaneously for the six East European countries, so that it can apply uniform statistical procedures as much as possible. When missing data for a country must be plausibly estimated, it is helpful to have an on-the-spot opportunity to check the information that might be available for other East European countries.

It was the consensus at the two workshops that the computations of the Research Project are documented, explained, and evaluated in a considerably less detailed and less readily accessible form than those published with the estimates for the U.S.S.R. In part the reason is the smaller scale of effort devoted to Eastern Europe. By "documentation" the workshop participants meant not mainly the citing of sources but specific information—for example, on the size and composition of the quantity and value series used in the samples, on prices, and on the intrasectoral weights employed, all on a comparative cross-country basis (that is, the kind of documentation summarized above for the U.S.S.R.). It is especially important for us to have this information comparatively for the East European countries for the industrial production index. (The documentation is better regarding the construction of the agricultural indexes, but even here, the summary of the methodology could be more detailed, so that it included, for example, information on the way in which expenses and depreciation were estimated to derive gross and net output.)

With respect to evaluation, the consensus was that it would be exceedingly useful to compare the Research Project's indexes and the official indexes in a more systematic and analytical fashion than has yet been done. Specifically, the suggestion was made that the differences between the official NMP and Research Project's GNP growth rate indexes be decomposed into coverage-induced, weighting-induced, and sector-index-induced differences (as has been done for the Soviet Union in Cohn 1972 and *U.S.S.R.* 1982) and that whenever possible the likely *specific* reasons for unusually large differences, for example, those identified in table 5-1, be indicated. Finally, the workshop participants believed that it would be helpful to have the results of a sensitivity analysis regarding the extent to which the independent estimates for particular countries might be biased by the presumed failure to account for improvements in quality and changes in product mix.

## Bulgaria

The authors of the country study noted the differences between the official and the Research Project growth rates and wished to calculate the contribution of the weighting-induced differences but did not know

*Table 5-6. Bulgaria: Variously Computed Growth Rates, 1970–80*
(percent per annum)

| NMP | 1965 official weights | 1975 Research Project weights |
|---|---|---|
| Official | | |
| 1970–75 | 7.3 | 7.6 |
| 1970–80 | 7.0 | 7.2 |
| Research Project | | |
| 1970–75 | 5.0 | 4.8 |
| 1970–80 | 3.2 | 3.0 |

*Source:* Singh and Park (1985).

the base year of the official series.[6] They deduced that the base year was 1965 because, when that year's sectoral weights were used, the index that was generated approximated the official NMP index the most closely (Singh and Park 1985, appendix 3). They found that the weighting does not account for much of the difference; see table 5-6. It might be added, however, that if weights were used in the official index for a more recent year, such as 1977, the weighting-induced difference would be more substantial, as can be seen by comparing the weights in table 4-9 of this book and in appendix 3 of the country study.

Next, the country authors proceeded to make two adjustments in the official NMP index. First, noting that the trade sector's contribution to NMP increased nearly six times between 1970 and 1980, far exceeding the growth of domestic and foreign trade turnover, they constructed a new trade index on the basis of Bulgaria's domestic and international trade volume and reestimated the growth of NMP using the original 1965 sector weights; see table 5-7. This adjustment thus lowers the official 1970–80 NMP growth rate by 1.6 percent per annum. Next they added nonmaterial services, using an index of the number of persons not privately employed in that sector, which yields the GNP growth estimates (compound growth formula from end-point index values) shown in table 5-7.

## Czechoslovakia

The country authors stress that there is upward bias in the official indexes due to concealed inflation and warn about a

---

6. The indexes of constant-price NMP sectoral series were computed until 1962 in the prices of 1957, and between 1963 and 1971 in the prices of January 1, 1962. Since 1972 they have been computed in the prices of January 1, 1971 (Singh and Park 1985, p. 4).

Table 5-7. *Bulgaria: Official and Adjusted NMP Growth Rates,*
*1970–80*
(percent per annum)

| NMP | 1970–75 | 1970–80 |
|---|---|---|
| Adjusted | 6.8 | 5.4 |
| Estimate of | | |
| country authors | 6.5 | 5.1 |
| Research Project | | |
| estimate | 4.7 | 2.9 |

*Source:* Singh and Park (1985).

paradoxical result—namely that the growth rate of NMP at official constant prices is faster than the growth rate computed from data at current prices, in spite of the fact that some inflation is officially admitted. This was achieved mainly by a simple statistical procedure: together with the change of price levels in 1976, a branch classification reform was performed. The effects of actual price changes thus cannot be traced at all [Havlik and Levcik 1985, p. 23].[7]

Prompted by the obvious problems with the official indexes of growth and some questions about the methodology underlying the Research Project index, the country experts made rough and ready alternative growth estimates, using a price index they had constructed to deflate GNP in national currency units. These may be compared with the GNP growth estimates of the Research Project, as shown in table 5-8. Both estimates are significantly lower than the official NMP growth rate (table 5-1). The difference between the Research Project's and the country authors' estimates is negligible during the first half of the 1970s but widens during the second half, when the Research Project shows a 2 percent annual growth tempo and the country experts 1 percent growth. Noting the fundamental differences in coverage and methods and the precarious nature of their own estimates of real price inflation (which required a series of assumptions), the country experts conclude that the exact source of the differences in the alternative estimates is difficult to trace.

### German Democratic Republic

The country expert considers the official growth rates strongly upward biased for the standard set of reasons. His independent estimate of the

7. The official indexes use the prices of January 1, 1967, until 1976 and the prices of January 1, 1977, since 1977.

*Table 5-8. Czechoslovakia: Country Experts' Growth Estimates versus Research Project's Growth Estimates, 1970–80*
(1970 = 100)

| Year | Country experts | Research Project |
|------|-----------------|------------------|
| 1970 | 100.0 | 100.0 |
| 1975 | 115.5 | 117.9 |
| 1976 | 117.1 | 119.9 |
| 1977 | 118.7 | 124.8 |
| 1978 | 120.3 | 126.9 |
| 1979 | 120.9 | 128.1 |
| 1980 | 121.1 | 130.2 |

*Source:* Havlik and Levcik (1985).

growth rate is based on that derived from two cross-section estimates of the ratio of per capita incomes of the German Democratic Republic to the Federal Republic of Germany in 1955 and 1980, a procedure that, after adjustment for changes in population, yields a 3.3 percent average annual growth of total GNP between 1955 and 1980. This growth tempo happens to be the same as that computed by the Research Project and can be compared with the official growth rate of 4.9 percent for the period.

A major reason for the upward bias in the official growth rates is inflation not captured by the official price indexes. A detailed study by another expert on the German Democratic Republic estimated, on the basis of purchasing power parity comparisons between the Federal Republic and the Democratic Republic over time, the extent of hidden inflation in the latter's official consumer price index (Keren 1982, table 5):

|         | Percentage |
|---------|------------|
| 1950–55 | 4.0 |
| 1955–60 | 2.2 |
| 1960–65 | 0.0 |
| 1965–70 | 0.0 |
| 1970–73 | 1.2 |
| 1973–77 | 2.0 |
| 1977–80 | 2.8 |

Using his estimates of hidden inflation for NMP, we may adjust the official growth rate and compare it with that computed by the Research Project (see table 5-9).

If a choice had to be made between the official growth rate and that computed by the research project, the country expert would consider the Research Project estimates to be the more realistic (Collier 1985, p. 44);

Table 5-9. The German Democratic Republic: Official Growth Rate
versus Research Project's Growth Estimates, 1965–80
(percent per annum)

| Growth rate | 1965–69 | 1969–73 | 1977–80 |
|---|---|---|---|
| Official | 5.2 | 5.3 | 3.9 |
| Official corrected for hidden inflation | 5.1 | 3.5 | −0.1 |
| Research Project | 5.2 | 3.4 | 1.0 |

Source: Keren (1982, table 6).

the estimate made by Keren, which became available as the country study
for the German Democratic Republic was being completed, is not discussed
in Collier (1985).

## Hungary

Hungary is the only centrally planned economy that officially publishes
not only NMP growth but also real GNP growth, following the SNA definition, so that a direct comparison can be made with the Research Project
series, eliminating the coverage-induced gap; see table 5-10. There is very
little difference between the official NMP and GNP growth rates; GNP in
fact has been growing slightly faster. During 1970–80, both the NMP
and the GNP series show a rate of growth almost twice as high as that
in the Research Project series: 5 percent versus 2.7 percent.

Table 5-10. Hungary: Official GNP Growth
versus Research Project's Growth Estimates, 1970–80
(1970 = 100)

| Year | Official | | Research Project |
|---|---|---|---|
| | NMP | GNP | GNP |
| 1970 | 100.0 | 100.0 | 100.0 |
| 1971 | 105.9 | 106.6 | 104.4 |
| 1972 | 112.4 | 112.7 | 106.6 |
| 1973 | 120.3 | 120.5 | 112.2 |
| 1974 | 127.5 | 127.6 | 115.1 |
| 1975 | 135.3 | 135.5 | 117.6 |
| 1976 | 139.3 | 140.3 | 118.0 |
| 1977 | 150.5 | 151.0 | 125.2 |
| 1978 | 156.9 | 157.7 | 128.7 |
| 1979 | 159.9 | 162.0 | 129.5 |
| 1980 | 158.6 | 162.4 | 130.2 |

Source: Hewett (1985).

Focusing on differences between the official GNP series and that produced by the Research Project during 1975–80, the country author concluded that differences in sectoral weights are not an adequate explanation, nor are obvious shortcomings in the Hungarian central statistical office's statistical methods. To be sure, it is possible that the CSO's indexes contain some upward bias on account of Hungary's chained price index, which may allow pseudo quality improvements to be recorded as output increases (Hewett 1985, pp. 13–14). On balance, however, the country author suspects that the Research Project's estimates are just as likely (and perhaps more so) to be downward biased as the Hungarian indexes are to be upward biased. He concludes: "Until more is known concerning these discrepancies, it will be a difficult choice . . . whether to rely on the [Research Project] or the Hungarian indices. Certainly these two indices set the bounds within which the actual GNP growth occurred" (Hewett 1985, p. 19).

Hungary's official publications show NMP but not GNP sectoral indexes; the latter series was obtained by the country expert from data that the Hungarian authorities submitted to the World Bank (Hewett 1985, appendix). It is interesting to note that, although the overall NMP and GNP series show approximately the same rate of growth, there seem to be large differences in the two series at the sectoral level, for example, in agriculture. Whereas the GNP series (which includes depreciation) increased by 24.1 percent between 1975 and 1980 (Hewett 1985, appendix), the NMP series for agriculture grew by 5 percent only (Központi Statisztikai Hivatal 1980, p. 87) during the same period. This in fact is a clue to the large discrepancy between the official series and the Research Project series for agriculture noted earlier (table 5-1). Clearly, more research is needed on these issues.

## Poland

Because the country author has computed GNP at official "constant 1977 prices," he is able to calculate GNP growth rates between the benchmark years 1970, 1975, and 1980. He stresses, however, that these officially based growth rates are subject to all of the known limitations of official data and statistical methods, including new product pricing and other sources of disguised inflation (Fallenbuchl 1985, p. 53). Table 5-11 compares the average annual growth of official NMP, officially based GNP, and the Research Project's GNP.

During 1970–75, GNP (official version) grew a little less rapidly than NMP because this was a period of rapid expansion of material production supported by large investments. During the second half of the decade the

Table 5-11. *Poland: Average Annual Growth of Official NMP,
Officially Based GNP, and the Research Project's Estimate of GNP*
(percent per annum)

| Years | Official | | Research Project GNP |
| | NMP | GNP | |
| --- | --- | --- | --- |
| 1970–75 | 9.8 | 8.4 | 6.6 |
| 1975–80 | 1.2 | 1.8 | 0.8 |
| 1970–80 | 5.5 | 5.1 | 3.7 |

Source: Fallenbuchl (1985, table V-5).

rapid decline in the growth of investment in material production reversed
this trend. The country expert repeatedly stressed the serious shortcomings of the official data, which incorporated all of the statistical problems
that CPE output, input, and price data are known to embody. He considers
the Research Project series more realistic, without endorsing its precise
numbers.

## Romania

The basic conclusion of the country expert is that Romania's official
growth rate is significantly upward biased. In addition to the factors
stressed for many of the countries, reliance on early year weights (1950
for 1950–59, 1955 for 1959–65, and 1963 for 1965–75) give the
Romanian indexes the most rapid growth possible. Further upward biases
are involved in the official scaling from NMP to GNP because of an apparently unrealistic series on depreciation (Jackson 1985, pp. 45–46).

New product pricing is clearly a major source of bias. Enterprises have
direct responsibility for determining the prices of some "new" products
on the basis of both costs and comparisons of "use values" with those
of standard "reference products." In view of the strong inducements for
producers to introduce new products in order to be able to raise prices,
it is certain that some of Romania's high industrial growth is really
unmeasured price increases. The scale of the problem (that pseudo new
products may be introduced at higher prices) is indicated by statistics
showing that as much as half of Romania's assortment of industrial
products changes every five years (Jackson 1985, p. 18).

The country specialist calls attention to several unconventional features
of Romanian statistics, including the application of different constant
prices for the same products in different sectors (Jackson 1985, p. 16)
and the requirement that firms outside agriculture report their output

and material expenditures in "current," "planning," and "constant" prices (Jackson 1985, pp. 17–18). These and other features of the Romanian price, planning, and statistical system make it impossible for an outsider to assess the meaning of the few "constant-price" series that are published.

A comparison of the official and Research Project series for 1975–78 shows that differences in sectoral weights are important (Jackson 1985, tables 41 and 42 and pp. 47–48). The enumerated problems with official data prompt the country expert to lean toward preferring the Research Project series. He notes also that the growth rate implied for 1950–73 by the physical indicators method, 5.9 percent per annum, is much closer to the Research Project's estimate of 4.8 percent than to the official figure of 8.5 percent. Moreover, the lack of published details and explanations of the methods used add considerable uncertainty to any Romanian data, whether official or independently calculated.

## Cuba

Constant-price series on aggregate production are not available after 1968 and cannot be constructed with reasonable accuracy, partly because of gaps in the availability of basic data and partly because of fundamental methodological problems. Even if acceptable time series on NMP or GNP could be constructed, it would not be possible at present to transform them into constant-price series. Although Cuba has a demonstrably significant rate of inflation (see chapter 4), price changes cannot be estimated accurately and certainly not for the economy's major sectors or for aggregate output.

Several industrial production and aggregate output series have been published in various official and private sources that purport to be (or were mistakenly accepted by secondary publications as) constant-price series. The authors of the country study demonstrate convincingly the reasons why none of them is acceptable (Mesa-Lago and Perez Lopez 1985). The authors warn especially about accepting the indexes of industrial production reported in the CMEA statistical yearbooks or those constructed by Swedish economist Brundenius for 1969–80, explaining the problems involved. Growth rates, mostly from current-price series, can be derived for different subperiods from various official and independently estimated data on some measure of aggregate output, but changes over time in concepts, methods, prices, and currencies make none of them acceptable for publication in official documents such as the *Atlas*. Between 1970 and 1975, for example, estimates of growth rate vary between 1 percent and 15 percent, depending on the series and method used, each requiring assumptions that introduce potentially very large margins for error.

## Conclusions

Although there are very important differences among the eight centrally planned economies, the experts generally agree that the systematic price distortions and methodological problems documented in chapter 4 and in this chapter result in a significant upward bias in their official growth rate statistics. The extent of the bias is believed to be so substantial as to lead to the conclusion that the official NMP growth rate or the NMP-based GNP growth rates of centrally planned economies *taken as a group* cannot be compared meaningfully with the GNP growth rates of market-type economies. The official growth rates have two very important sets of problems: distorted prices, and methods of index number construction that tend to yield a significant upward bias.

Economic theory states that, for prices to be proper weights for output aggregation, they must bear a certain relationship to costs. Although this requirement is not met perfectly in market-type economies, the deviations from the theoretical norm of prices in centrally planned economies are much more substantial, largely because of the often large and arbitrary taxes and subsidies on products. Distorted domestic prices are more likely to affect the growth rates of countries undergoing major structural transformation, that is, with some sectors growing significantly faster than others, which has typically been the case for centrally planned economies during the postwar period.

There are two basic statistical approaches to growth rate computations. One is to aggregate physical production series into branch and sectoral indexes and eventually into a GNP index by using constant prices and value-added weights. Many market-type economies employ this method (Cohn 1972, p. 122). The other method, on which all centrally planned economies and many other countries rely, is double deflation: the value of gross output and the value of inputs are both deflated by relevant price indexes. It has convincingly been demonstrated that the way in which the double-deflation method is typically implemented in CPEs leads to an upward bias in their statistics on growth. The main reasons are that the gross value is typically overstated and the price indexes used to deflate them are downward biased, so that the resulting constant-price series will be upward biased. The reasons for this are systemic (for example, managerial incentives), political (legitimacy is tied to economic achievement), and the absence of a strong, independent scientific tradition in the central statistical offices of some countries. There are notable differences among the CPEs regarding the relative importance of these factors, with corresponding impact on their growth rate statistics.

Prompted by these and other shortcomings of the official indexes, economists in the West have devoted considerable effort to developing and refining alternative estimating methods, using official data exclusively but replicating as much as possible commonly accepted standards of valuation and index number construction. The basic Western approach is to aggregate the physical output series of CPEs into branch, sector, and GNP indexes, using weights constructed from official data according to the AFC standard, which was pioneered during the 1950s by Abram Bergson, a consultant on this project. There is a clear consensus in the Western community of experts about the theoretical validity of this approach.

Implementation of the Western approach is not, however, without serious problems. To apply it successfully and on a timely basis, a great deal of detailed current information on physical production—as well as reliable data on wages, prices, the capital stock, depreciation, and so forth by sector—are essential. The information made public by CPEs is almost always less, in some cases very considerably less, than would be desirable, so that it is necessary to estimate and to rely upon assumptions during implementation.

The other major problem is that the approach, if applied "purely," does not adequately measure quality improvements and the introduction of new products. The resulting growth indexes will therefore be downward biased. In actual application, the method will not be pure because physical product samples either are not available or cannot be used in some subsectors. In these cases, official value indexes will be used, which contain a significant upward bias, especially in the industry and construction sectors. Thus, in actual fact, Western estimates are a hybrid in which some component series are upward biased, whereas others are downward biased. Whether the biases approximately cancel out can be estimated only after examining the data that were available and the methods used (including the bases for the estimates and the assumptions), which vary a great deal from country to country and in some cases also over time in a given country.

Conceptually, the differences between the generally available official NMP and Western-computed GNP growth indexes can be decomposed into (1) coverage-induced gap (differences in the treatment of services and depreciation); (2) intersectoral weighting-induced gap (differences in the weights for sectors); and (3) sector-index-induced gap (differences in the sectoral indexes). The basic finding of the country studies is that, for most countries, the third gap accounts for much of the difference and that this gap is by far the most important in industry, although there are notable differences among the countries.

Romanian official indexes appear to be particularly suspect and strongly upward biased because they incorporate most of the systemic, political, and methodological problems typical of CPEs as well as of developing countries that lack a strong tradition of independent data collection and statistical analysis. To be sure, none of the other CPEs, with the possible exception of Hungary, is exempt from most of the problems identified for Romania. Although the country expert on Hungary has not been able to gather sufficient information to give the Hungarian central statistical office a clean bill of health on its growth rate computations, the evidence he presents suggest that, for a variety of historical, political, and systemic reasons, Hungarian data and statistical methods are subject to less bias than are those of the other centrally planned economies, at least since the introduction of comprehensive reforms in 1968.

The view that the official growth rates are significantly upward biased is unequivocal for all centrally planned economies except Hungary; the country expert on Hungary is not certain. Most country experts, however, stopped short of endorsing the alternative growth computations available in 1982, mostly because the country specialists were not able to resolve satisfactorily various concrete questions about the application to their countries of the method, which involves a complex set of calculations. The general view is that Western computations would be preferable provided that (1) the construction of the sectoral indexes is transparently documented with country-specific information; (2) the differences between the official and independently computed indexes are decomposed, as mentioned above; (3) in case of very large differences between the official and alternative branch or sectoral indexes, the gap is explained and resolved in favor of the Western index (in many cases the issue can be decided easily if the documentation is transparent); and (4) there is an objective evaluation, if possible including some sensitivity analysis, of the strengths and weaknesses of the alternative indexes, by country.

For the U.S.S.R., the basic data available from official sources, although not without gaps, have been fundamentally sufficient for the task of constructing independent growth estimates. Very considerable resources have been devoted to the making of those estimates, which in the main sectors are transparently documented and evaluated against the official indexes, with sensitivity analyses for the estimates in the problem subsectors. These considerations have led the country expert unequivocally to prefer the independent Western estimates to the official series.

The country experts on Czechoslovakia, the German Democratic Republic, Poland, and Romania consider the recomputed Western indexes more plausible than the official ones but stop short of endorsing their use at this time until various issues, discussed above, have been satisfactorily resolved. The experts on Bulgaria—a country strongly deficient in the amount of statistical information and methodological detail it provides—made whatever adjustments they could, which significantly reduced the official growth rates. They imply that the adjusted figures may still contain a significant upward bias. The country author on Hungary leans toward a preference for the official index unless it can be demonstrated in concrete terms that the alternative is the superior one. The country authors on Cuba have insufficient basis for recommending the use of any set of growth statistics.

It is to be hoped that in the future the Bank will receive substantive cooperation from the central statistical offices of all centrally planned economies. Specifically, it is to be hoped that the central statistical offices will be responsive to requests for additional information and will also take note of the problems with growth rate computations that I have summarized in this book and that are described also in the country studies. As long as cooperation is not possible, the best long-term strategy for obtaining internationally comparable growth rates for CPEs would be to improve the application, but especially the documentation and evaluation, of the alternative computations that already are available and will continue to be so. This general approach should not preclude the possibility that the official growth statistics of selected CPEs will be accepted for inclusion in publications designed to facilitate international comparisons, such as the *Atlas*. Hungary's growth rate statistics are an obvious candidate for such treatment.

# Appendix A

# Atlas *Methods Applied to CPEs*

Since 1966 the Bank has published data on the CPEs' dollar GNP (covering the period since 1964) and growth rates (since 1961) in its annual *Atlas*. Figures A-1 through A-8 present the current-dollar per capita GNP of the eight CPEs annually for 1964–80. Figures A-9 through A-12 plot the real per capita GNP growth rates of the same countries for 1961–79, compiled from the annual issues of the *Atlas*.

Table A-1 summarizes our knowledge about the evolution of *Atlas* methods of estimating per capita GNP of CPEs in national currency units. Table A-2 compiles the evolution of *Atlas* methods of the conversion of benchmark year per capita GNPs of CPEs to U.S. dollars and procedures employed to move the benchmark estimates forward to current dollars. Table A-3 summarizes the data base and the statistical formula used to compute real growth rates.[1]

The following three sections summarize the key facts concerning *Atlas* data and methods used to obtain per capita GNP in national currency units, conversion coefficients to dollars, and growth rates.

## GNP in National Currency

Very little is known about the definition and year-to-year or inter-CPE comparability of the data published. Evidence revealed by the data and certain phrases used in the *Atlas* technical notes suggest the following.

---

1. To compile and present *Atlas* data and methods in this summary form, I had to rely on the map notes and Technical Notes published in various issues of the *Atlas*, on unpublished technical background papers prepared by the Bank's staff, and on estimates revealed by the data's own logic. The Bank's methods of computing GNP and its data sources changed frequently. Little substantive information is provided in the Bank documents for the period before 1973.

*1964–65*

Gross material output or net material product rather than GNP data were published (except in the cases of Bulgaria and Romania), that is, essentially excluding the service sectors and (in NMP) depreciation. For all centrally planned economies, the GNP data for 1964–66 appear inconsistent from year to year (see figures), and there is no explanation as to why.

*1966–69*

GNP at factor cost was published; sources and methods are not indicated.

*1970–72*

GNP at market prices was published. For 1970, however, the GNP estimates for some centrally planned economies included intermediate consumption for the material sectors, evident from the sharp increases in per capita GNP estimates from 1969 to 1970 for most countries, from the significant decline in the 1971 GNP of each of seven centrally planned economies (some by as much as 25 percent), and from an *Atlas* note explaining that adjustments recognized that the original data of some countries were gross, not net, material product. For Bulgaria a large adjustment was made in 1972 (when its GNP jumped by 73 percent); for Romania no similar adjustment appears near that time.

*1973–76*

The GNP data—except those of Romania—are based on 1965 benchmark GNP estimates obtained through the United Nations Economic Commission for Europe physical indicators global method, moved to 1973 and annually moved forward to 1976 by growth rates *computed in the West* (by the Research Project on National Income for the East European countries and the Joint Economic Committee of the U.S. Congress for the Soviet Union; *U.S.S.R. 1982*). Romania's GNP is either that obtained directly from Romania or its official NMP scaled to GNP by an unknown method (see note *c* on figure A-6).

*1977–80*

The GNP estimates—except those of Romania—are based on official NMP data scaled to GNP on the basis of the average (regression) relationship found between the 1970 NMP and GNP for a group of West

European countries. The benchmark per capita GNP estimates were extrapolated forward by the GNP per capita growth rates as estimated through another equation that relates growth rates of per capita GNP and per capita NMP for the West European countries.

## 1981–

No *Atlas* was published in 1982 and 1984. The 1983 *Atlas*, reporting 1981 and revised 1980 data, omitted dollar per capita GNP estimates for the CPEs reviewed in this study except for Hungary and Romania. The 1983 *Atlas* gives the reason that "a number of methodological issues concerning the estimation of per capita GNP for centrally planned economies remains unresolved. Until a broadly acceptable methodology is developed, GNP per capita estimates for nonmember countries with centrally planned economies will not be shown."

Hungary's 1981 (and revised 1980) GNP estimates were derived from the official estimates of GDP by adding net factor income (from the balance of payments). The same method was followed to obtain estimates for subsequent years also. When Hungary joined the Bank in 1980, a World Bank mission undertook an evaluation of the country's official national accounts estimates in forints and concluded: "It is the judgment of the mission that the quantity and quality of statistical information made available to it by the Hungarian authorities compares very favorably with that available for other developing countries" (World Bank 1984, p. 137). At the same time, the mission recommended improvements to estimate GDP fully in accordance with the method suggested by the United Nations system of national accounts (World Bank 1984, p. 143).

Romania's 1981 (and revised 1980) GNP estimate was obtained from the government authorities, which did not adjust the official NMP data. In the 1985 *Atlas* no data were published for Romania because information on the methodology and basic data was not sufficient to permit the Bank to evaluate the government's GNP data fully.

## Converting GNP to Dollars

### 1964–72

No information is available on the exchange rates that were used and the kinds of adjustments that were made (statements in the *Atlas* indicated that some had been made).

### 1973–76

No conversion coefficients are required, because the physical indicators method was used. Romania is the exception. Its *commercial* exchange rate, that is, the weighted average of effective exchange rates for foreign transactions in convertible currencies, was used.

### 1977–80

For all CPEs except Romania, the 1970 *noncommercial* (that is, tourist) exchange rates were used to convert to 1970 dollars. In the case of Romania, the *commercial* exchange rate (as defined in the previous paragraph) was used. The 1970 benchmark GNP was then extrapolated to 1979 and 1980 by the use of the growth rates estimated from another equation. The 1981 *Atlas* notes: "This method [of estimation] is proving increasingly unsatisfactory. The figures shown here differ very much from such other estimates as derived from official GNP estimates converted at the annual average exchange rates. In view of such wide variations among alternative per capita GNP estimates, the Bank is undertaking research to improve the methodology" (p. 18).

### 1981–

Hungary's official *commercial* exchange rate was used to obtain dollar values, relying on the standard *Atlas* method employing a three-year weighted average of prices and exchange rates (see the 1983 *Atlas*, pp. 27–28). Whereas in the 1981 *Atlas* Hungary's 1980 per capita GNP in dollars was $4,180, the 1983 *Atlas* estimate for the same year is $1,930; that is, it shows a decline of more than 50 percent, due largely to the exchange rates used. (See the discussion of Hungary's alternative exchange rates in this volume.) The Bank notes, "Several factors may influence both the level and the comparability of [Hungary's per capita dollar GNP] ... estimate with those of other countries, and the Bank is aware of other estimates that have been made in Hungary's case. These have used methodologies that attempt to take account, severally, of price and wage distortions, subsidies and taxes, and possible distortions introduced through the exchange rate, and have provided a range of alternative results" (1983 *Atlas*, p. 22; and World Bank 1984, p. 144).

Romania's GNP estimate in national currency units was converted to dollars at the *commercial* exchange rate, that is, at the effective exchange rate for foreign trade transactions in convertible currencies. The latest year for which data for Romania are published in the *Atlas* is 1981.

## Growth Rates

Because the *Atlas* publishes not year-to-year growth rates but only average growth tempos covering a span of years (see figures A-9 through A-12), we must separately identify the data base (that is, the growth of the aggregate that is being measured), the index number method (the problems and how they were handled), and the growth rate averaging formula. The *Atlas* did not publish growth rates of per capita GNP through 1966.

### 1967–73

The data base is unknown. The numbers (figures A-9 through A-12) suggest that they are official numbers. We may strongly suspect that not all growth rates refer to the same definition of national income across countries (see the discussion above on GNP in national currency units), not even in the case of the same country in all years. To give just one example: from 1971 to 1972, Bulgaria's GNP in current dollars as reported in the *Atlas* jumped 73 percent (so obviously there must have been a change in the definition of the aggregate reported), whereas its average growth of 7.5 percent (1965–71) declined to 5.9 percent (1965–72). Either the data base for computing the growth rate changed (there was no change in the averaging formula), or there was a negative growth rate in 1972 that lowered the seven-year average by 1.6 percent. Because Bulgaria's NMP growth was 10 percent in 1972 (Alton 1974, p. 277), there had to be a change in the data base. Similar anomalies are found also for Czechoslovakia, the German Democratic Republic, Hungary, and Poland.

### 1973–76

Western computations of CPE growth rates (by the Research Project for the East European countries and by the Joint Economic Committee for the U.S.S.R.) were used except in the case of Romania, whose data are obviously official growth rates of some national income aggregate.

### 1977–79

The official NMP growth rates were scaled to estimated GNP growth rates on the basis of a regression relationship found for 1970–76 between the NMP and GNP growth rates for a group of West European countries.

Thus once again the *Atlas* publishes what in essence are official growth rates.

### 1980–

Official growth rates of per capita GNP in constant prices were used. For Romania, 1980 is the latest year for which growth rates are published.

Regarding the averaging formula, for data covering the period before 1970 (that is, up to and including those published in the 1971 *Atlas*), for all countries the compound rate between the initial and the current year was used; for data covering the period since 1970 (that is, beginning with the 1972 *Atlas*), they were computed by fitting trend lines to the logarithmic values for each year of the time period.

## Conclusions

### Per Capita Dollar GNP

Estimates for 1964–72 should be considered highly tentative, containing potentially large margins of error. They should not be used for analytical purposes without first clarifying for each country the definition of the original national income aggregate and its method of computation, the kinds of adjustments made to derive the GNP, and the meaning of the exchange rate used for converting to dollars. No direct comparisons can be made of the level of per capita GNP of any individual CPE with that of any other CPE or non-CPE country.

The GNP (GDP) estimates for 1973–76 for individual centrally planned economies except Romania are roughly comparable with each other and with market-type economies. The degree of confidence that can be placed in the level and cross-country comparability of these estimates depends upon our assessment of the strengths and shortcomings of the physical indicators method, discussed in chapter 3 of this volume.

Estimates for 1977–80 (the last year represents preliminary data published in the 1981 *Atlas*) for individual CPEs except Romania should be considered tentative, with potentially large margins of error. They should not be used for analytical purposes without first clarifying for each country the definition of its official national income aggregate (said to be NMP) and its method of computation, the validity of the *Atlas* method used to scale NMP to GNP, and the meaning of the 1970 NCU/ dollar commercial exchange rates used for dollar conversion. Comparisons of the levels of per capita dollar GNP of any individual centrally planned economy with those of other centrally planned or market-type economies should be considered very tenuous, involving substantial error margins.

Estimates since 1980 (for the year revised very substantially for Hungary, as I noted) are applicable only in the case of Hungary and (through 1981 only) Romania. Regarding the estimates for Hungary, the discussion above in this appendix should be noted.

Certainly since 1973 and possibly before 1973, Romania's per capita dollar GNP has been estimated on the basis of methods that differ in several highly significant respects from those employed for other centrally planned economies. Romania's original data base, the *Atlas* method of adjustment (if any), and the meaning of its commercial exchange rate should be clarified. In any event, however, Romania's dollar GNP data published in the *Atlas* until now cannot be compared with those of any other CPE or non-CPE country because the discrepancies are fundamental.

## Growth Rates

The estimates covering the period 1960–72 should be considered highly tentative, containing potentially large error margins. They should not be used for analytical purposes without first clarifying for each country which national income aggregate is being measured by the official data and the index number problem. The growth rates of individual CPEs cannot be directly compared with each other or with those of MTEs.

Growth rates covering the period 1973–76 are based, except for Romania, on Western computations, which are roughly comparable among CPEs and are probably comparable in a rough and ready way also with those of non-CPEs. The degree of confidence we place in these estimates depends upon our assessment of the strength and shortcomings of the official data on which Western estimates are based as well as on expert assessments of the application of the adjusted factor cost method to the particular CPE country. The general and country-specific conclusions of the experts involved in this project have been summarized in chapter 5, "Conclusions."

Growth rates covering the period 1977–81 are essentially official statistics, which are based on methods that incorporate, depending on the CPE, modest to possibly large error margins, for reasons discussed in chapter 5. *Atlas* figures for non-European CPEs were derived by ad hoc methods that often vary from year to year, depending on the availability of data that are in large part exceedingly poor.

## Figure A-1. Bulgaria's GNP per Capita in Current U.S. Dollars, 1964–80

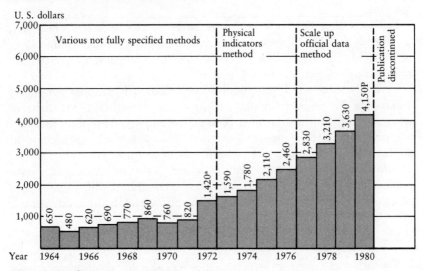

*Note*: P = preliminary.
a. Not comparable to 1971.
*Source*: World Bank, *Atlas*, 1966–81, 1983.

## Figure A-2. Czechoslovakia's GNP per Capita in Current U.S. Dollars, 1964–80

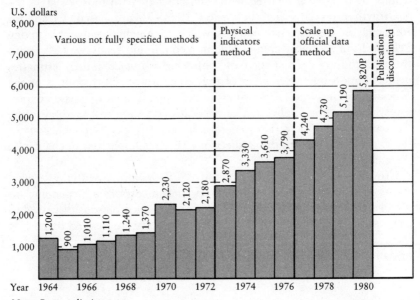

*Note:* P = preliminary.
*Source:* World Bank, *Atlas*, 1966–81, 1983.

Figure A-3. *The German Democratic Republic's GNP per Capita in Current U.S. Dollars, 1964–80*

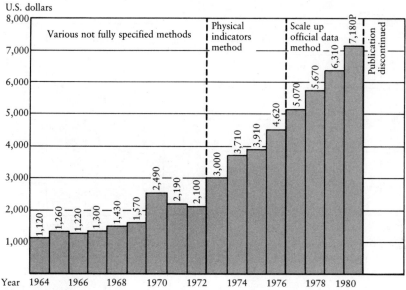

*Note:* P = preliminary.
*Source:* World Bank, *Atlas*, 1966–81, 1983.

Figure A-4. *Hungary's GNP per Capita in Current U.S. Dollars, 1964–81*

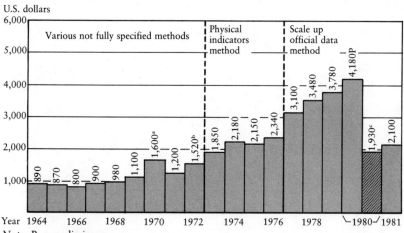

*Note:* P = preliminary.
a. Not comparable to 1969.
b. Not comparable to 1971.
c. Revised.
*Source:* World Bank, *Atlas*, 1966–81; revised 1980–81 data, World Bank, *Atlas*, 1983.

*Figure A-5. Poland's GNP per Capita in Current U.S. Dollars,*
*1964–80*

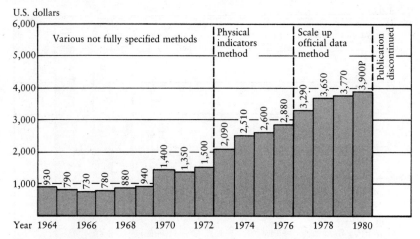

*Note*: P = preliminary.
*Source*: World Bank, *Atlas*, 1966–81, 1983.

*Figure A-6. Romania's GNP per Capita in Current U.S. Dollars,
1964–81*

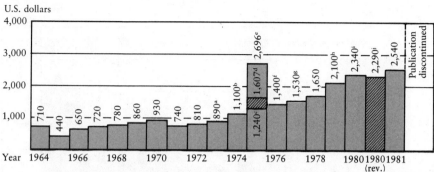

U.S. dollars

a. 1973: No figure is published in the *Atlas* table; a note reads: "The calculation of the figures was under discussion when *Atlas* went to press. Based on information supplied by Romanian Government and using a currency conversion rate of 20 lei to the U.S. dollar, the per capita GNP would amount to $890 for 1973 and the preliminary estimate for 1974 would be $910. These figures are, however, not comparable with those for other countries" (1975 *Atlas*).

b. 1974: The number is published in text table without any note regarding comparability with other countries. Romania thus appears to be treated statistically as if it were a non-CPE, that is, dollar GNP is published on the basis of GNP in lei and the exchange rate provided by Romania. The *Atlas*'s technical note states: "The GNP per capita estimates (*Atlas* methodology equivalent) for the East European CPEs *other than Romania* were . . ." (1976 *Atlas*, emphasis added).

c. 1975: Note to data in text table: "This estimate is not comparable to those for other CPEs. It has been arrived at, following the Bank *Atlas* methodology, by adjusting [no explanation how and by whom] official Romanian national accounts data and converting them into U.S. dollars at the effective exchange rate for foreign trade transactions, which approximates lei 20 per U.S. dollar" (1977 *Atlas*).

d. Background note by Bank staff dated May 9, 1978 (not published or mentioned in *Atlas*), indicates that if Romania's GDP were estimated on the same basis as those of the other CPEs, it would have been $1,607.

e. The note mentioned in *d* above also calculates that if Romania's official growth rate (which one is not specified) were used to extend the ECE's 1965 GNP estimate for Romania to 1975, it would yield $2,696, 68 percent higher than the estimate shown in note *d* and 117 percent higher than the figure published in the *Atlas* (similar computations are not shown for the other CPEs).

f. 1976: Same note in *Atlas* as that mentioned in note *c* above.

g. 1977–79: Same note in *Atlas* as that mentioned in note *c* above except that the exchange rate is not given.

h. Note in *Atlas*: "The estimates are not comparable to those for other centrally planned economies. They have been arrived at, following the *Atlas* methodology, by using official national accounts data and converting them to U.S. dollars at the effective exchange rate for foreign trade transactions. The basis for Romanian estimates, as also for other centrally planned economies, is under study. These figures should be treated as tentative. The Government of Romania has recently revised the GNP data series for 1977–79."

i. 1980: Preliminary. Method and warning as stated in *h* (1981 *Atlas*).

j. 1980: Revised. Method essentially as stated in *h*. No specific warning is given with Romania's data (1983 Atlas).

*Source*: World Bank, *Atlas*, 1966–81, 1983; World Bank, Economic Analysis and Projections Department, Background Note, May 8, 1982.

*Figure A-7. U.S.S.R.'s GNP per Capita in Current U.S. Dollars, 1964–80*

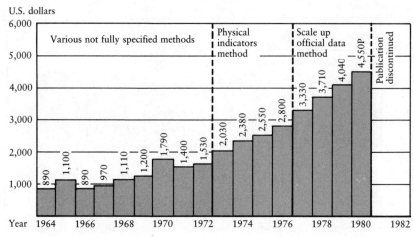

Note: P = preliminary.
Source: World Bank, *Atlas*, 1966–81, 1983.

*Figure A-8. Cuba's GNP per Capita in Current U.S. Dollars, 1964–78*

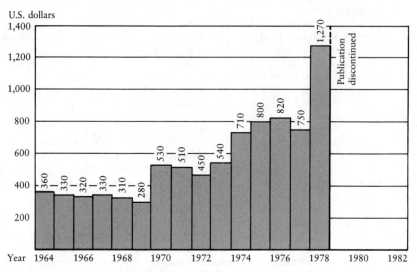

Note: For an explanation of data and methods, see Mesa-Lago and Perez-Lopez (1985).
Source: World Bank, *Atlas*, 1966–80.

*Figure A-9. Bulgaria and Romania: Average Annual Growth Rates of Real GNP per Capita, 1961–80*

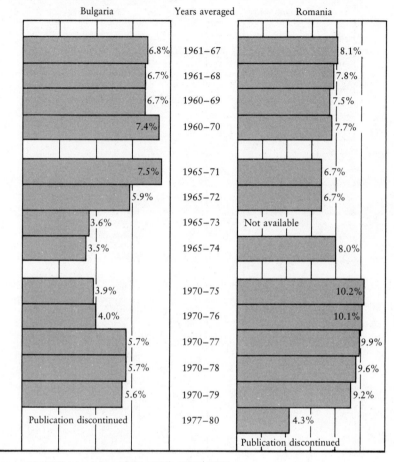

*Source*: World Bank, *Atlas*, 1969–1981, 1983, 1985.

*Figure A-10. Czechoslovakia and the German Democratic Republic: Average Annual Growth Rates of Real GNP per Capita, 1961–79*

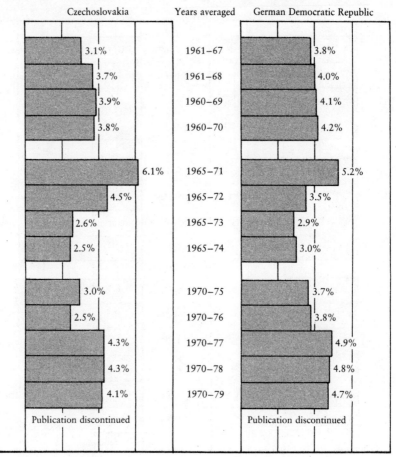

| Czechoslovakia | Years averaged | German Democratic Republic |
|---|---|---|
| 3.1% | 1961–67 | 3.8% |
| 3.7% | 1961–68 | 4.0% |
| 3.9% | 1960–69 | 4.1% |
| 3.8% | 1960–70 | 4.2% |
| 6.1% | 1965–71 | 5.2% |
| 4.5% | 1965–72 | 3.5% |
| 2.6% | 1965–73 | 2.9% |
| 2.5% | 1965–74 | 3.0% |
| 3.0% | 1970–75 | 3.7% |
| 2.5% | 1970–76 | 3.8% |
| 4.3% | 1970–77 | 4.9% |
| 4.3% | 1970–78 | 4.8% |
| 4.1% | 1970–79 | 4.7% |
| Publication discontinued | | Publication discontinued |

*Source*: World Bank, *Atlas*, 1969–81, 1983.

Figure A-11. Hungary and Poland: Average Annual Growth Rates
of Real GNP per Capita, 1961–80

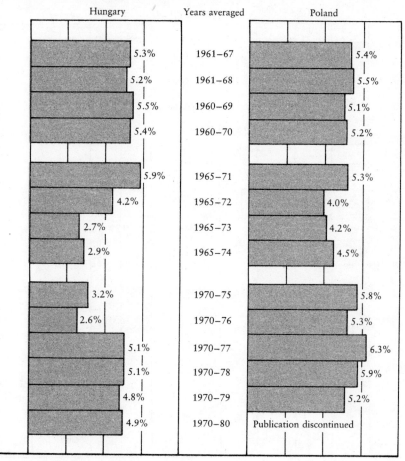

| Hungary | Years averaged | Poland |
|---|---|---|
| 5.3% | 1961–67 | 5.4% |
| 5.2% | 1961–68 | 5.5% |
| 5.5% | 1960–69 | 5.1% |
| 5.4% | 1960–70 | 5.2% |
| 5.9% | 1965–71 | 5.3% |
| 4.2% | 1965–72 | 4.0% |
| 2.7% | 1965–73 | 4.2% |
| 2.9% | 1965–74 | 4.5% |
| 3.2% | 1970–75 | 5.8% |
| 2.6% | 1970–76 | 5.3% |
| 5.1% | 1970–77 | 6.3% |
| 5.1% | 1970–78 | 5.9% |
| 4.8% | 1970–79 | 5.2% |
| 4.9% | 1970–80 | Publication discontinued |

Source: World Bank, Atlas, 1969–81, 1983.

*Figure A-12. U.S.S.R. and Cuba: Average Annual Growth Rates of Real GNP per Capita, 1961–79*

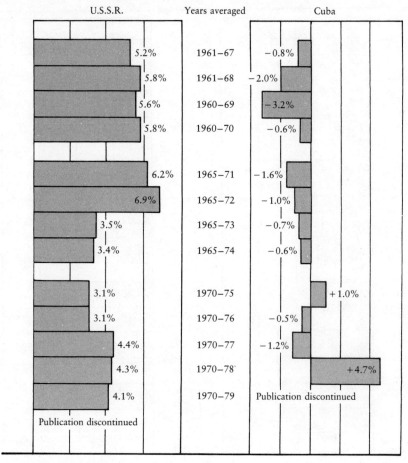

| U.S.S.R. | Years averaged | Cuba |
|---|---|---|
| 5.2% | 1961–67 | −0.8% |
| 5.8% | 1961–68 | −2.0% |
| 5.6% | 1960–69 | −3.2% |
| 5.8% | 1960–70 | −0.6% |
| 6.2% | 1965–71 | −1.6% |
| 6.9% | 1965–72 | −1.0% |
| 3.5% | 1965–73 | −0.7% |
| 3.4% | 1965–74 | −0.6% |
| 3.1% | 1970–75 | +1.0% |
| 3.1% | 1970–76 | −0.5% |
| 4.4% | 1970–77 | −1.2% |
| 4.3% | 1970–78 | +4.7% |
| 4.1% | 1970–79 | Publication discontinued |
| Publication discontinued | | |

*Source*: World Bank, *Atlas*, 1969–81, 1983.

Table A-1. *"Atlas" Methods of Estimating per Capita GNP or GDP in NCUs*

| CPE countries | Non-CPE countries |
|---|---|
| **A.** 1964–65 | 1964 |
| "For certain Sino-Soviet countries the data relate to net material product." (1967) | 1. In most cases, national product at factor cost. |
| **B.** 1966–69 | 1965–69 |
| 1. Point of departure is NMP data.<br>2. Adjustments (not explained) are made to estimate GNP at factor cost.<br>3. Warning: "in the absence of market conditions, the internal cost and price relationships are even more than usually out of line with international prices." (1968–71) | 1. GNP estimates are based on revised 1964 national accounts data at factor cost.<br>2. 1964 dollar estimates extrapolated to the current year by the index of (real) GNP per capita growth rates. (1968) |
| 1970 | 1970 |
| 1. GNP at market prices. Adjustments have been made to include product originating in public and private services to derive approximate estimates of GNP. (1972)<br>2. GNP includes intermediate consumption. | 1. GNP at market prices expressed in weighted average prices of the base period, 1965–71. (1972–73) |
| **C.** 1971–72 | 1971–72 |
| 1. GNP at market prices. Adjustments (not explained) have been made for a few CPEs, subtracting intermediate consumption, recognizing that data for those countries was gross rather than net material product. (1973)<br>2. Warning: "note that the estimates for Bulgaria and Hungary differ substantially from last year's estimates." (1974) | Same as above. |
| **D-1.** 1973–76[a] | 1973 |
| 1. 21 "physical indicators correlated with the levels of per capita GDP in 22 nonsocialist countries for 1965. The resulting estimating equations are applied to CPEs to obtain GDP estimates for 1965." (TN, March 1976) | The multiyear base period is updated from 1965–71 to 1972–74. (1975) |

(Table continues on following page.)

*Table A-1 (continued)*

| CPE countries | Non-CPE countries |
|---|---|
| 2. The set of 1965 estimates is moved to 1973 (and to the subsequent years) by means of GNP and population growth indexes of CPEs (yielding current-year GDP in 1965 dollars). | |
| 3. The weighted average GNP deflator for the 22 non-CPEs is used to convert into current dollars. (TN, March 1976) | |
| 4. The above estimates are further adjusted as follows. For the 22 nonsocialist countries there are two sets of GNP estimates for 1973 (and subsequent years): one based on the physical indicators method and another based on the SNA method. The relationship between these two estimates is established through a linear regression and the same relationship applied to the seven CPEs (including Romania). (TN, March 1976) | |
| 5. Warning about comparability with non-CPEs. (1975–78) | |
| D-2.  *1974–75* <br> Method remains the same as in D-1 with the following modifications. (1976) <br> 1. Estimates for 1965 are moved forward by means of indices of real GNP and population growth, and the weighted average GNP deflator for the 18 European market economies (included in the original ECE study). <br> 2. In D-1.4, substitution of a second degree polynomial relationship for the linear regression. | *1974–81* <br> Multiyear base period shifted to 1973–75 and the base period is moved annually for the years up to 1980. (1983) |
| D-3.  *1976* <br> Two sets of estimates, both based on the physical indicators method, are averaged, one with a 1965 base (ECE method and results), the other with a 1973 base (modified ECE method carried out by the Bank). (1978) | |

## Table A-1  (continued)

| CPE countries | Non-CPE countries |
|---|---|

E.   *1977–81*[b]

1. Official NMP data in NCUs is used as point of departure. (1979–1981)
2. The 1970 National Accounts data of 12 West European countries are used to develop the relationships between
   a. NMP per capita and GNP per capita;
   b. Average annual growth rates of NMP per capita and GNP per capita for 1970–76. (1979–1981)
3. For each CPE, GNP per capita for 1970 was obtained by entering NMP per capita to E.2.a, above.
4. 1970 base GNP extrapolated to the current year by using the growth rates obtained from E.2.a, above.
5. Warning about comparability with non-CPEs. (1979–81)

F.   *1982–*

No data published for the countries reviewed in this study except for Hungary, for which official GDP (adjusted for net factor income from abroad) is used. (1983)

*Note:* Quoted passages appear in Technical Note in each *Atlas*. Years in subheadings are calendar years covered by the data; years in parentheses indicate date of *Atlas* publication; TN = technical note by the staff of the Bank's Economic and Social Data Division.

a. D-1 describes the basic method employed for 1973–76; D-2 and D-3 indicate the modifications in the method for 1974–75 and 1976, respectively. Romania's GDP is not computed in the same way as that of other CPEs. See notes for figure A-6.

b. 1981 preliminary data published in 1983 *Atlas*. No *Atlas* was published in 1982 and 1984.

*Source:* World Bank, *Atlas,* 1967–81, 1983.

## Table A-2. *"Atlas" Methods of Converting GNPs to U.S. Dollars and Moving Forward to Current Dollars*

| CPE countries | Non-CPE countries |
|---|---|
| **A.** *1964*<br>Method not explained. | *1964*<br>The figures have generally been converted into U.S. dollars at official exchange rates. (1966) |
| **B.** *1965*<br>1. Method not explained.<br>2. Warning: wide margin of error due to difficulties in "selection of the most appropriate ERs." (1967) | *1965–69*<br>1. GNP from NCUs is converted on the basis of ERs prevailing in 1974—official or par value.<br>2. In some instances rough adjustments are made to approximate an equilibrium ER.<br>3. Implicit U.S. GNP price deflator is used to move to current dollars. (1968) |
| *1966–70*<br>1. Method not explained. (1968–72)<br>2. Warning: selecting an ER is problematical, "since 'basic' rates maintained by these countries are frequently far removed from hypothetical 'equilibrium' rates." (1968) | *1970–72*<br>1. GNP from NCUs (in weighted average prices) converted to U.S. dollars at a weighted average ER for the base period, 1965–71.<br>2. This is adjusted for U.S. inflation (via implicit GNP deflator) between the base period and the current year. (1973) |
| **C.** *1971*<br>"Adjustments [not explained] have been made in the various ERs used by a number of countries with CPEs before linking them to the U.S. dollar through an adjusted dollar-ruble rate." (1973)<br>*1972*<br>"Adjustments [not explained] are made in the various ERs used by CPEs to arrive at 'reasonable' conversion rates before linking them to the U.S. dollar." (1974) | |
| **D-1.** *1973*[a]<br>1. No conversion required, as figures are obtained in dollars.<br>2. Moved to current dollars using the weighted average GNP deflator of the 22 nonsocialist countries. (1975) | *1973–*<br>1. Converted to U.S. dollars at the GNP-weighted average ER for the 3-year base period (progressively moved forward).<br>2. Converted to current dollars by the implicit U.S. GNP deflator for that year. (1975) |

## Table A-2 (continued)

| CPE countries | Non-CPE countries |
|---|---|
| D-2. *1974–76*[a] <br> Except for Romania, method remains the same as in D-1, with the following modification: moved to current year by the weighted average GNP deflator of the 18 European market economies included in the ECE study. (1976) | |
| E. *1977–80*[a] <br> 1. Conversion to 1970 U.S. dollars by the 1970 noncommercial ERs. (1979–81) <br> 2. Moved to current dollars by multiplication by the U.S. implicit GNP deflator with 1970 as the base. (1979–81) <br> 3. Warning about comparability with non-CPEs because of, among other things, price and exchange rate problems. (1979–81) | |
| F. *1981–* <br> Only Hungary and Romania are included; their prevailing commercial exchange rates are used. (1983) | |

*Note*: Quoted passages appear in the Technical Note in each *Atlas*. Years in subheadings are calendar years covered by the data; years in parentheses indicate date of *Atlas* publication; TN = technical note by the staff of the Bank's Economic and Social Data Division.

a. Between 1973 and 1980 conversion of Romania's data into U.S. dollars is different from that for other CPEs. See notes for figure A-6.

*Source*: World Bank, *Atlas*, 1966–81, 1983.

*Table A-3. "Atlas" Data Base and Methods*
*for Computing Growth Rates*

| CPE countries | | Non-CPEs, growth rate averaging formula |
|---|---|---|
| Data base | Growth rate averaging formula | |
| A. *1964–66* No growth rates published. (1966–68) | | |
| B. *1967–69* Source of data not indicated. (1969–71) | *1967–69* Compound rates between the initial (1960) and current year. (See figures for years averaged.) (1969) | *1967–69* Same as CPEs. |
| C. *1970–71* Source of data not indicated. (1972–73) | *1970–71* Trend lines fitted to the logarithmic values of population and the real GNP per capita over time for (a) 1960 to current year and (b) 1965 to current year. Figures show growth rates obtained in (b). (See figures for the years averaged.) For more detailed explanation of formula, see Note. | *1970–81* Same as CPEs 1970–71, except for changes in the period covered by the indexes. |
| D. *1972* Source of data not indicated but published growth rates (see figures A-9 through A-12) suggest strongly that data base or formula was changed. (1974) | *1972* Probably the same as above, but see comment on data base. (See figures for years averaged.) | |
| E. *1973–76* Bulgaria, Czechoslovakia, German Democratic Republic, Hungary, Poland: growth rates computed by Alton. (1974) U.S.S.R.: publications of the Joint Economic Committee of the U.S. Congress. (Source: background note by World Bank | *1973–76* Probably the same as 1970–71. (See figures for the years averaged.) | |

## Table A-3 (continued)

| CPE countries | Non-CPE countries |
|---|---|
| staff dated May 9, 1978.) | |
| Romania: official data provided by Romania (not further specified). (1975–78) | |
| F. *1977–80* | *1977–* |
| For all but Romania: the official NMP growth rates were scaled to estimated GNP growth rates on the basis of a regression relationship found between the NMP and GNP growth rates of 12 West European countries for 1970–76. (Source: methodological note by World Bank staff dated October 1980. See also 1980, 1981 *Atlas*.) | Same as above. (See figures for the years averaged.) |
| Romania: same as 1973–76. | |
| G. *1981–* | |
| The official data of Hungary and Romania. (1983) | |

*Note*: Average annual growth rates "were computed by fitting a trend line to the values of population and GNP per capita over time. The trend line was computed by transforming the compound rate equation:

$$x_t = x_0 (1 + r)^t$$

where

$x$ = population or GNP per capita
$t$ = time
$r$ = rate of growth

into the log form.

$$\log x_t = \log x_0 = t \log (1 + r)$$

and regressing the values of population and GNP per capita on time using the least squares method. By considering all available observations in the relevant periods, the real growth rates obtained by the regression method reflect general trends rather than cyclical or irregular factors present in any particular year" (TN, March 1976). Years in subheadings are calendar years covered by the data; years in parentheses indicate the date of *Atlas* publication; TN = technical notes by the staff of the Bank's Economic and Social Data Division.

*Source*: World Bank, *Atlas*, 1969–81, 1983.

# Appendix B

# *Physical Indicators Used in the ECE Study of GDP Growth Rates*

| Physical indicator | Core study | Extended exercise |
|---|:---:|:---:|
| **I. Industry** | | |
| 1. Steel consumption, kg/head | + | + |
| 2. Cement consumption, kg/head | + | + |
| 3. Sulphuric acid consumption, kg/head | + | − [a] |
| 4. Nonferrous metals, consumption, kg/head | + | − [a] |
| 5. Energy consumption, kg coal equivalent/ head | + | + |
| 6. Electricity consumption, kWh/head | + | + |
| 7. Electricity consumption in industry, kWh/ head | + | − [a] |
| 8. Plastic materials consumption, kg/head | + | − [a] |
| 9. Manufacturing employment, percentage of total employment | − [b] | + |
| **II. Agriculture** | | |
| 10. Agricultural employment, percentage of total employment | + | + |
| 11. Milk yield per cow, liters | + | + |
| 12. Tractors, stock per person employed in agriculture, units | + | − [a] |
| 13. Fertilizer consumption, per person employed in agriculture, kg | + | + |
| **III. Food consumption** | | |
| 14. Animal protein, grams/day/head | + | + |
| 15. Cereals, grams/day/head | + | − [b] |
| 16. Meat, percentage total calorie intake | + | + |
| 17. Sugar consumption, kg/head/year | + | + |
| 18. Food expenditure as percentage of private consumption expenditure | + | − [a] |
| **IV. Clothing** | | |
| 19. Textile yarn consumption, units/head | + | + |
| **V. Consumer durables** | | |
| 20. Passenger cars, stock per thousand inhabitants | + | + |

228

| | | |
|---|:---:|:---:|
| 21. Television receivers, stock per thousand inhabitants | + | + |
| 22. Radio receivers, stock per thousand inhabitants | + | + |
| VI. Communications | | |
| 23. Paper consumption, kg/head | + | + |
| 24. Domestic letters, per thousand inhabitants | + | + |
| 25. Telephones, per thousand inhabitants | + | + |
| 26. Daily newspapers, circulation per thousand inhabitants | − [b] | + |
| VII. Housing | | |
| 27. Rooms, per thousand inhabitants | + | + |
| 28. Dwellings with fixed bath or shower, percentage of total dwellings | + | − [a] |
| 29. Water supply, percentage of population with easy access | − [b] | + |
| VIII. Health | | |
| 30. Infant mortality, per thousand live births | + | + |
| 31. Death rate due to infections and parasitic diseases, per 100,000 population | + | + |
| 32. Hospital beds, per thousand inhabitants | + | + |
| 33. Expectation of life at birth, years | − [b] | + |
| IX. Education | | |
| 34. Student enrollment in higher education per 100,000 inhabitants | + | + |
| 35. Literate, percentage of the population aged 15 and over | − [b] | + |
| 36. Combined primary and secondary education enrollment, percentage of population aged 5–19 | − [b] | + |
| Total | 30 | 28 |

*Note:* See chapter 3, "Comparison of Alternative Convertors," for a description of the ECE study. Plus sign means covered. Minus sign means not covered.

a. No adequate data available.

b. The correlation is not sufficiently strong.

*Source:* United Nations/ECE (1980*a*, table II-3).

# References

An asterisk indicates a study commissioned or made available for the World Bank research project, Evaluation and Estimation of National Accounts Statistics of Centrally Planned Economies; this volume is the main report of that project.

Ahmad, Sultan. 1980. Approaches to purchasing power parity and real product comparisons using shortcuts and reduced information. Staff Working Paper 418. Washington, D.C.: World Bank.

Alton, Thad. 1974. Economic growth and resource allocation in Eastern Europe. In Joint Economic Committee, U.S. Congress. *Reorientation and commercial relations of the economies of Eastern Europe.* Washington, D.C.: U.S. Government Printing Office.

————. 1981. Production and resource allocation in Eastern Europe: Performance, problems, and prospects. In Joint Economic Committee, U.S. Congress. *East European economic assessment,* pt. 2. Washington, D.C.: U.S. Government Printing Office.

————. 1982. *Occasional papers of the Research Project on National Income in East Central Europe.* New York: L. W. International Financial Research.

Balassa, Bela. 1982. *The Hungarian economic reform, 1968–81.* Occasional Paper 506. Washington, D.C.: World Bank.

Beckermann, W. 1966. *Comparaison internationale du revenue réel* [International comparison of real national income]. Paris: Organisation for Economic Co-operation and Development (OECD).

Bergson, Abram. 1961. *The real national income of Soviet Russia since 1928.* Cambridge, Mass.: Harvard University Press.

Bornstein, Morris. 1976. Soviet price policy in the 1970's. In Joint Economic Committee, U.S. Congress. *Soviet economy in a new perspective.* Washington, D.C.: U.S. Government Printing Office.

———. 1977. Economic reform in Eastern Europe. In Joint Economic Committee, U.S. Congress. *East European economies post Helsinki.* Washington, D.C.: U.S. Government Printing Office.

Botos, Katalin. 1980. A transzferábilis rubel reális árfolyama [The realistic exchange rate of the transferable ruble]. *Közgazdasági szemle* 27 (Budapest), September 1980.

Bundesministerium für innerdeutsche Beziehungen. 1979. *DDR Handbuch* [GDR handbook]. Cologne: BIB.

Campbell, Robert W. 1966. *Soviet economic power: Its organization, growth, and challenge.* Boston: Houghton Mifflin.

*———. 1985. *The conversion of national income data of the U.S.S.R. to concepts of the System of National Accounts in dollars and estimation of growth rate.* World Bank Staff Working Paper no. 777. Washington, D.C.

Central Statistical Office of Hungary. 1982. Information on the Hungarian system of balances of the national economy. Paper presented to the Working Party on National Accounts and Balances, Conference of European Statisticians, Geneva, June.

Central Statistical Offices of Austria and Poland. 1982. Comparison of prices and gross domestic expenditure between Poland and Austria 1975 and 1978. Report presented to the thirtieth plenary session of the Conference of European Statisticians, May.

Cohn, Stanley. 1972. National income growth statistics. In Vladimir G. Treml and John P. Hardt, eds. *Soviet economic statistics.* Durham, N.C.: Duke University Press.

*Collier, Irwin L. 1985. *The estimation of gross domestic product and its growth rate for the German Democratic Republic.* World Bank Staff Working Paper no. 773. Washington, D.C.

Csikós-Nagy, Béla. 1980. *A magyar árpolitika* [Hungarian price policy]. Budapest: Közgazdasági és Jogi.

Csikós-Nagy, Béla, and László Rácz. 1982. Az árszinvonal emelkedése és tényezöi [Increases in the price level and their causes]. *Gazdaság* (Budapest), 16:2.

Drechsler, Lászlo. 1982. The measurement and performance of Hungary's economy in international perspective. Paper presented at the Conference on the Hungarian Economy and East-West Relations, Indiana University, Bloomington, March (revised version).

Ehrlich, Éva, and Gyula Pártos. 1979. A fejlettség inhomogenitása: Egy kisérlet [The nonhomogeneity of development: An experiment]. *Gazdaság* (Budapest), nos. 2–3.

*Fallenbuchl, Zbigniew M. 1985. *National income statistics for Poland, 1970–1980.* World Bank Staff Working Paper no. 776. Washington, D.C.

Gerschenkron, Alexander. 1947. The Soviet indices of industrial production. *Review of economics and statistics*, 29:4 (November).

Gregory, Paul R., and Robert C. Stuart. 1981. *Soviet economic structure and performance*. New York: Harper and Row.

Havlik, P. 1983. *A comparison of purchasing power parity and consumption levels in Austria and Czechoslovakia*. Working paper no. 87. Vienna: Institute for Comparative Economic Studies.

*Havlik, Peter, and Friedrich Levcik. 1985. *The gross domestic product of Czechoslovakia, 1970–1980*. World Bank Staff Working Paper no. 772. Washington, D.C.

Heston, Alan. 1982. The price structure of expenditures of Poland, Hungary, and Romania based on ICP results. Washington, D.C.: World Bank; processed.

Hewett, Edward. 1980. Foreign trade outcomes in Eastern and Western economies. In P. Marer and J. M. Montias. *East European integration and East-West trade*. Bloomington: Indiana University Press.

*———. 1985. *The gross national product of Hungary: Important issues for comparative research*. World Bank Staff Working Paper no. 775. Washington, D.C.

Hungary, Ministry of Finance. 1982. *Hungarian state budget in the seventies*. Budapest: Ministry of Finance.

*International Financial Statistics*. Various issues. Washington, D.C.: International Monetary Fund (IMF).

International Monetary Fund (IMF). 1982. *Hungary: An economic survey*. Occasional paper no. 15. Washington, D.C.: IMF.

*Jackson, Marvin R. 1985. *National accounts and the estimation of gross domestic product and its growth rates for Romania*. World Bank Staff Working Paper no. 774. Washington, D.C.

Jánossy, Ferenc. 1963. *A gazdasági fejlettség mérhetősége és új mérési módszerei* [The measurability of economic development and its new measuring methods]. Budapest: Közgazdasági és Jogi.

Keren, Michael. 1982. The use of purchasing power parities in the measurement of consumer price changes in Eastern Europe: An example from East Germany. Philadelphia: University of Pennsylvania; processed.

Kohn, Martin J. 1981. Consumer price developments in Eastern Europe. In Joint Economic Committee, U.S. Congress. *East European economic assessment*, pt. 2. Washington, D.C.: U.S. Government Printing Office.

Központi Statisztikai Hivatal. *Statisztikai évkönyv*. 1955–84.

Kravis, Irving B. 1984. Comparative studies of national incomes and prices. *Journal of economic literature* 22 (March).

Kravis, Irving B., A. Heston, and R. Summers. 1978. Real GDP per capita for more than one hundred countries. *Economic journal* 88(June).

————. 1981*a*. New insights into the structure of the world economy. *Review of income and wealth*, ser. 27, no. 4 (December).

————. 1981*b*. The share of services in economic growth. Paper prepared for the seventeenth conference of the International Association for Research in Income and Wealth, Gouveux, France.

————. 1981*c*. An approximation of the relative real per capita GDP of the People's Republic of China. *Journal of comparative economics* 5(March).

————. 1982. *World product and income: International comparisons of real gross product*. Baltimore: John Hopkins University Press for the World Bank.

Marer, Paul. 1972. *Soviet and East European foreign trade, 1946–1969: Statistical compendium and guide*. Bloomington: Indiana University Press.

————. 1981. Economic performances and prospects in Eastern Europe: Analytical summary and interpretation of findings. In Joint Economic Committee, U.S. Congress. *East European economic assessment*, pt. 2. Washington, D.C.: U.S. Government Printing Office.

————. 1982. Alternative approaches to estimate national income statistics of centrally planned economies. Background paper for first workshop on CPE national income statistics, Washington, D.C., June 1982.

Marer, Paul, and John Tilley. 1974. Tourism. In Joint Economic Committee, U.S. Congress. *Reorientation and commercial relations of the economies of Eastern Europe*. Washington, D.C.: U.S. Government Printing Office.

*Mesa-Lago, Carmelo, and Jorge Perez-Lopez. 1985. *A study of Cuba's Material Product System, its conversion to the System of National Accounts, and estimation of gross domestic product per capita and growth rates*. World Bank Staff Working Paper no. 770. Washington, D.C.

*Monthly Bulletin of Statistics*. New York: United Nations.

Pártos, Gyula. 1982. A gazdasági fejlettség szinvonala 1977-ben: Egy nemzetközi összehasonlitás [Economic development levels in 1977: An international comparison]. Budapest: Hungarian Academy of Sciences, Institute of World Economy; processed.

Research Project on National Income in East Central Europe (RPNI). 1982. Agricultural output, expenses and depreciation, gross product, and net product in Eastern Europe, 1965, 1970, and 1975–1981. New York: L. W. International Financial Research; processed.

*Singh, Shamsher, and Jong-goo Park. 1985. *National accounts statistics and exchange rates for Bulgaria*. World Bank Staff Working Paper no. 771. Washington, D.C.

Statistisches Bundesamt. 1970–81. *Internationaler Vergleich der Preise für die Lebenshaltung* [International comparison of prices for the cost of living]. Series 17. Wiesbaden.

Steiner, James E. 1982. Disguised inflation in Soviet industry. *Journal of comparative economics*, September.

Sysakova, Viera. 1981. *Súbor opatreni zameranych na zvýšenie účinnosti ceneveho systému a vonkajších ekonómichych vzt'ahov* [Measures designed to increase the effectiveness of the price system and of external economic relations]. *Finance a uver* (Prague), no. 12. Translated in *Soviet and East European foreign trade* 19:1 (Spring 1983).

Szilágyi, György. 1978. A gazdasági színvonal és struktúra összehasonlitása faktoranalizissel [The comparison of economic level and structure via factor analysis]. *Statisztikai szemle* (Budapest), February.

———. 1979. Az értékmutató-összehasonlitások módszertani fejlödése a KGST-ben [Evolution of the methods of comparing value indices in the CMEA]. *Statisztikai szemle* (Budapest).

Szombathelyi, Ferenc. 1982. Bulgária gazdasági fejlődésének új vonásai [New aspects of Bulgaria's economic development]. *Külgazdaság* (Budapest), June.

Theriot, Lawrence H., and JeNelle Matheson. 1979. Soviet economic relations with non-European CMEA: Cuba, Vietnam, and Mongolia. In Joint Economic Committee, U.S. Congress. *Soviet economy in a time of change*, vol. 2. Washington, D.C.: U.S. Government Printing Office.

Treml, Vladimir, and Barry Kostinsky. 1982. *The domestic value of Soviet foreign trade: Exports and imports in the 1972 input-output table.* Foreign Economic Report no. 20. Washington, D.C.: U.S. Bureau of the Census, Foreign Demographic Analysis Division.

United Nations. 1948. *Economic survey of Europe.* New York: UN.

———. 1971. *Basic principles of the system of the national accounts.* New York: UN.

———. 1980. *Yearbook of national income statistics.* Vol. 1. New York: UN.

———. 1981. *Comparisons of the system of national accounts and the system of balances of the national economy,* pt. 2: *Conversion of aggregates of SNA to MPS and vice versa for selected countries.* Doc. ser. F., no. 20. New York: UN.

———. Economic Commission for Europe. 1980a. Comparative GDP levels. In *Economic bulletin for Europe.* New York: UN, ECE.

———. 1980b. *Economic survey of Europe, 1979.* Geneva: UN, ECE.

———. 1983. *International comparison of gross domestic product in Europe, 1980.* Geneva: UN, ECE.

*U.S.S.R.: Measures of Economic Growth and Development, 1950–80.*

1982. Studies Prepared for the Joint Economic Committee, U.S. Congress. Washington, D.C.: U.S. Government Printing Office.

*van Brabant, Jozef M. 1985. *Exchange rates in Eastern Europe: Types, derivation, and application.* World Bank Staff Working Paper no. 778. Washington, D.C.

Wädekin, Karl-Eugen. 1982. *Agrarian policies in Communist Europe.* Totowa, N.J.: Allanheld, Osmun.

Wharton Econometric Forecasting Associates. 1981. *Romanian Crisis or Turning Point.* Washington, D.C.: WEFA.

Wolf, Thomas A. 1982. Computing exchange rate deviation indices. Memorandum to Paul Marer. October 18.

———. 1983. Guidelines for departure from the standard *Atlas* methodology for calculating dollar GNP per capita. Washington, D.C.: World Bank; processed.

*———. 1985. *Exchange rates, foreign trade accounting, and purchasing-power parity for centrally planned economies.* World Bank Staff Working Paper no. 779. Washington, D.C.

World Bank. 1966–81, 1983, 1985. *Atlas.* Washington, D.C.: World Bank.

———. 1982. *World Development Report 1982.* New York: Oxford University Press for the World Bank.

———. 1984. *Hungary: Economic developments and reforms.* Washington, D.C.: World Bank.

# Index

Administratively set prices, 20, 27, 28, 59, 121, 155, 160

AFC. *See* Factor costs (adjusted)

Agricultural costs, 59, 167

Agricultural procurement prices, 121–22, 153, 154, 159, 167

Agricultural production, 20, 23, 186; index of, 174, 182–83, 191–92, 198

Agricultural products, 11, 191; pricing of, 72, 122–23, 143, 147, 149

Agriculture, 177, 179; subsidization of, 122, 135

Alton, Thad, 178

Arbitrage, 27, 32, 75

Austria, 25, 89, 132; compared with Czechoslovakia, 5, 45, 48–49, 82; compared with Hungary, 106, 108, 109; compared with Poland, 36, 62, 63, 65, 102; exchange rates in, 45, 49

Balance of payments, 57, 70, 77, 156

Balance of trade, 21–22, 29n2, 57

Bergson, Abram, 12, 174, 177, 202

Bias: in country statistics, 194, 195, 202–03, 204; in estimates, 24, 39, 124, 198, 202–03, 204; in methodology, 11–12, 22, 35–37, 96–98, 106–07, 167–68, 175, 191, 201; in net material product, 25, 171

Black market, 36, 67, 158–59

Borenstein, I., 93

Branch indexes, 12, 174, 191, 201, 203

Brundenius indexes of industrial production, 200

Budget, 126, 129; of Czechoslovakia, 138, 140; of German Democratic Republic, 142; of Hungary, 149; of Romania, 157; of U.S.S.R., 135

Bulgaria, 4, 5, 6, 16, 17; exchange rates in, 28, 41–43, 161; foreign trade with, 111, 194; foreign trade multiplier for, 43; gross national product of, 101–02, 106; growth rates of, 193–94, 203–04; net material product of, 25, 182; prices in, 43, 137–38; purchasing power parity for, 43

Capital formation, 48–50, 63

Capital goods, pricing of, 141, 157

Central Intelligence Agency, PPP estimates by, 41

Centrally planned economies (CPEs): exchange rates in, 27; national accounts of, 3–5

China, 5

CMEA. *See* Council for Mutual Economic Assistance

Commercial exchange rates, 8, 31, 71–72, 109, 111, 114, 123; of German Democratic Republic, 50–51; of Hungary, 161, 164; of Poland, 57–59, 70; of Romania, 64

Comparative advantage, 128

Conference of European Statisticians, 35

Consumer price indexes, 38, 43, 130, 196

Consumer prices. *See* Retail prices

Consumption, 38–39, 48–50, 56, 62–63, 65, 73, 97, 101–02, 179

Cost-of-living comparisons, 33; by Federal Republic of Germany, 38; by United Nations, 38–39, 43, 56, 63

Costs, 59, 146, 201. *See also* Agricultural costs; Factor costs; Industrial costs

Paul Marer is professor of international business at the School of Business of Indiana University and a consultant to the World Bank.